NO BOSTON OLYMPICS

NO BOSTON OLYMPICS

HOW AND WHY SMART CITIES

ARE PASSING ON THE TORCH

Chris Dempsey and Andrew Zimbalist

ForeEdge

ForeEdge
An imprint of University Press of New England
www.upne.com
© 2017 Chris Dempsey and Andrew Zimbalist
All rights reserved
Manufactured in the United States of America
Designed by Mindy Basinger Hill
Typeset in Minion Pro

For permission to reproduce any of the material in this book, contact
Permissions, University Press of New England, One Court Street, Suite 250,
Lebanon NH 03766; or visit www.upne.com

Library of Congress Cataloging-in-Publication Data

Names: Dempsey, Chris, author. | Zimbalist, Andrew S., author.
Title: No Boston Olympics: how and why smart cities are passing on the torch /
    Chris Dempsey and Andrew Zimbalist.
Description: Lebanon NH: ForeEdge, an imprint of University Press
    of New England, [2017] | Includes bibliographical references and index.
Identifiers: LCCN 2016049141 (print) | LCCN 2016054863 (ebook) |
    ISBN 9781512600582 (cloth) | ISBN 9781512600704 (epub, mobi & pdf)
Subjects: LCSH: Olympic host city selection. | Olympic host city selection—2024.
    | Olympics—Finance.
Classification: LCC GV721.5 .D448 2017 (print) | LCC GV721.5 (ebook) |
    DDC 796.48—dc23
LC record available at https://lccn.loc.gov/2016049141

5 4 3 2 1

TO BOSTON'S JOURNALISTS,

whose coverage of Boston 2024 set a model,

and who are a crucial part of the history told herein

AND TO THE CITIZENS OF MASSACHUSETTS,

who know a bad deal when they see one

The Montreal Olympics can no more have
a deficit than a man can have a baby.

MONTREAL MAYOR JEAN DRAPEAU, JANUARY 29, 1973

(The 1976 Montreal Olympics
would close with a deficit
of more than $1 billion on an
original estimated total budget
of $310 million.)

CONTENTS

Illustrations follow page 106

JIM BRAUDE

FOREWORD

The question we were left with after it all fell apart: Is Boston simply the City of No?

Can the place that produced the first public school and newspaper ever again embrace an endeavor on the scale of the Olympic Games? Or is there an even bigger message in Boston 2024's defeat?

No Boston Olympics: How and Why Smart Cities Are Passing on the Torch provides the answers.

The book takes us back to the beginning—even before the shocking moment on January 8, 2015, when the United States Olympic Committee designated Boston as its choice to host the Summer Games in 2024.

The authors, Chris Dempsey and Andrew Zimbalist, take us behind the scenes of events that played out on a grand public stage. And they paint so many pivotal moments the public wasn't aware of in rich, gold-medal-worthy detail.

They had great material to work with, too. The real-life cast of characters in this David and Goliath epic would make the producer and director behind Chariots of Fire envious.

The politicians: a new, populist mayor, all-in, looking for a defining moment. An even newer governor (sworn in just hours before the USOC's decision was announced) playing hard to get. Both men against a backdrop of mostly mute lower-level public officials.

You want athletic greats? How about Red Sox slugger David Ortiz and Celtics legend Larry Bird?

And masters of the universe aplenty: the most powerful and decent, it should be noted, men and women, well men, anyway, in Boston, championing the effort. Then hiring scores of consultants, community leaders, former government officials—virtually all the potential opposition except Zimbalist and Dempsey—to try to get the bid to the finish line (as you'll learn, they even tried to convince Zimbalist to join the team).

Then there was a press corps that did its job relentlessly (I doubt I deserve that adverb, but I covered it too, on WGBH, public radio, and TV. We proposed a debate, but only the "no" side said yes. Boston 2024 asked if they could appear in the studio monthly to take questions from callers—we said yes, but they never showed. Callers did, though. Every time we uttered the word "Olympics," the phone lines were jammed.) Add a snowstorm of biblical proportions. Then throw in a healthy dose of arrogance, corruption, and even indictments in foreign capitals, and you'll get a feel for what this story is all about.

Actually, I omitted one set of actors, the most important ones: ordinary people who asked tough questions and wouldn't take "trust me" for an answer. A public, a stunningly well-organized, hungry-for-information public. So many more than #10peopleontwitter, as one leading booster described the opposition. An uprising that surprised Boston 2024's high-profile leadership team, though it shouldn't have.

Remember, most in town were still suffering from a hangover courtesy of the Big Dig (at one time the largest urban public works project in the nation's history), the project originally budgeted at $2 billion that ended up costing taxpayers eight times that much in an effort to speed traffic under the city.

Let me predict this: Throughout your reading of this book, you'll shake your head and ask, Was Boston 2024's goal to find the dwindling number of those who still were on their side and hand them over to the opposition?

Boston 2024 said it wanted public input but held no public meetings until after the bid was awarded and the five-ring train appeared to have left the station. At first its backers wouldn't agree to voter input via ballot, then they said they would. The mayor said that he read the bid that he literally and figuratively signed on to, but then we learned that no, he hadn't. The Games were to be walkable, but even the hardiest Olympians, much less attendees, were unlikely to walk the ninety miles to watch whitewater kayaking in the western part of the state.

"Not a penny of public funding" was the mantra, but no guarantee ever followed that the boosters could honor the pledge. Boston 2024 promised to improve the physical infrastructure of the city, expand opportunity for communities of color, and leave behind a physical and human legacy that would make a great city even greater. One mistake and misstatement after another eroded the public's willingness to listen.

Boston 2024's attempts to paper over a deplorable Olympic history in prior host cities and an incomplete, risky proposal for this city was undone at every turn by people like Zimbalist and Dempsey who were then and in these pages armed with nothing more than facts.

Writing a history of a charged debate from which the feelings are still palpable can be a dicey proposition. Is it too soon? Are emotions still too current for any retelling to be dispassionate, to have the proper amount of perspective? Should anyone who was involved in the story tell the story?

With *No Boston Olympics*, the post-Rio timing is perfect and the tour guides are just the right ones. Andrew Zimbalist is a world-renowned academic who has chronicled what can—and usually does—go wrong with huge international sporting events. But unlike most reporters of events, he was a player in this one. His collaborator in the effort, Chris Dempsey, was the man at the center of the underfunded, understaffed just-say-no campaign, a guy whose sole prior experience with the Olympics was to sit on his couch and watch them on NBC.

For whom is this excursion through two hundred often-surreal days written? Everyone! The powerful who want to do really big but potentially disruptive things in their communities. The often powerless, who seek an active voice in important initiatives that affect their lives. And those on the sidelines, hard-working average taxpayers who want to be treated fairly and honestly. The book is far more than a behind- and in-front-of-the scenes history; it's a primer on how to do and how not to do big things that matter.

There's only one part of the story that Zimbalist and Dempsey were unable to tell: Will the sponsors' commitment that, win or lose, the bid effort itself would enrich the debate over the future direction of the city and region ever be realized? We'll have to leave that to the book's sequel.

So is Boston the City of No? Finish reading and I think you'll conclude that we're not. We're just the city that says no to well-intended but not very good ideas.

The authors of this book first met in January 2015, just days after the United States Olympic Committee's (USOC) decision to choose Boston 2024 as the sole US bid to host the 2024 Summer Olympics. The setting for that initial face-to-face conversation was a dimly lit church on Marlborough Street in Boston's historic Back Bay neighborhood. On short notice, No Boston Olympics had paid $700 to rent the church's main sanctuary space for its first organizing meeting. The event drew a crowd of about 150 interested and curious citizens from across eastern Massachusetts and a dozen or more media outlets from around the region and the world. They came to hear a long-tenured economics professor, Andrew Zimbalist, share his research on why the costs of an Olympic bid generally far outweigh the benefits, and to hear what the young, politically engaged leaders of No Boston Olympics, including Chris Dempsey, planned to do to stop Boston 2024's juggernaut of powerful, well-connected, and wealthy boosters from imposing those net costs on Massachusetts taxpayers and residents. It was a successful early test of an effective collaboration between the academic and the activists. That collaboration seemed to culminate and conclude six months later in a live prime-time televised debate that pitted Zimbalist and Dempsey against the chairman of Boston 2024's bid, Steve Pagliuca, and a member of the USOC, Dan Doctoroff. The USOC withdrew its support on July 27, 2015, just a few days thereafter.

But that fall, in October 2015, we found ourselves reunited over schnitzel and beer in a hotel bar in the booming harbor district of Hamburg, Germany. That northern port city was considering its own 2024 Olympic bid. Hamburg's HafenCity University had invited the American academic to give a lecture on the pros and cons of Hamburg's proposal. That very same week, student leaders at the University of Hamburg, whose student government had voted to oppose Hamburg's bid, were hosting No Boston Olympics. The student organizers had assembled a panel of Olympic-bid opponents from Boston, Munich, and Kraków, cities where organized opposition had successfully defeated Olympic proposals. In Hamburg, we concluded that there was a broader audience interested in understanding why and how Bostonians had turned down the "once-in-a-lifetime" opportunity to host Olympic Games. No matter where in the world they might live, the same kinds of curious and engaged citizens who filled those church pews on Marlborough Street for that initial No Boston Olympics organizing meeting in January 2015 might very well sit down to read a book that delved deeper into Boston's story.

We find at least three compelling reasons to share our view on what happened in Boston. First, as was the case in Hamburg, the Boston 2024 bid holds some clear lessons for civic leaders in other places that might be considering hosting the Olympic Games. Perhaps it is inevitable that boosters in some cities will continue to be drawn to the glittery promises of the International Olympic Committee. We want both proponents and opponents of those prospective bids to be better informed about why the citizens of Boston rejected the Games. Second, some of the lessons from the Boston 2024 proposal and public debate may be more broadly applicable to important conflicts and conversations around infrastructure, growth, and democratic governance. The debate in Boston raised essential questions about who gets to decide how a region should change and who should pay for those changes. Every region in the world must grapple with these same questions. Therefore, a reader who lives in a place that will never bid on hosting Olympic Games still has something to learn from Boston's story. Third, the story of Boston 2024 provides a revealing look at Massachusetts politics and civic life in the second decade of the twenty-first century. The authors are observers of, and participants in, this distinctive and peculiar political culture, and we wish to contribute to its chronicling and recording.

We acknowledge that our treatment and descriptions of the events, decisions, and individuals described in the following pages contain inherent biases. We do not claim that the narrative portions of this book are impartial. Nonetheless, we have endeavored to approach the subject as fairly and dispassionately as is possible for two people who were deeply engaged in the issue and who played a role in its outcome.

We are in the uncomfortable and challenging position of needing to describe friends, loved ones, opponents, allies, and onetime rivals—even more awkward is that sometimes the very same people play more than one of these roles! But our experience was that our participation in the public debate about Boston 2024 built and strengthened far more friendships than it destroyed, even with those on the opposite side of the issue from us. We hope the words in this book do the same.

Perhaps most challenging is that this book requires us to describe our own actions and roles. We use the third-person point of view rather than the first-person for two reasons: (1) because this work is coauthored, it would have been difficult to differentiate between instances when the first-person perspective was that of one coauthor, the other, or both; and (2) our goal in this work was to describe the general history and broader implications of the Boston 2024 debate, rather than just create an account of our part in it.

To be clear, writing a historical narrative in which one has taken part is fraught with peril. Done poorly, it becomes self-aggrandizing hagiography, like the narrative carvings and sculptures on a Roman triumphal arch. Even when done thoughtfully, it cannot provide a complete and impartial retelling of what occurred. Then again, probably no historical account can. With this book, we seek to make a self-aware and modest contribution to existing and future interpretations and analyses of the Boston 2024 tale, while also providing fodder for discussions already occurring around the world about the costs and benefits of bidding for and hosting the Olympics.

NO BOSTON OLYMPICS

INAUGURATION DAY

Thursday, January 8, 2015, was a dry but bitterly cold day in New England. The winter wind whipped among the brick and granite civic and commercial buildings massed on Boston's Beacon Hill, prodding the familiar collection of legislators, lobbyists, and bureaucrats to dart quickly from automobiles and subway head houses to their offices and appointments. At noon, under the golden dome of the centuries-old State House at the very top of the hill, businessman and former state budget chief Charlie Baker was inaugurated as Massachusetts's seventy-second governor, the victor two months prior in a hard-fought election against the state's attorney general, Martha Coakley. Baker was a Republican in a Democratic state. His margin of victory had been just forty thousand votes out of more than two million cast—the Commonwealth's closest gubernatorial race in fifty years.[1] In his inaugural address, Baker pledged to set aside partisanship, make government more efficient, improve transparency and accountability, and work always in the public interest.[2] It would take monumental news to push the inauguration and the new governor's first words from above the fold of the front page of Friday's *Boston Globe*, but the results of a secretive, closed-door meeting in a conference room at Denver International Airport would do just that.

At 6:29 p.m. Eastern Time, the Twitter account of the United States Olympic Committee declared that the USOC's board of directors had chosen a bid from Boston as the official US bid for the 2024 Olympics: "*BREAKING: The USOC selects #Boston2024 as US bid to host the 2024 Olympic & Paralympic Games.*"[3] The USOC's board, composed largely of former Olympic athletes and business executives with ties to Olympic sponsors, had voted for an underdog bid from Boston over alternatives from Washington, D.C., San Francisco, and the favorite and two-time Olympic host, Los Angeles. Once

Boston Magazine's List of Boston's Ten "Most Powerful People," April 2015

NAME	POSITION OR ASSOCIATION	AFFILIATION WITH BOSTON 2024
John Fish	Suffolk Construction chairman and CEO	Boston 2024 chairman.
Charlie Baker	Governor of Massachusetts	
John Henry	Owner of *Boston Globe* and Boston Red Sox	Made public statements in support of the bid and allowed Boston 2024 to use Fenway Park for PR events, but never formally associated with the bid.
Elizabeth Warren	U.S. Senator	
Robert Kraft	Owner of the New England Patriots	Boston 2024 executive committee.
Marty Walsh	Mayor of Boston	Boston 2024's most important political supporter.
Jim Davis	Chairman of New Balance	New Balance contributed between $100k and $500k to Boston 2024.
Karen Kaplan	Hill Holiday chairman and CEO	Member of Boston 2024 Advisory Council. Hill Holiday contributed between $500,000 and $999,999 to Boston 2024.
Jeffrey Leiden	Vertex chairman and CEO	Member of Boston 2024 Advisory Council. Vertex donated Class A office space to Boston 2024.
Barbara Lee	Philanthropist	

Source: Based on Carly Carioli and George Donnelly, eds., "Boston's 50 Most Powerful People," *Boston Magazine*, May 2015, accessed July 28, 2016, www.bostonmagazine.com/news/article/2015/04/28/most-powerful-people-in-boston/.

the decision had been made and the news had been shared with the world, USOC chairman Larry Probst, CEO Scott Blackmun, and other USOC staff immediately boarded a plane for Boston's Logan Airport. A press conference was scheduled for early Friday morning at the Boston Convention and Exhibition Center in the city's fast-growing Seaport District. The massive, 2.1-million-square-foot convention center also happened to be the site of Governor Baker's inaugural ball on Thursday evening, and attendees were buzzing with the news that the Olympic rings might come to Massachusetts.

Within hours of the USOC's announcement, Boston 2024, the private group organizing the Olympic bid, convened a congratulatory and euphoric conference call for its lengthy roster of business, political, and institutional supporters. Boston 2024's boosters included many of greater Boston's largest corporations, six of the city's "ten most powerful" individuals (according to the annual ranking by *Boston Magazine*), and the city's popular new mayor, Martin J. "Marty" Walsh, who had given the bid his enthusiastic backing. Many of the companies, civic institutions, and wealthy donors supporting the bid had made six-figure financial contributions to the effort, fueling a campaign that by January 2015 already had spent more than $10 million on staff salaries, communications and political consultants, Class A office space, and design and planning services.[4]

About one hundred yards down Beacon Street from the State House, a small team of volunteers opposed to Boston 2024's Olympic bid huddled around laptops in a cramped conference room in temporary, makeshift headquarters. Boston's Olympic boosters had dismissed the group, known as No Boston Olympics, in bid documents submitted privately to the USOC: "Polling data shows that they do not represent the majority of public opinion, no elected official has publicly endorsed the group, they have not received significant financial backing and their efforts have been limited to social media."[5] It wasn't an entirely unfair description. Although the group had been founded more than a year earlier, No Boston Olympics had raised less than $5,000—to Boston 2024's $10 million—and could point to only a handful of sympathetic elected officials. Just one month prior, one of its three cofounders had publicly and conspicuously flipped sides to become a backer of the bid. Polling done by local media outlets showed that most voters in Boston, and in Massachusetts more broadly, supported the idea of a Boston Olympic Games. And while the group's efforts might have extended beyond just social media, No Boston Olympics hadn't yet held a single organizing meeting, nor did it have full-time staff, office space, or even a post office box to receive mailed contributions.

Exactly two hundred days after that cold winter evening, when the USOC's choice of Boston pushed Governor Baker's inauguration from the headlines, Boston 2024 and the USOC jointly terminated the bid in the face of organized public opposition that USOC chairman Larry Probst would later call unprecedented for an American city.[6] The narrative that follows explains how No Boston Olympics and allied groups mobilized that public opposition, forever changing the course of Boston's history and dealing a shocking defeat to Boston 2024's boosters, the USOC, and the International Olympic Committee.

ONE

CITIUS, ALTIUS, FORTIUS

Faster, higher, stronger. The Dominican priest Henri Didon, one of the great French preachers of the late nineteenth century, kicked off a scholastic athletic competition in France with these words in 1891.[1] In attendance was his friend Pierre de Coubertin, the father of the modern Olympics and of the International Olympic Committee (IOC). Coubertin was born into an aristocratic family in Paris on New Year's Day 1863. The Frenchman was an intellectual and an academic. He was deeply interested in the development of young men through both education and athletics. On his first trip to England, in 1883, Coubertin made a special visit to the Rugby School, the birthplace of rugby football, famous for combining physical education with academic instruction. Coubertin believed that athletics could help build a nation or even an empire: "There can be no reasonable doubt about [athletics] effecting a strong and vigorous education of body and character. To the merits of this education we may ascribe a large share in the prodigious and powerful extension of the British Empire in Queen Victoria's reign," he wrote in 1896.[2]

Coubertin also had a passion for ancient Greece; he saw the ancient Greeks' famed Olympic Games as the quintessential intersection of civilization and athletics. By the time he heard Father Didon's three-word phrase, which would become the Olympic motto, Coubertin was well on his way to reviving the ancient Olympic Games for the modern era. In June 1894, Coubertin organized the Congress on the Revival of the Olympic Games at the Sorbonne in Paris, which led to the creation of the International Olympic Committee. A Greek businessperson living in Paris, Demetrius

Vikelas, became the IOC's first president. Coubertin became the organization's secretary general. The committee's central charge was to organize the first modern Olympic Games, to be held in Athens in 1896.

The 1896 Games shared the fate of many of its successors: they were beset by cost overruns, the construction of otherwise unneeded facilities, and logistical failures. A Greek diplomat and early member of the IOC, Stephanos Skouloudis, filed a report that concluded that the budget had soared to more than three times Coubertin's initial cost estimates. The cost of the Panathenaic Stadium, the signature venue, had risen from 585,000 to 920,000 drachmas.[3] Skouloudis, who would later become prime minister of Greece, resigned from the IOC in protest. Other members of the committee followed him, upset and embarrassed by how the IOC had conducted its affairs. At first, private funds had been eyed for the construction of the velodrome and shooting gallery. But when those funds didn't materialize, Coubertin and the IOC fell back on a guarantee that they had secured from the Greek government to complete the construction of these venues. Then, as now, the International Olympic Committee was asking host governments to pick up the tab when things didn't go according to plan.[4]

But the Games went on. A Bostonian, James Connolly, was awarded the very first Olympic medal, for winning the triple jump (then known as the "hop, skip and jump").[5] Newspapers such as the *London Times*; the *St. Paul Daily Globe*; the *San Francisco Call*; and the *Times*, the *Tribune*, and the *Sun* of New York were among the many that reported on the events and competitions. The *Boston Herald* noted on May 8, 1896, that Connolly and other Olympic athletes had received a hero's welcome on their return to the United States. Even in a world not yet connected by modern telecommunications, the inaugural Olympic Games achieved one of their most important goals: producing riveting popular content for the international media.[6]

At the conclusion of the 1896 Games, King George I of Greece pleaded with the International Olympic Committee to make Athens the permanent home of the modern Olympics. After all, the country had just built all the stadiums and venues needed to play host—it made practical sense to reuse them in the future.[7] But Coubertin had other ideas. He wanted to bring the Games first to Paris, his hometown, and then to "every large capital of the world in turn."[8] The World's Fair—an earlier nineteenth-century creation—had used this model with great success.[9]

Perhaps Coubertin's plan had some merit in an era before radio, television, the Internet, or air travel. Maybe in the 1890s it made sense to move the Games around, even if that did require the wasteful construction of new facilities that often lacked a legitimate long-term use. But since that time, the Olympics have become a blockbuster television event—for every individual watching the Olympics in a stadium, hundreds of thousands more do so on a screen. Billions of people can now enjoy the events in real time no matter where the competitions might be held. Today, unlike in 1896, those who want to experience the competitions in person can hop on a plane. No weeks-long ocean voyage is needed. A century of technological innovation has made Coubertin's business model antiquated.[10]

Yet the International Olympic Committee, buoyed by its unregulated, worldwide monopoly of the Games, has clung to the only approach it has ever known. And why wouldn't it? The roughly one hundred IOC members, hailing from countries large and small around the world, are in an enviable position.[11] Few experiences are more luxurious than being a member of the IOC in an Olympic host city. According to a document shared with the Oslo 2022 bidding committee, the IOC demands that local host committees pay for IOC members' lodging and meals in the host city's finest hotels; provide security; cover the costs of vehicles and personal drivers that have access to exclusive lanes on local roads and highways; welcome each IOC member with gifts of seasonal fruits, cakes, and Coca-Cola products; and be given special entrances and exits to the local airport. These demands struck many in Norway as condescending and outrageous—they contributed to a refusal by the country's ruling party to back the Oslo bid.[12] But there is no evidence that the IOC has modified them for future hosts.

And the costs associated with pampering IOC members pale in comparison to the IOC's requirements for shiny new sporting venues, a gleaming media and press center, and an Olympic village that can host more than ten thousand athletes and five thousand coaches and trainers at the Summer Games. Most important, the IOC requires host cities to provide a financial backstop for all construction and operations associated with the Games. If things don't go according to plan, it is the host government, not the IOC, that must pay for the cost overruns—just as it was in Athens in 1896.

The IOC can perpetuate this system because every two years bidding committees in at least a handful of cities decide they want a shot at Olympic glory. The idea of seeing one's own city stand proudly on the world stage as an Olympic host holds obvious allure. The opportunity often proves particularly compelling to those in the business of construction, real estate development, investment banking, hospitality, or insurance. After all, well-connected firms and individuals in these industries stand to benefit greatly from the billions of dollars of spending required of Olympic hosts. Local bidding committees convince themselves that the Games will deliver vast and incalculable benefits for themselves and for their communities. The IOC then plays these overeager bidding committees off one another and extracts ever-more-lavish concessions, proposals, and promises from prospective hosts.

Of course, even monopolists can run afoul of their consumers by pushing their advantage too far. This happened to the IOC in the 1970s. Denver, the capital city of Colorado, had won the right to host the 1976 Winter Games. But the organizing committee lacked transparency and had failed to consult with the Denver City Council on its plans. Olympic skeptics pushed for a referendum in November 1972 that would bar public funds from being used on the Games. Despite being outspent by a 7.3 to 1 margin, the opposition easily defeated the Olympic bid by a 60/40 vote. Colorado's citizens had decided that the financial cost and potential environmental damage of hosting were not worth it.[13] Spurned by its chosen host city, the IOC had to ask Innsbruck, the 1964 host, to replace Denver. Three consecutive Summer Games in that era were financial or political debacles. Mexico City 1968 was plagued by political repression, militant protests, and air pollution. Munich 1972 was haunted by the terrorist attack at the Israeli compound of the Olympic village. Montreal 1976 suffered from incompetence and corruption, resulting in a final cost that rose to more than nine times the original estimates. Two years later, in 1978, when it came time to bid for the 1984 Games, only two cities expressed interest. One was Los Angeles. The other was Tehran, which dropped out of the running in the months leading up to the Iranian Revolution. The IOC found itself in the unenviable position of being an auctioneer with only one bidder. Understanding that it had unusual and unique leverage over the IOC, Los Angeles offered to host with three conditions: first, that taxpayers would not have to backstop the Games financially in the event of a cost overrun or revenue shortfall; second, that it would be able to reduce costs by using some of the same facilities used for the 1932 Olympics; and, third, that instead of constructing an athletes' village, it would be allowed to lodge athletes at the dormitories at the University of California–Los Angeles and the University of Southern California. Without the capacity to play one bidder against another, as it typically would, the IOC was forced to drop its standard conditions and agree to Los Angeles's terms. Sound management, good fortune, and dramatically reduced requirements for infrastructure and venue construction permitted the Los Angeles Games to accrue a genuine surplus of $215 million.[14]

The success of Los Angeles was enough to turn the tide for the IOC's standing, and from 1984 to the early 2000s, the committee enjoyed crowded fields of bidders for its Games. Thanks to more competition among the world's cities, the IOC was able to extract promises of more and more elaborate venues and accommodations. Eventually, as hosting costs rose above $5 billion, then $10 billion, then $20 billion, the bubble burst again. Beginning in the early 2000s, the number of cities bidding began to fall, leading to a veritable crash of bidders for the 2022 Winter Games during 2013 and 2014.

At the beginning of 2013, bidding groups in eight applicant cities expressed interested in hosting the 2022 Games. By the end of that year, St. Moritz/Davos and Munich both dropped out of the process following defeats in public referenda. In 2014, a referendum in Kraków led that city to drop its bid. The Stockholm City Council soon opted out, as did the government in Oslo. Lviv also exited, owing to the political turbulence in the Ukraine following Russia's invasion. Only two cities remained: Almaty, Kazakhstan, and Beijing, China. We discuss China's plans for the 2022 Winter Games in a later chapter.

The IOC was in crisis mode again, and its new president, former German Olympic fencer Thomas Bach, sprang into action. Bach pushed through a program of reforms intended to promote a more flexible bidding process and a reduced financial burden on host cities. The reform program was passed at the IOC convention in Monaco in December 2014 and was cleverly dubbed Agenda 2020—a play on words that suggested perfect 20/20 vision, a roadmap for the future, full enactment by the year 2020, and the list of forty actual reform proposals. With bold and hopeful language, Agenda 2020 restated the IOC's alleged commitment to human rights, to sustainability, and to economic sanity.

But will Agenda 2020 actually lead to better outcomes for host cities? A closer look at the forty reform items is enlightening. Remarkably, just seven of these items are germane to bidding and hosting committees. The remaining thirty-three deal with other IOC goals and objectives, such as eliminating the use of performance-enhancing drugs by Olympic athletes, strengthening the value of the IOC's television rights, and spreading the values of "Olympism." Of the seven relevant items, some can hardly be seen as creating significant opportunities for cost savings. For example, Item #3 includes a provision that calls for boosters to submit their Olympic bids electronically, rather than by the traditional method of delivering printed versions. This change in the IOC's bidding process might save bidding committees a few *thousand* dollars on airfare or shipping, at a time when just *bidding* on the Games typically costs $60 million to $100 million.[15]

More promising is Item #1, which states the IOC's desire to "actively promote the maximum use of existing facilities and the use of temporary and demountable venues." Such an approach *could* reduce the costs of hosting. But the historical precedent on this commitment is discouraging; it turns out the IOC has made this pledge before.

The IOC's own 2002 Olympic Games Study Commission acknowledged that "the size and complexity of the Olympic Games have reached a point where they present significant operational and organizational risks which need to be addressed," and urged IOC members to choose bids that relied on lower-cost existing and temporary facilities.[16] But less than three years later, in a frenzied auction environment that included bids from Paris, New York, Madrid, and Moscow, these same IOC members voted for a London 2012 bid that proposed building a brand-new Olympic stadium, velodrome, aquatics center, Olympic village, media and broadcast center, and other facilities. London's 2012 Olympics ended up costing more than three times the estimates submitted to the IOC—an overrun of more than $10 billion. Two years after that, the IOC chose an ostentatious bid from

Sochi, Russia, where almost none of the required venues or infrastructure were in place. It became the most expensive Olympics in history, with a total cost estimated at over $50 billion.[17]

Given the IOC's disappointing track record, Agenda 2020 should be viewed skeptically by potential hosts. Until proven otherwise, it amounts to nothing more than spin—an obvious attempt to regenerate interest from potential host cities and assuage well-founded fears that the Games will lead to waste and overspending. Boston 2024's boosters, for example, frequently cited the passage of Agenda 2020 as evidence that the IOC would reject expensive bids. Yet these same boosters still proposed building almost all the most expensive Olympic venues and facilities from scratch, including the major venues that had led to those billions of dollars of overruns in London. Similarly, IOC president Bach praised all four of the remaining 2024 bids (Paris, Rome, Budapest, and Los Angeles) as consistent with Agenda 2020, even though some of the bids require construction that easily will amount to billions of dollars. Rome has since dropped out.

Until and unless a comprehensive reform to the IOC's long-standing auction process takes place, the general trend of uneconomic, budget-busting bids is likely to continue. With the exception of Los Angeles in 1984, the International Olympic Committee has required each host city to guarantee that any overruns associated with the Games will be borne by the hosts, not by the IOC. As long as they are not the ones taking on the financial risks of cost overruns, the IOC's members will be drawn to more extravagant bids that promise to attract more television viewers or leave behind a feel-good "legacy" of glistening new venues that glorify the Olympic movement. These considerations, along with political leanings, personal connections, and backroom logrolling, ultimately hold far greater sway with IOC members than whether a bid's cost estimates are accurate, or whether the Games fit into a city's long-term development plans.

In the end, the IOC accepts no responsibility for determining whether the bid meets the needs of the host city. That job falls to the bidders and their political backers. In Boston and other places where citizens have demanded accountability from bidding committees, the IOC's predilection for grandiose, garish, made-for-TV Games, the demands for exclusive access to roads and parks, and the mandate for a financial guarantee from taxpayers to cover overruns, have put the boosters in an uncomfortable position. In these cases and others, the interests of the public conflict with the interests of the IOC. The bidding committees are caught in the middle—pulled in opposite directions. We call this dynamic the Boosters' Dilemma and reference it a number of times in the narrative that follows.

In Boston, as the public learned more and more about the details of Boston 2024's proposal, support for the bid dropped. Yet the actions that the boosters could have taken to improve public support—most notably, eliminating the request for taxpayer financial backing of the Games—were deemed unacceptable by the International Olympic Committee. The Boosters' Dilemma meant that any major concessions to the public equated to a repudiation of the IOC's demands; it ultimately left Boston's Olympic boosters paralyzed.

Of course, the Boosters' Dilemma exists only when Olympic bids are scrutinized appropriately by an engaged, educated, and organized populace, an energetic and hungry press, or perhaps an antiestablishment political party. In 2014 and 2015, Boston was fortunate to have the right mix of these ingredients to ensure that the boosters would not be able to submit a bid that elevated the desires of the IOC over those of the region's residents.

I'm not in this to lose.

BOSTON 2024 CHAIRMAN JOHN FISH, INTERVIEW
WITH THE *BOSTON GLOBE*, SEPTEMBER 2014

TWO

2013 AND 2014

Eric Reddy and Corey Dinopoulos, both Massachusetts natives and young professionals living in the Boston area, were the Leibniz and Newton of Boston 2024's Olympic dream. In the fall of 2012, each learned that the United States Olympic Committee would be seeking applicant cities to bid for the 2024 Summer Olympics and thought that the Athens of America, as locals sometimes call Boston, would make an ideal host. Reddy had many years of experience in sports marketing, and Dinopoulos was a visual design professional and Olympic aficionado. Many years earlier, Dinopoulos had undertaken a college project that contemplated how the mega-event might fit with Boston's global brand as a historic city that was now a hub of education and innovation. Introduced to each other because of their mutual interest in a potential Boston bid, Reddy and Dinopoulos met for the first time at the Omni Parker House, the celebrated hotel two blocks down Beacon Street from the State House.[1]

SPRING 2013—A FALSE START FOR BOSTON 2024

Reddy and Dinopoulos were unknown in Massachusetts politics, but they found some initial support for their notion from Eileen Donoghue, a state senator from the historic mill city of Lowell, twenty-five miles northwest of Boston. Donaghue cochaired the legislature's Committee on Tourism, Arts, and Cultural Development and believed the Olympics could be a boon to those interests. But Boston mayor Tom Menino—a towering figure in the city—gave the duo a cool reception. Menino, who by 2013 had held sway over the city of Boston for twenty years, was no stranger to Olympic bids. In 1992, the year before city council president Menino would assume the mayor's office upon the resignation of mayor Ray Flynn, a group of Boston business leaders led by sports agent Stephen Freyer had pitched an Olympic bid to city hall. Mayor Flynn, a former All-American basketball player at Providence College, was supportive of the effort. He had once posed holding the Olympic torch in front of the famous Paul Revere statue in Boston's North End. But in 1993, Flynn was appointed by President Clinton to be ambassador to the Vatican and he soon gave way to Menino. At first, the new mayor supported the bid, telling the *Boston Globe*, "I will work with the Olympics Committee. I will promote it. This is good for Boston, good for its people."[2] After further examination, Menino turned away from the Olympic bid, concluding that his priorities should be the day-to-day needs of the city's residents, rather than the demands of a three-week sporting event. He ultimately supported the construction of a new convention center in the city, but not the accompanying baseball and football stadiums that many saw as precursors to playing Olympic host. "Stadiums do not revive cities," he said in a later State of the City speech. "People do."[3]

Twenty years after that initial Olympic pitch, Mayor Menino seemed as convinced as ever that Boston would be better off passing on a bid. On February 19, 2014, when the USOC sent his office—and that of thirty-four other mayors around the country—a letter soliciting bids for the 2024 Summer Games, Menino dismissed it. Perhaps a diligent staffer in Menino's office read the insightful piece by longtime Olympic observer and writer Alan Abrahamson (somewhat perplexingly reposted on the USOC's website) explaining the subtext of the USOC's letter: "If you, Mr. or Ms. Mayor, would like to play in the Olympic space, be crystal clear going in you will do so as the junior partner."[4] That is, in any American bidding process, the USOC calls the shots and the host city is just along for the ride. More likely, Abrahamson's piece went unnoticed, because for Menino and his seasoned staff, the letter needed no translation. The mayor was famous for adopting a direct, hands-on approach to proposals that might alter his beloved city. In one instance that became lore in Boston's real estate community, the mayor had personally chosen the architectural design of the crown of a new building that was to grace the city's skyline from a set of options presented by an obsequious developer eager for a green light from city hall. To Menino, playing "junior partner" held little appeal if outsiders from the USOC were going to take a lead role in organizing a three-week sporting event that would bring generational, monumental, and disruptive changes to Boston.

On March 5, 2013, Menino panned a Boston Olympic bid as "far-fetched" in a radio interview with public radio station WBUR, saying, "I need every penny I have to make sure we continue the services to the people of Boston."[5] A *Boston Herald* article published the next day, titled "Hub Olympics Idea Torched," quoted Menino's close friend and ally, John Fish, the chairman and CEO of Suffolk Construction. "We're coming out of the greatest economic recession and I don't think our resources should be diluted by going after something so far out," said Fish, the city's most successful builder. "If someone wanted to pour $1 billion into our health care or education system or the life sciences industry, I'd be all for that discussion." Fish had supported Stephen Freyer's bid in the early 1990s but now told *Herald* reporters Dave Wedge and Erin Smith: "Our perspective has changed."[6] Led by the earnest but insignificant duo of Reddy and Dinopoulos and lacking the support of the incumbent mayor and power players like Fish, a Boston 2024 bid was, for all intents and purposes, stillborn.

BOSTON 2024 GETS OFF THE STARTING BLOCKS

Just three weeks after the *Herald* report had seemingly ended the city's Olympic prospects, the political landscape in Boston experienced a tectonic shift: Mayor Menino announced that he would not be seeking reelection. The pronouncement created a once-in-a-generation political vacuum and touched off a feverish race to replace the only mayor that many Bostonians had ever known. More than a dozen candidates, including the eventual finalists—a state representative and union organizer from Dorchester named Marty Walsh, and city councilor John Connolly—would vie to be Boston's first new mayor since 1993.

The political vacuum also created new life for the idea of a Boston Olympics. Its new champion was someone who just a few weeks prior to Menino's decision had panned the bid to the *Herald*. John Fish's perspective had changed again. Fish grabbed the reins from Reddy and Dinopoulos and began to meet quietly with other civic leaders about the idea of bringing the Olympics to Boston in 2024. He persuaded a still-reluctant but now lame-duck Menino to allow him to respond to the USOC's forlorn February solicitation letter. He invited USOC officials to town in October 2013 for a private meeting at the Mandarin Oriental, perhaps Boston's most luxurious building, where Fish owned a $7 million condominium. Among those in attendance were Dinopoulos and Mayor Menino, who by then had just a few months remaining in office and was no doubt curious about the bid's prospects. In that meeting, USOC officials told Fish that a host city's priority should be to determine its long-term plans for development, and to submit a bid only if hosting the Olympics fit into those plans. (This spin—"we really care about the city's development"—is the standard rhetoric. Note that the USOC eventually turned to Los Angeles, whose bid has little to do with city building.) The idea captivated Fish, a prolific builder who recognized a unique opportunity to remake parts of the city over the following decade. As he put it to *Boston Magazine*, "I start with the question: What is the city of Boston going to look like in 30 to 40 years? It involves thinking big—not just thinking about where we've been and where we're going, but thinking a little abnormally. We may never realize the Olympics in 2024, but the opportunity to bring the community together to talk about the future is a powerful thing."[7]

Fish was perhaps the only person in Massachusetts positioned to attempt something as ambitious as an Olympic bid. He had been named the most powerful Bostonian by *Boston Magazine* in 2012—even ahead of the governor and the mayor—and with his deep connections in the city's political, business, and philanthropic spheres, had an unmatched reputation as the person to go to when one wanted to get things done in Boston. Among other civic and institutional roles, Fish was the incoming chairman of the *Greater Boston* Chamber of Commerce; the deputy chairman (and future chairman) of the Federal Reserve's Boston branch; the founder of the Massachusetts Competitive Partnership, which advocated for business interests at the State House; and the incoming chairman of the board of trustees at Boston College, one of the city's most influential universities. Fish had created an unrivaled platform for influencing the direction of the region in the coming decades. His competitive intensity was the stuff of legend in Massachusetts business circles. Fish was known for arriving at work at 4:30 a.m. He had ruthlessly outcompeted rival construction firms, including one owned by his own brother, to become the dominant builder in New England. Bringing the Olympics to Boston would be a crowning achievement, cementing Fish's position as his generation's ultimate Boston power broker.

Fish also must have understood that leading a successful Olympic bid would bring him benefits far beyond Massachusetts's borders. A successful bid offered unprecedented international exposure for its leaders. Peter Ueberroth, the president and CEO of Los Angeles's 1984 bid, had used the Games to catapult himself from a successful but nationally unknown regional businessperson to become *Time* magazine's Man of the Year in 1984, and later commissioner of Major League Baseball. Billy Payne, who spearheaded Atlanta's 1996 bid, would later become chairman of Augusta National Golf Club, home of the Masters tournament. The bidding process alone would provide Fish the chance to use his private jet to travel the world to rub shoulders with royalty, former Olympic athletes, and the ultrawealthy who made up the International Olympic Committee. It was the opportunity of a lifetime for a businessperson and philanthropist who had spent two decades gradually amassing power in Massachusetts's capital city. John Fish was hooked.

Fish began to put his immense political capital to work building the foundation of an Olympic bid. He and his allies helped orchestrate the passage of a legislative resolution, first filed in January 2013 by Senator Donoghue, establishing a commission to investigate the "feasibility of hosting the summer Olympics [in Massachusetts] in 2024." Governor Deval Patrick signed the resolution on October 31, 2013—a Halloween treat for Olympic boosters. Despite its significance, the resolution received only minimal coverage from the media, as the news cycle focused on the Red Sox World Series win on October 30 and the final dramatic days of Boston's mayoral election. The stated purpose of the commission, for which no funding was appropriated, was to review "all aspects of a prospective summer Olympics in the Commonwealth" with a focus on requirements and impacts in the areas of (1) infrastructure, (2) transportation, (3) tourism, (4) lodging, (5) location for events (venues), (6) costs, and (7) benefits.[8]

Massachusetts's wealth of universities and think tanks meant that State House leaders could choose from a long list of professors and academics with the experience and expertise to weigh the costs and benefits of a potential bid, as was called for in the resolution. In fact, Massachusetts was home to noted economists whose research focused specifically on the impacts of sporting mega-events. One of these economists, Professor Victor Matheson of the College of the Holy Cross in Worcester, proactively reached out to the commission and volunteered to serve. Another, Andrew Zimbalist at Smith College in Northampton was contacted by his state senator, Stan Rosenberg (a powerful figure who was in line to become the next senate president). After receiving Zimbalist's blessing, Rosenberg submitted the professor's name to Governor Patrick for consideration. Either Matheson or Zimbalist would have been a logical choice for inclusion if the governor were looking for a balanced and serious assessment. Zimbalist had written a bookshelf's worth of books and studies on the economics of sports and had examined the International Olympic Committee's business model closely. Matheson had authored a score of peer-reviewed academic articles on sporting mega-events and had conducted econometric studies assessing the true economic impact of hosting an Olympic event. Another logical choice would have been Judith Grant Long, an urban planning professor at Harvard University, who was a leading scholar on sports facilities and economic development and was working on a manuscript on the Olympics and urban design. Zimbalist recommended her to Senator Rosenberg. Despite their expertise and eagerness to serve on the commission, not one of the three scholars was asked to serve.

Instead, the appointees to the commission were a cast of characters whose qualifications had more to do with their political connections and ties to the tourism and construction industries than their economic knowhow. Among them were State House political staffers and the CEO of Boston's Duck Boats, made famous for parading the city's professional athletes down Boylston Street after championship victories (the Red Sox championship parade that year was Saturday, November 2). Appointees also included the sports agent Stephen Freyer (the bid leader who had won Mayor Flynn's support in 1992), Dan O'Connell (a former secretary of economic development for Governor Patrick who later had been hired by John Fish to run the Massachusetts Competitive Partnership), state senator Donoghue (who had supported the 2024 bid from its early days), and John Fish himself, who became the commission's chairman. Thus, while the commission's stated goal was to study the feasibility of a bid, it also served another purpose: demonstrating to the USOC that Fish and his allies could successfully pull the levers of power in state and local government—a necessary precondition to advancing an Olympic bid.

Boston voters went to the polls on November 5, 2013, and handed Marty Walsh a slim electoral victory. By then, Fish and his allies in the political and business communities were artfully executing the early stages of the traditional Olympic booster playbook: leaking to the media venue possibilities that conjured images of world-class athletes competing in locations familiar and famed (such as Fenway Park and Harvard Stadium), promising that with careful planning Boston's Games would avoid the issues of cost overruns and white elephants that had plagued prior host cities, and pitching the bid as a "once-in-a-lifetime" opportunity to think big about the city's future and to upgrade its infrastructure. Among those Fish had recruited to the effort were Mitt Romney, former Massachusetts governor and organizer of Salt Lake City's 2002 Winter Games, who spoke hopefully about the idea on a visit to NBC's *Meet the Press*; Ed Davis, the former Boston police commissioner, who had gained acclaim for his response to the 2013 Boston Marathon bombings; and Robert Kraft, the dapper owner of the New England Patriots. In a front-page *Boston Globe* story, perfectly timed to appear in the slow news cycle that followed the captivating and exhausting city election, Romney, Davis, and Kraft all praised the idea of a bid, while Fish outlined his approach to the civic effort that might ultimately bring the Games to Boston: "It has to be done thoughtfully. It has to be based on analytics. It has to be slow and deliberate. It has to be done with consensus. And we need to sit at the table and have this discussion constructively—or we'll never know."[9]

THE ORIGINS OF OPPOSITION

Marty Walsh's victory over John Connolly by fewer than five thousand votes was a disappointing loss for thirty-something Massachusetts natives Liam Kerr and Chris Dempsey. Kerr, who lived in a small first-floor condominium on the "Back of the Hill" in the shadow of the State House, had run an education-focused political action committee that had spent more than $1.3 million in support of Connolly's election. Dempsey, a management consultant at Bain & Co., had been a member of Connolly's finance committee, organizing "Young Professionals" fundraisers and canvassing efforts for a candidate he had supported since they were first introduced in 2008.

They were in Kerr's living room commiserating over the loss just days after the election when the two first discussed the prospect of a Boston Olympic bid. Although they both recently had earned MBAS, Kerr and Dempsey had public policy backgrounds and a lifelong interest in Massachusetts's civic affairs. They were eager to stay involved, notwithstanding the loss of their favored mayoral candidate.[10] Articles like the one in the *Globe* that quoted powerful boosters Fish, Romney, Davis, and Kraft alarmed the duo. A Boston 2024 bid seemed to be barreling ahead without opposition and without sober reflection, despite some glaring drawbacks and a troubling history of poor outcomes in prior host cities. While the boosters were talking about a "frugal" bid, early inklings of their plans were anything but frugal. As *Boston Globe* Olympics reporter John Powers pointed out in November 2013: "Except for TD Garden, the city would have to build all of the big-ticket venues from scratch: the main stadium (Gillette [Stadium] lacks the required track), an aquatics complex with a 10-meter diving platform, a velodrome, and an Olympic village (no, college dorms don't qualify)."[11] The boosters were also highlighting the idea that the bid could be an exercise in planning for Boston's future. Kerr and Dempsey both aspired to careers that might help shape the region's future, but they didn't see the wisdom in letting those civic plans be driven by the needs of a three-week event. That unfortunate result seemed inevitable if the IOC awarded Boston the Games at the conclusion of the bid process in 2017.

Dempsey grew up in Brookline Village, the son of two public school educators who had met in the late 1970s while teaching at the Martin Luther King, Jr. School, in Boston's gritty Grove Hall neighborhood. His father, a social studies teacher, had often shared the story of Boston's Stop the Highways movement in the 1960s and 1970s. In that proud and prescient moment in Boston's history, neighborhood groups had joined together to oppose a proposal for an "Inner Belt" circumferential highway and arterial "Southwest Corridor" highway that would have cut through neighborhoods in Roxbury, Fenway, Cambridge, and Somerville, among others. The construction of these highways had been supported by major business leaders, contractors, and labor unions, and had the strong backing of the Republican governor, Frank Sargent, a former Department of Public Works commissioner. But years of committed activism and opposition by neighborhood and grassroots groups had turned the tide—culminating in an address by Governor Sargent on live television in February 1970 in which he said, "Nearly everyone was sure that highways were the only answer to transportation problems for years to come. But we were wrong."[12] To Dempsey, the Stop the Highways movement provided hope that a "No" campaign could succeed against powerful interests—at least that had been true in 1970. More important, it was also evidence that saying "No" could have an immensely positive legacy for the region he loved. By 2013, more than forty years after its victory, the Stop the Highways movement was still seen as a dramatic step forward for smarter, better, more sustainable planning and growth. The highway naysayers hadn't stopped the city's progress—they'd defended their city from a damaging plan, and turned it toward a brighter, more prosperous future.

Like Dempsey, Kerr had grown up in the suburbs of Boston in a middle-class family. Kerr was a political junkie with an entrepreneurial mind. While he appreciated and understood the role that personal relationships played in politics, he despaired over the fact that these relationships were often the primary driver of policy outcomes in Massachusetts. Kerr and Dempsey had read the independent economic analysis that consistently found that "winning" an Olympic bid was typically a losing proposition for the host community. But Massachusetts's political leaders seemed to be letting a few powerful and well-connected individuals lead the state down this potentially harmful path.

Kerr contacted his friend and associate Conor Yunits, another Massachusetts native in his early thirties. Yunits had helped advise Kerr's political committee from his post at the public affairs consulting firm Liberty Square Group, where Yunits was a vice president. Like Kerr, Yunits was a political junkie—he had run unsuccessfully for state representative in his native Brockton, where his father had once served as mayor. Yunits had been following the potential bid's developments closely and shared Kerr and Dempsey's concerns with the strong momentum behind it.

Many Bostonians dismissed Boston 2024 as a lark. The conventional wisdom was that the USOC and IOC would never pick Boston over larger, wealthier, higher-profile cities like Washington, D.C., Los Angeles, Paris, or Rome. At a Chamber of Commerce event in June 2014, US Senator Ed Markey joked that a Boston Olympics should include condo flipping and synchronized double parking as official sports.[13] Even with powerful boosters behind it, the bid seemed like a long shot and made for a reliable punch line.

But Dempsey, Kerr, and Yunits knew that Boston had some natural advantages. Chief among them was Boston's position on the East Coast, the most valuable time zone in the world for live television events. And Boston's rivers, harbor, parks, monuments, historic neighborhoods, and stately downtown provided an appealing backdrop for television. Boston was also home to two brands whose value even Olympic sponsors such as Coca-Cola and Toyota would envy: Harvard and MIT. The IOC would salivate at the chance to associate itself with these prestigious universities. Finally, Boston's political and business communities were just large enough to rally the resources needed to support an Olympic bid, and just cozy enough that they might be able to squelch any substantive dissent. The USOC and IOC wanted cities to present a united front. These factors made Boston 2024 a credible bid to advance at the USOC level over bids from places like Los Angeles (been there, done that), Washington, D.C. (too political), or Dallas (too Texas).

Olympic prognosticators had reason to believe that whichever bid emerged from the USOC's process would be the favorite to win when the IOC voted in 2017. The IOC's single-largest source of revenue was its contract with NBC television for the rights to air the Games in the United States. Yet the Olympic Committee's premier event, the Summer Olympics, hadn't been hosted in the United States since Atlanta in 1996. Surely NBC was eager to have the Games back on US soil and had communicated that desire to the IOC in its negotiations to extend its ownership of those television rights. That deal, completed in May 2014, will pay the IOC $7.75 billion between 2021 and 2032.[14] Further strengthening a US bid's chances was a May 2012 settlement of a long-standing disagreement between the USOC and IOC about how Olympic media and sponsorship funds would be distributed. Now the USOC and IOC were on better terms. With all of these points taken as a whole, Boston 2024 seemed anything but a lark—even as early as the fall of 2013, proponents could reasonably argue that Boston was the front-runner—ahead of any city in the world—to host the 2024 Summer Games.

Some saw the 2024 Games as an opportunity to showcase Boston to the world, but Dempsey, Kerr, and Yunits saw the bid as a threat to their city's bright future. The trio zeroed in on the fundamental problem with the International Olympic Committee's bidding process: the IOC's Olympic "auction" was designed to produce bids that led to great outcomes for the IOC, but couldn't guarantee the same for the bid cities. Winning cities almost always overbid for the right to host the Games, even while Olympic boosters tried to reassure skeptical residents that they were getting a good deal on a "once-in-a-lifetime" opportunity. The three friends concluded that the exact same dynamics were at play in Boston.

Just as troubling to Dempsey, Kerr, and Yunits was the fact that the civic institutions and watchdog organizations that normally might raise concerns about a costly megaproject seemed to be staying silent. Sam Tyler, president of the Boston Municipal Research Bureau, a watchdog organization, had told the *Boston Herald* that an Olympics was "a cost we cannot afford" when Menino and Fish had first opposed the concept in March of 2013.[15] Now that powerful figures in Boston's business community were lining up behind the bid, Tyler and others in similar positions were mum. Some of Boston 2024's boosters sat on the boards of directors of these organizations and provided them with substantial funding. (For example, Fish's Suffolk Construction had a seat on the board of Tyler's organization.) Even Olympic skeptics in the business community were too polite, or too intimidated, to publicly question the wisdom of a bid. Few elected officials seemed eager to take on some of the most powerful men in the state. Opposition to Boston 2024 would have to come from the grass roots. There in Kerr's living room, Dempsey, Kerr, and Yunits decided to organize an effort to oppose the bid. They settled on a straightforward name for their effort: No Boston Olympics.

From the very start, the self-titled cochairs of No Boston Olympics knew that they would never come close to matching the resources that Boston 2024's boosters would marshal in support of the bid. The boosters would be able to hire dozens of full-time staff and a small army of consultants.

No Boston Olympics organizers would have perhaps five or ten hours a week each to dedicate to the cause, as they balanced the responsibilities of full-time jobs and young families. The bid's opponents would have to fight asymmetrically. They spent a few dollars to register www.NoBostonOlympics.org, pulled together some basic data on the cost of prior Games, and began posting stories and articles about the downsides of Olympic bidding and hosting. They also created a No Boston Olympics Twitter account (@NoBosOlympics), through which they started to engage with supporters, detractors, and those just interested in learning more about Boston 2024's bid and its nascent opposition group.

Dempsey, Kerr, and Yunits reasoned that even if they didn't succeed in stopping the bid, their opposition might force the boosters to develop a proposal that was more responsible (or at least less irresponsible). They endeavored to provide consistent, balanced, factual responses to Boston 2024's more emotional, impassioned sales pitch. As Boston 2024 tried to appeal to Bostonians' hearts, No Boston Olympics would appeal to their heads. Given Boston's long tradition of healthy, substantive civic debate, the group felt that this was a strategy with some promise.

A crucial component of this strategy was the so-called earned-media exposure made possible by a symbiotic relationship with Massachusetts's deep roster of savvy and dedicated reporters, columnists, and political pundits. The press was eager to tell both sides of the Olympic story. Reporters are taught that good journalism means seeking out comment from opposing perspectives. This provides a balanced news story, but it also has other benefits. Conflict is far more compelling than conformity: it sells papers and draws eyeballs to screens (and, thus, advertisements that support that journalism). As editors and journalists in newsrooms around the region received Boston 2024's boastful press releases, they asked: "What does the other side think of this?" No Boston Olympics was ready with answers. Yunits had strong professional and personal relationships with many members of the press and Kerr knew others from his work in politics. All three co-founders made themselves available to the media for statements and broadcast appearances. They also worked behind the scenes to provide reporters with scholarly articles and data that challenged the boosters' optimistic claims.

Boston Magazine reporter Steve Annear was the first to write about the burgeoning conflict that No Boston Olympics' Twitter engagement and website had sparked. In February 2014, Annear laid out the arguments of three different groups: Boston 2024, No Boston Olympics, and Boston 2026, a small group of volunteers advocating for Boston to bid on the Winter Games (that group would fold after the USOC's selection of Boston 2024 in January 2015). Dinopoulos, who was still running Boston 2024's social media, was dismissive of both of the rival efforts, but especially of No Boston Olympics. He told Annear, "They have 36 followers, we have like 3,000.... To be quite honest, they don't faze me at all."[16]

The outrageous $50 billion-plus price tag and the high-profile, humorous failures of the February 2014 Winter Games in Sochi, Russia, provided compelling material for both sides of Boston's Olympic debate.[17] To bid proponents, a Boston Games would be an opportunity to reclaim the Olympic tradition from the clutches of authoritarian regimes like Russia and China, which attempted to use them to project political power and control. In contrast to Sochi, boosters claimed, a Boston bid would be sustainable, frugal, innovative, and pluralistic. To opponents, Sochi was a reminder that the International Olympic Committee valued grand promises over responsible plans, encouraging host countries to shower resources on a three-week event, rather than to make sound, sensible investments that might contribute to long-term economic growth. Statements about Sochi by the IOC's president, Thomas Bach, demonstrated to bid opponents that the IOC was still unwilling to confront these realities. Bach claimed to be bringing a reform mindset to the IOC, but nevertheless called Sochi "a great success" and touted the event's operational profit (a "profit" that was only possible on paper, owing to massive financial transfers from the Russian treasury to the Sochi organizing committee). Bach's statements had a jarring incongruity with Sochi's price tag and the conspicuous waste and overbuilding widely reported by the international media.

A week after Annear's article and just four days after Sochi's closing ceremonies, the Feasibility Commission created by Donoghue, chaired by Fish, and populated by political insiders released its fifty-seven-page report. The commission's unsurprising conclusion was that a Boston Olympic bid was not only feasible but also potentially beneficial, offering an opportunity to invest in economic growth, infrastructure, and international attention that would position Massachusetts for global success:

> The Commission finds that it would be feasible for Massachusetts to host the 2024 Summer Olympic Games based upon its initial assessment that suggests that the Commonwealth fares comparatively well against many of the IOC criteria. But the Commission does recognize that pursuing a bid would be an enormous task, and that infrastructure and venue requirements would need to be addressed. The Commission does not, however, see the prior two points as prohibitive, rather, the Commission views these challenges as an opportunity to leverage an Olympics to catalyze and accelerate the economic development and infrastructure improvements necessary to ensure that Massachusetts can compete globally now and into the future.[18]

The document was peppered with facts and figures about the Massachusetts economy, the state's abundant tourism amenities, and the immense resources of its colleges and universities. It painted an appealing picture of the region—making it clear that *Greater Boston* could compete with any city in the world in the areas of business, culture, education, innovation, and sport.

Despite the explicit charge of the enabling resolution to do so, the report failed to address the potential costs of hosting the Olympic Games. It acknowledged, "an accurate estimate into the future can be difficult," but resolved, "any cost-benefit analysis or specific recommendations as to budget are beyond the scope of this Commission." Actually, costs were noted specifically as part of the commission's scope—the politically connected members of the commission had just decided that raising them as a concern or assigning to them a dollar figure would be inconvenient.

The release of the report was No Boston Olympics' first major opportunity to execute on its responsive strategy. Dempsey, Kerr, and Yunits had anticipated the commission's unwillingness to seriously address the potential costs of the Games—it wasn't the conversation the boosters wanted to have—so No Boston Olympics jumped into the void. A day *before* the commission released its report, No Boston Olympics released a report of its own that estimated the costs of a Boston Olympics at $10 to $20 billion.

The analysis wasn't very sophisticated—it simply located reliable cost figures for recent Games and adjusted them to 2014 US dollars—but it was also simple to understand and difficult to refute. No Boston Olympics found that since Sydney in 2000, the average cost of the Summer Games was $19.2 billion dollars, and the median cost was that of London, at $15 billion (though subsequent analysis showed London's costs to be $18 billion plus).[19] No Boston Olympics concluded that the Boston Games were likely to cost between $10 and $20 billion. That put the total bill in the range of Boston's infamous Big Dig, a $15 billion highway project that had gone wildly over budget and disrupted the city for more than a decade.

When the media reported on the release of the commission's report, they also injected No Boston Olympics' rough price tag—exactly the conversation the commission had tried to avoid. Alison King of New England Cable News offered Kerr an on-screen opportunity to cite economic studies that had found that the Games did not leave the economies of host cities better off. And reporter Michael Levenson from the *Boston Globe* gave Kerr the final word in his coverage of the commission's report (which, like many of the boosters' documents over the course of 2014 and 2015, was leaked to the *Globe* ahead of other outlets). Kerr said, "We don't need the IOC to give us a deadline for how to shape the future of our city and state."[20] It was an early test of No Boston Olympics' responsive, grounded, fact-based strategy—and it had worked.

"THE RIGHT PEOPLE ARE ALL QUOTED"

Boston 2024 and No Boston Olympics continued their skirmishes through the spring and summer of 2014. On June 13, the USOC created its "shortlist" of American cities, ruling out bids from San Diego and Dallas and leaving the four final bids still in play: Boston, Los Angeles, San Francisco, and Washington, D.C. A week later, Yunits and Dempsey wrote an op-ed published by the *Boston Globe*, laying out one of No Boston Olympics foundational arguments. The article began:

> Boston is absolutely capable of hosting the Olympics. Let's settle that
> question right away and shake off the moniker of "cynic" used by Olympic

boosters to describe anyone opposed to bringing the games here. With our brilliant engineers, dedicated civic leaders, and strong sporting traditions, we would build beautiful venues and run a smooth, safe international event.[21]

The acknowledgment that Boston *could* host the Olympics was important and intentional. The key question for No Boston Olympics was not "*Can* Boston host an Olympics?" but "*Should* Boston host an Olympics?" This reframing achieved at least two objectives for No Boston Olympics: (1) it dulled criticism of bid opponents as small-minded naysayers, instead positioning them as believers in a confident, capable, world-class Boston with little to prove; and (2) it reminded readers that a potential Olympics was not a competition or a lottery to be won, but rather a policy choice that must be made only after a proper weighing of the costs and benefits.

The choice to appeal to Boston's proud self-image came naturally to Dempsey, Kerr, and Yunits, but it contrasted with the message of at least one prior group of Olympic opponents. No Games Chicago, which opposed the Windy City's 2016 Olympic bid, had at times chosen to focus on Chicago's failures, predicting an inability to successfully "pull off" the Games. The group sent the IOC a book of news clippings that cataloged Chicago's "corruption, incompetence, decaying infrastructure, and more pressing priorities."[22] A similar message of the inevitability of "corruption" and "incompetence" might have appealed to a segment of the Massachusetts population. Many in the Bay State were skeptical of the close ties between the city's business and political establishment and were still weary from the Big Dig. But that segment of the population likely would have been opposed to Boston 2024 under almost any circumstances. No Boston Olympics could already count on their support. Bid opponents needed to appeal to citizens who, while they were still cautious about how public resources might be spent, didn't want to see the complicated history of the Big Dig as an excuse to never again think boldly about the city's future. As No Boston Olympics often put it, "We have to think big. But we also have to think smart."

No Boston Olympics added a fourth cochair in August 2014, when Kelley Gossett, also in her early thirties, joined Dempsey, Kerr, and Yunits. Gossett was a graduate of Boston College and Suffolk University Law School. She had worked as a staffer in the Massachusetts legislature and as a policy advocate for social service nonprofits and foundations. In early 2014, Gossett had watched an HBO *Real Sports* special on the tremendous costs borne by prior Olympic host cities and was troubled that boosters were trying to bring the Games to her city. In her job as a social services advocate, Gossett had fought hard for the legislature to pass $250,000 earmarks for family-service organizations—now it might spend *billions* on a three-week sporting event? In the summer of 2014, she was introduced to Kerr at a political event for Martha Coakley, the Democratic candidate who eventually would lose to Baker. She immediately expressed interest in joining the No Boston Olympics team. Gossett's high-energy, direct style reinvigorated the group and brought an important new dimension to No Boston Olympics. Gossett's strong state house relationships and her ease and experience working the halls of power on Beacon Hill would prove essential as the bid advanced.

But even as No Boston Olympics added the politically savvy Gossett, the powerful players backing Boston 2024 were also building strength and momentum. The indispensable man for Boston 2024 was Boston's new mayor, Marty Walsh. Walsh was a native of Boston's working-class Dorchester neighborhood, the son of two Irish immigrants. He had overcome childhood cancer and, as an adult, alcoholism, to become a union official in the building trades. He was simultaneously a state representative, representing the neighborhood in which he had grown up. Walsh was both a forceful supporter of the construction industry and a rabid sports fan. Thus, the idea of a Boston Olympics—and a potential legacy as "the Olympics Mayor"—held great appeal to Walsh. Certainly billions of dollars' worth of Olympic construction would be a boon to Walsh's union political base. Boston 2024 chairman John Fish had already pledged that 100 percent of the facilities would be constructed with union labor (although the enormity of Olympic-related construction projects would have necessitated that a good portion of this labor would have come from outside Boston and, most probably, outside Massachusetts. Moreover, the eventual Boston 2024 plan involved importing prefabricated facilities with a dubious guarantee at best that nonunion labor would be excluded). The bid also presented an opportunity for Walsh to cement his relationship with Fish and other business leaders. During the 2013 election, political pundits had argued that the downtown business community was wary of seeing a onetime union official occupy city hall. Walsh's rival Connolly had received most of the business community's support. Backing the bid seemed to ensure that Walsh would enjoy a warm reception at the chamber of commerce, where John Fish was chairman. By embracing the bid, Walsh could at once please his base, protect his political Achilles' heel, and build a mayoral legacy.

Walsh's advisors in city hall also urged him to support the bid. The administration's most prominent cheerleader for the Games was Dan Koh, the mayor's chief of staff and a Harvard Business School classmate of Dempsey. With a background in entertainment, media, and sports, Koh was predisposed to supporting Boston 2024. His support for the bid was fortified when his girlfriend and soon-to-be fiancée, Amy Sennett, joined Boston 2024. Sennett started in an unpaid role and then was hired in a permanent position dealing with strategic initiatives at a salary of $120,000. Employing those with powerful personal relationships in city hall was not an unfamiliar practice for Fish, who had put Mayor Menino's son *and* brother on the payroll at Suffolk Construction. Despite the potential for a conflict of interest, Koh was named the Walsh administration's point person for Boston 2024, coordinating the city's efforts as early as August 2014, within weeks of when Sennett joined the bid committee staff.[23]

By October 12, 2014, less than a year after his election, Walsh was "all-in" on the bid, telling the *Globe*: "I'm cautiously enthused about where we're heading. If we got chosen as an Olympic site? I think it would be a tremendous opportunity for the city of Boston in so many different ways."[24] It was Boston 2024's most important endorsement yet. The bid now had the backing of the city's most powerful business figure, Fish, and its most powerful political figure, Walsh. The resources of city hall were firmly behind the bid, providing Boston 2024 with broad leeway to develop a proposal that could beat out bids from Los Angeles, San Francisco, and Washington, D.C., and win the support of the USOC.

While the boosters refused to share many details of their plans, they maintained a consistent set of talking points: the Boston Games would be "frugal" and wouldn't use any taxpayer dollars beyond those needed for infrastructure and security; they would rely on Boston's wealth of university resources, making use of college athletic fields and dormitories; they would be compact and walkable, with "the city as the Olympic Park"; they would be a catalyst for making improvements to the city's infrastructure, especially its under-resourced public transit system; and they would leave a "legacy" of enhanced sporting infrastructure, increased tourism, vibrant new neighborhoods, and stronger long-term economic growth. The boosters pegged the costs of the Games at only $4.5 billion—a fraction of what Games had cost in Beijing, Sochi, or London. Bostonians would be getting a great deal.[25]

Boston's lengthy roster of world-class universities played a critical role in Boston 2024's pitch. A glowing Associated Press article in late November 2014 bore the headline "Boston Wants to Take Olympics Back to School," touting venue locations at Harvard, MIT, and Tufts. "The University Games," as the Associated Press called them, would "harness the resources of the Boston area's 100 colleges and universities to keep the Games affordable and compact." The article even suggested that local universities would share their donor and alumni lists with Boston 2024 to raise money for Olympic venues. One of Boston 2024's promotional videos, titled "Believe in Boston" and debuted for a USOC delegation, featured Harvard University basketball coach Tommy Amaker, Berklee College of Music president Roger Brown, Joi Ito of the MIT Media Lab, and MIT executive vice president Israel Ruiz. Boston 2024's apparent ties to the region's universities made for an appealing story to both the USOC's board members and the public.[26]

For many Boston residents, the most attractive part of Boston 2024's pitch was that hosting the Olympics would force the state and the city to upgrade the city's infrastructure—especially its faltering transit system, the Massachusetts Bay Transportation Authority (MBTA). Over the course of 2014, Boston 2024 positioned its bid as an opportunity to finally address the MBTA's shortcomings. It was a natural association in the eyes of many residents—all that Olympic construction and activity, and all those Olympic tourists, surely would require an upgrade to the city's infrastructure. For all of its faults and excesses, the Big Dig undoubtedly had improved some of the city's roads and highways. Perhaps the Olympics could do the same for the MBTA. The boosters often talked about their bid as a "catalyst" for transit improvements. As Dan O'Connell told the *Globe*: "The games will act as a catalyst. We can really upgrade the system as part of this."[27] According to the boosters, the bid would force a discussion about how to make transit improvements. Hosting the Games in 2024 would provide a deadline for getting those improvements done. A similar case was made by writer Garrett Quinn, in a widely read *Boston Magazine* piece in early 2014: "There's only one way Massachusetts is ever going to be smart enough to fix the MBTA—and that's by doing the stupidest thing possible."[28] For Quinn and others, the waste associated with the Olympics was a small price to pay if it meant the T would benefit from dramatic improvements. The sentiment was echoed widely in the message boards and comment sections of early articles about Boston's Olympic bid.

Perhaps the boosters' most crucial claim was that the Games would be financed privately: they were insistent that public dollars would be spent only on infrastructure improvements and security. But when pressed, the boosters also acknowledged that the IOC requires host cities to guarantee that they will cover cost overruns, meaning that if the Games don't go as planned, the public would be on the hook to make a financial contribution. To address these concerns, Boston 2024 touted its plans to purchase insurance that would cover any overruns and protect the public. They also asserted that the federal government would pick up the billion-dollar-plus security tab.

The back-and-forth between bid proponents and opponents continued in the press and on social media—with Boston 2024 working to generate excitement and allay concerns and No Boston Olympics reliably responding and raising questions about costs and transparency. Zimbalist joined in with op-eds in the *Globe*, writing in October that "Governor Patrick appointed a committee of 10 construction and related industry executives to investigate the feasibility of the hosting the Games. The construction industry will benefit mightily from all the contracts. The rest of us will pay the bills."[29]

Despite being the only one of the four bid cities with an organized opposition group, Boston's boosters felt that they were still the USOC's favorite. On September 10, 2014, Fish said he estimated Boston 2024's chances of winning the USOC bid at 75 percent. "I'm not in this to lose," he told the *Boston Globe*. "I would never bet against myself."[30] The boosters knew that they had a bid the USOC would find attractive and they were brimming with confidence.

But the opposition was clearly having an impact. On at least one occasion,

Boston 2024's frustration with No Boston Olympics caused its leadership to lash out. Reached directly on the phone by a *Boston Herald* reporter in late October, without the filter his public relations team normally might provide, John Fish called No Boston Olympics cochairs "grandstanders," asking, "Who are they and what currency do they have? What have they done to help Boston, and help make the Commonwealth of Massachusetts a better place?"[31] Quotations like these only proved counterproductive to the Boston 2024 cause. In this case, the *Herald* story inspired a response by *Boston Globe* columnist Yvonne Abraham, who pointed out that Dempsey had served as a Massachusetts Assistant Secretary of Transportation, writing: "[Dempsey] and his allies are young, but they have plenty of currency. And no Olympics critic deserves to be dismissed like that."[32] The *Herald* article also prompted a letter from State Senator Jamie Eldridge, who had known Gossett for many years through her work with the legislature. He praised Gossett and told the *Herald* that he was "outraged" by Fish's remarks.[33] The boosters had tried to diminish No Boston Olympics, but lashing out had only elevated the opposition's standing in the debate.

No Boston Olympics also made its case directly to the USOC's board members. The group mailed them collections of newspaper articles and added their email addresses to No Boston Olympics' email list, so that the members received regular updates on the opposition's activities. Dempsey personally and politely reached out to USOC board members Whitney Ping and Angela Ruggiero, both former Olympians, with whom he had friends in common. Ruggiero ignored Dempsey's outreach. Ping declined a conversation, citing a "conflict of interest," but forwarded Dempsey's email to the USOC's chief bid officer, Chris Sullivan. Sullivan never responded to multiple requests from No Boston Olympics to meet with the USOC.

That fall's arguments crystallized in a *Boston Globe*–sponsored debate on December 8, 2014, between Dempsey and Juliette Kayyem, a Boston 2024 executive committee member. Kayyem had been a Democratic gubernatorial candidate earlier in the year and was an experienced debater. But she had difficulty making the case that the Games would be good for Boston. As MassLive's Garrett Quinn wrote, "[Kayyem] struggled mightily when repeatedly confronted by [Dempsey] on the negatives of hosting the games in Boston. The bulk of the forum had Kayyem on the defensive as Dempsey referenced over and over the white elephants and headaches that have been left behind in previous Olympic host cities around the world with the notable exception being Barcelona in 1992."[34] (MassLive would have done well to reference Los Angeles in 1984 as well.) At multiple points in the debate, Kayyem unintentionally reinforced perceptions of the organizing committee as an elite, insular group that felt little need to incorporate public opinion into its plans for the city. In one instance, Kayyem questioned Dempsey's understanding of the Olympic process, stating flippantly, "I have been to five Olympics, I don't know if you've been to any." No Boston Olympics supporters in the crowd chortled and Dempsey pounced, asking whether the implication was that those who hadn't been to an Olympics shouldn't have the right to have an opinion on whether they were right for Boston. Later, Kayyem defended Boston 2024's efforts at transparency by indicating that its well-orchestrated stories in the *Globe* were sufficient, saying, "There seems to be a front-page story on it in the *Boston Globe* where the right people are all quoted." The "right people." It smacked of an insider's game. But perhaps Kayyem's most stunning statement of the night was that she hadn't read the bid herself. Dempsey noted that the bid already had been approved by Mayor Walsh and submitted to the USOC but wasn't available for review by the public or the media. "So who *has* read the bid?" he asked.

BETRAYAL AND REINFORCEMENT

The *Globe* debate had shown that No Boston Olympics could hold its own against the bid's boosters. But behind the scenes, the bid's opponents were preparing for a major public setback. Hours before the debate, cofounder Conor Yunits had informed Dempsey, Gossett, and Kerr that he would be dropping his affiliation with No Boston Olympics and would announce support for the Boston 2024 bid in an interview with *Boston Globe* columnist Shirley Leung. Leung's column laid out Yunits's reasons for his conversion: that No Boston Olympics had successfully forced the bid to be more transparent, that the more he learned about the bid the more he liked it, and that Mayor Walsh's forceful support gave Yunits confidence that costs would be kept in line. It wasn't the most convincing case. Leung sensed that the conversion had occurred under pressure. "So who got to you, Conor?" she asked rhetorically.[35] Though Yunits declined to admit it publicly, it was clear to his former cochairs that his decision had more to do with personal preservation than with any substantive improvements to the bid or the bidding process. Yunits was a political professional whose paycheck depended on having good relationships with city hall. By opposing the mayor and the city's biggest power brokers on their signature initiative, Yunits, a father of two young daughters, put his livelihood at risk. Yunits's flip was a calculated maneuver—whether the bid died or advanced at the USOC level and no matter his view of the merits of the proposal, Yunits believed he would be better off if he sided with the boosters. Indeed, Yunits had informed his cochairs of his decision to convert only a few days after his attendance at Mayor Walsh's holiday party.

But while No Boston Olympics was losing a cofounder, it was gaining more allies committed to fighting the bid. They came in the form of another group of grassroots organizers that would eventually come to be known as No Boston 2024. The group's leaders were Robin Jacks and Jonathan Cohn, residents of Boston's Jamaica Plain and Fenway neighborhoods, respectively, who had backgrounds in progressive and antiestablishment political organizing. Jacks and Cohn could be brash and unyielding on Twitter and other social media, but they were also adept at rallying support from socially conscious, progressive citizens, many of whom lived in neighborhoods of Boston such as Jamaica Plain or across the Charles River in the cities of Cambridge and Somerville. No Boston 2024 became the first group—on either side of the debate—to hold a public meeting on the Boston 2024 bid. In November 2014, they met in the hallway (they couldn't afford to rent the main hall) of a community church in Jamaica Plain, asking attendees for cash contributions to cover the $75 rental fee.

No Boston 2024 worked to raise public consciousness about some of the social costs associated with hosting the Olympics. They partnered with the ACLU's Kade Crockford, a Boston resident and native, to highlight the erosion of civil liberties that inevitably accompanied the billions spent on security in conjunction with the Games. They worked with Cassie Hurd of the Boston Homeless Solidarity Committee to draw attention to the sad history of how previous Olympic Games have caused the displacement of residents to make way for Olympic venues and to sanitize the city before its appearance on the world stage. Atlanta, for example, had displaced the residents of two low-income neighborhoods and then purged the streets of homeless in the days leading up to the 1996 Games there. Rio engaged in an urban cleansing project for the 2014 World Cup and 2016 Olympics that has resulted in the displacement of over seventy thousand favela residents from their homes. Jacks was adept at tapping into a network of activists not just in Boston but around the world—for example, she arranged for Dave Zirin, a progressive sportswriter for the *Nation* and a fierce critic of the IOC, to give a well-attended talk at a meeting hall in Jamaica Plain. The fastidious Cohn later would prove particularly effective at filing complicated Massachusetts Public Records Law requests with public agencies, forcing them to hand over emails and other documents that provided insight into Boston 2024's dealings with city and state officials.

No Boston Olympics welcomed these needed reinforcements, but also saw good reason to keep them at arm's length. Jacks had been an outspoken member of Boston's Occupy Wall Street effort, a movement that was broadly unpopular with moderate and conservative voters in the region. This unpopularity reached a fever pitch in January 2015, when former members of Occupy Boston chained themselves to concrete-filled barrels placed on Interstate 93, one of Boston's major highways, causing immense disruption to the city on a busy work day. No Boston Olympics leaders breathed a sigh of relief when they learned that those protesters had no direct ties to No Boston 2024. But the potential to be associated with radical, disruptive activities like shutting down a highway made the leaders of No Boston Olympics anxious. If the public perceived Olympic opponents as the same people who would occupy Boston or shut down a highway, Boston 2024's opposition would be doomed to fringe status. No Boston Olympics made the decision early on not to incorporate these new allies into their group, but instead to encourage them to work as a separate entity. That way, No Boston Olympics could disavow and distance themselves from any action these activists might take that would be counterproductive to the organization's efforts.

But as the months went on, the two groups developed a trusting partnership. Jacks and Cohn proved to be reasonable and level-headed leaders of their own grassroots movement. No Boston 2024 would form a loose but influential coalition with the more centrist, establishment-oriented No Boston Olympics. The existence of separate organizations enabled the creation of two unique opposition brands with distinct but complementary tactics. The *Globe* debate between Dempsey and Kayyem provided a good example: while the business-suit-clad Dempsey faced off with a Boston 2024 executive committee member inside, No Boston 2024 protested the bid outside, wielding megaphones and homemade signs. Later, in 2015, No Boston Olympics was eager to cultivate a relationship with Mayor Walsh and his team at city hall. That ruled out tactics such as filing public records requests, which would have antagonized the mayor and his staff. No Boston 2024, in contrast, took a much more aggressively contrarian approach to the Walsh administration. They were free to file requests that forced city hall to make public hundreds of emails, while they relentlessly critiqued Mayor Walsh and the administration on social media. This two-pronged attack had grown out of No Boston Olympics' fear of association with the more radical No Boston 2024, but had the unintended result of broadening the tactics available to Olympic opponents and enhancing the effectiveness of both groups.

In the six weeks between No Boston 2024's first meeting in Jamaica Plain and the USOC decision on January 8, 2015, the two groups pestered Boston 2024 and the USOC with an assortment of demonstrations, op-eds, letters to USOC officials, and media interviews. The groups' public relations efforts were aimed at poking holes in Boston 2024's narrative, raising concerns about costs, and asking for a more transparent, more democratic selection process. No Boston 2024's grassroots energy had given Boston's opposition movement new strength.

BEHIND CLOSED DOORS

Boston 2024's refusal to hold public meetings or solicit public input was a significant source of frustration, distrust, and skepticism both for members of the Boston media and for bid opponents. At various points, the boosters had indicated that they intended to hold meetings; in June 2014, the Walsh administration had said: "We intend to engage Boston residents, businesses, and community and neighborhood groups as we begin to discuss what it could mean for our neighborhoods and region."[36] That same month, John Fish had said his next step in the bid process was "to begin a series of community meetings across the Commonwealth to gather information and solicit feedback."[37] But no summer meetings materialized. Then, in October, Fish told the *Boston Globe* that public meetings would be held in November.[38] Then on November 21, Walsh said on WGBH Boston Public Radio that Boston 2024 was putting together plans for citizens to have input on the bid before the USOC decision in January. But the fall or early-winter meetings never materialized either. The bid committee didn't hold a single public meeting until after the bid was submitted and the USOC decision was made.

Observers later would label the decision to forgo these meetings as political malpractice on the part of Fish and Walsh. But surely these bid leaders knew that the appearance of avoiding public meetings created significant political risk, reinforcing a growing narrative that the bid was being driven by an elite and connected group with special access to city hall. The decision provided bid opponents with an effective and straightforward talking point that helped undermine public trust: a bid that would have immense impact on Boston was being developed behind closed doors.

It's safe to say that Fish and Walsh, and their political advisors, would have preferred to hold at least a few perfunctory public meetings to dull this attack. But USOC leaders in Colorado Springs had told Boston's boosters that public meetings were unwelcome. To USOC chairman Larry Probst and CEO Scott Blackmun, public meetings must have felt like an unnecessary hazard, one that would give a vocal opposition group such as No Boston Olympics a platform for dissent. And public meetings in Boston would only draw more attention to the fact that the bids in all four cities were being kept secret (the bids endorsed by the mayors of San Francisco and Washington, D.C., still have not been made public as we write in August 2016). As long as each city's mayor supported the bid, the USOC saw no need for additional public process at that early stage.

Fish and Walsh knew that holding public meetings against the USOC's will would effectively mean the end of Boston 2024's bid. To advance to the next round of competition, they needed to prove to the USOC leadership that they could be trusted to follow orders from Colorado Springs. After all, the USOC's process in 2013 and 2014 was really just a trial run for the far more demanding bidding process the IOC would administer. (The selection of the US entry in early 2015 would be followed by two years of competition among prospective host cities from around the globe, culminating in a final decision by the IOC in September 2017.) The Boosters' Dilemma had reared its head. What the Olympic movement wanted—in this case an opaque and secretive bidding process—was inconsistent with the expectations and demands of Boston's residents, who like to be heard from early and often on policy matters. The content of the bid aside, it was all too clear to bid opponents that by refusing to hold public meetings, Boston's boosters already were placing the USOC's priorities over those of the city's residents.

Another key concern for the USOC was the prospect of a ballot initiative that might block the Games. Over recent years, many Olympic bids have been put to public vote. More often than not, citizens vote down the "honor" of hosting the Games. The International Olympic Committee has become so fearful of public referenda that it now actively pressures bid cities not to conduct them. One can't blame the IOC—they want to avoid the embarrassment of yet another democratic city dropping out of their auction process. Indeed, the very notion that bidding is worth a vote, to be made after a careful and clearheaded weighing of the pros and cons, is entirely inconsistent with the IOC's preferred message—that bidding is a "competition" or a "race" to be won by the best bid from the most worthy city.

Here, too, the USOC had given Walsh and Fish their marching orders. On December 11, Walsh told WGBH reporter Adam Reilly that no public referendum was needed: "I don't necessarily think we need a vote on it. There will be a lot more dialogue if we get to the next round."[39] The unredacted bid documents released just days before the demise of the bid, in July 2015, showed that the USOC put the question of a referendum directly to each of the bid committees: "Could you be forced into a referendum by opponents to the bid? If so, what would the legal implications be if the referendum were negative?" Boston 2024's answer was telling—it downplayed the possibility that No Boston Olympics or another group could

Recent Olympic Referenda

CITY	YEAR OF GAMES	YEAR OF VOTE	SUPPORT BID (%)	OPPOSE BID (%)
Hamburg	Summer 2024	2015	48	52
Kraków	Winter 2022	2014	30	70
Oslo*	Winter 2022	2013	55	45
Munich	Winter 2022	2013	48	52
St. Moritz and Davos	Winter 2022	2013	47	53
Vancouver	Winter 2010	2003	64	36
Bern	Winter 2010	2002	21	79

Sources: Based on the following articles (listed by city). Hamburg: Justin Huggler, "Hamburg Withdraws Bid to Host 2024 Olympics," *Telegraph,* November 30, 2015, www.telegraph.co.uk/news/worldnews/europe/ germany/12025211/Hamburg-withdraws-bid-to-host-2024-Olympics.html; Kraków: David Wharton, "Krakow, Poland, Says No to Bidding for 2022 Winter Olympics," *Los Angeles Times,* May 26, 2014, www.latimes.com/ sports/sportsnow/la-sp-sn-bidding-for-2022-winter-olympics-20140526-story.html; Oslo: Gwladys Fouche, "Oslo Votes to Bid for 2022 Winter Games," Reuters, September 10, 2013, www.reuters.com/article/us -olympics-norway-referendum-idUSBRE98907M20130910; Munich: Karolos Grohmann, "Munich 2022 Games Bid Ruled Out by Referendum Loss," Reuters, November 10, 2013, www.reuters.com/article/us -olympics-munich-idUSBRE9A90FH20131110; St. Moritz and Davos: Brian Homewood, "St. Moritz and Davos Winter Games Bid Rejected by Public," Reuters, March 3, 2013, www.reuters.com/article/us-olympics-swiss -idUSBRE9220CK20130303; Vancouver: "Vancouver Votes Back Bid for Olympics," *New York Times,* February 24, 2003, www.nytimes.com/2003/02/24/sports/olympics-vancouver-voters-back-bid-for-olympics.html.

*Oslo later would drop the bid in the face of significant political and public opposition in the Norwegian city. The Stockholm city council voted to drop the Swedish city's bid to host the 2022 Winter Games in January 2014.

marshal the resources needed to get a question placed on the ballot, and pointed out that the boosters would be able to challenge the referendum process and potentially file lawsuits against it. Once again, the USOC was hearing what it needed to hear from Boston's boosters—in this case, that they would steamroll any opposition and do everything in their power to prevent citizens from having a vote on the bid.

Thus the USOC's due diligence on each city's prospective bid was about much more than venue locations or plans for the opening ceremonies. It was also about testing the leadership behind the bid—namely bid chairman John Fish and Mayor Walsh. Could the leaders of the bids be trusted to meet the exacting requirements of the IOC? Would they pledge to meet all of the IOC's demands—not just in terms of venue construction but also a pledge of taxpayer backing for cost overruns and revenue shortfalls? Would they adhere to a secretive process that kept details of the bids out of public view until after the decision had been made? Would they agree to block a potential referendum on the Games? It was all a test—and both Boston 2024's chairman and the mayor of Boston were passing with flying colors.

On December 1, Boston 2024 submitted its bid book to the United States Olympic Committee. The text of the bid itself, signed by Fish and Boston 2024 CEO Dan O'Connell, described Mayor Walsh as an "ardent advocate" of the bid. Walsh's unbridled support was reiterated in two other documents that held the mayor's signature and were included in the bid package. The first was a joinder agreement (discussed below) between the City of Boston and the USOC, spelling out the terms of the relationship between the two entities should the USOC select Boston 2024. The second was a letter from Walsh to USOC CEO Scott Blackmun written on October 24, 2014. The letter indicated that Walsh had "reviewed the most recently available Host City Contract," was "cognizant of what responsibilities a 2024 designation would entail," and confirmed his support for the overall bid.[40] Neither the Boston city council nor the state legislature had endorsed the bid. Not more than a handful of Bostonians had even been granted the opportunity to read it. Nonetheless, Boston 2024's private bid documents had become "Boston's" bid.

The documents and the accompanying joinder agreement had been signed by Mayor Walsh, but neither the Walsh administration, nor Boston 2024, nor the USOC were willing to share "Boston's bid" with the public or media. When No Boston Olympics publicly asked Mayor Walsh to tell Boston 2024 to make the bid available, his spokesperson responded evasively and lamely, issuing a statement that said: "Boston 2024 is the driving entity behind the Olympic bid. At every step, Mayor Walsh has encouraged a robust public process, and we know that the Boston 2024 committee will make the bid public when appropriate."[41] And the boosters certainly weren't eager to share the bid. With Walsh steadfastly at their side, Boston 2024 felt immune to any public pressure the opponents might muster. The bid documents would remain secret.

Despite the immensity of the decision to submit a bid, Mayor Walsh and his team clearly had not engaged very deeply on the subject matter. (In fact, Mayor Walsh later would say that he hadn't read the bid before signing off on it.) Jim Braude and Margery Eagan's November interview with Mayor Walsh on Boston Public Radio, less than two weeks before the bid would be submitted, had been revealing. "We're working on the contracts to make sure the safeguards are in there so we aren't picking up the tab. I've made it perfectly clear to the USOC . . . I was given guarantee from them that there was no obligation. That was from the past. When you look at the Olympics bids in the United States—the cities that's [sic] hosted it. I'm not aware of any United States city that's actually lost money on an Olympic bid . . . on having an Olympic Games in their city," Walsh said.[42] The statement was one inaccuracy built on another. First, the USOC very clearly was requiring the City of Boston to bear responsibility for cost overruns—it was a fundamental part of the IOC's host city contract, a contract that Walsh's letter to Blackmun had said the mayor had reviewed. Second, Olympic bids in the United States *had* placed significant costs on taxpayers—for when it comes to hosting Olympic games, there is no such thing as American exceptionalism.

Since 1980, the United States has hosted four Olympic Games. Each of these had cost overruns, and only Los Angeles, in 1984, did not rely on significant support from taxpayers. Organizing committees in Lake Placid 1980, Atlanta 1996, and Salt Lake City 2002 all relied on substantial infusions of public dollars. In the case of Lake Placid, the State of New York had to step in after the Games had ended to stave off bankruptcy by the bid committee. New York State purchased the venues from the committee at inflated prices, allowing the group to close out its books quietly, but leaving state taxpayers with a bevy of overbuilt venues that would need public funds for ongoing maintenance. If Mayor Walsh or his team had conducted a simple Google search for "Lake Placid overrun 1981" they would have found that the first result was a *New York Times* article that clearly laid out these facts.[43]

Despite this and other clear evidence to the contrary (see chapter 11), the statement that US cities didn't lose money on their Olympics was a popular refrain for Boston 2024 and its boosters. Boston 2024 CEO Dan O'Connell often used this talking point. "Every game that's been held in the US, winter or summer—that's Salt Lake City, Los Angeles, Atlanta, Lake Placid—have been cash flow positive," he told Fox 25 on December 2.[44] That Walsh and O'Connell would stick so blithely to these inaccurate assertions made it clear to No Boston Olympics that one of two things were true about the mayor and Boston 2024: (1) either they hadn't done much research on prior bids, or (2) they were willing to overlook inconvenient facts to advance their bid. Neither possibility was very flattering.

On December 16, Mayor Walsh led a delegation of boosters and public officials to make Boston 2024's pitch to the USOC's Board of Directors. The meeting was held at the headquarters of videogame maker Electronic Arts (EA), in Redwood Shores, California, in Silicon Valley. EA's chairman was Larry Probst, who also served as chairman of the United States Olympic Committee. The delegation included Walsh, Fish, Koh, UMass-Boston chancellor Keith Motley, Paralympian and Boston Marathon champion Cheri Blauwet, and David Manfredi, a Boston-based architect whose firm was being paid to lead much of the design work behind the bid.

Because the meeting was held behind closed doors, we can't know all the details of what was said. But thanks to Public Records Law requests by No Boston 2024's Jonathan Cohn and the *Boston Examiner*'s Andrew Quemere, the public now has a copy of Mayor Walsh's prepared remarks, written by his speechwriter Eoin Cannon. (The Public Records Law request also revealed that Boston 2024 staff members were given the opportunity to provide input on Walsh's remarks before they were finalized.) After some stirring words about Mayor Walsh's interaction with Boston schoolchildren, Walsh mentioned the opposition to the bid. "I've spent my life building bridges between communities—on the front lines, standing up against things that were wrong," he said. "I know what community opposition looks like. I don't dismiss it lightly. So believe me when I tell you, we don't have real opposition in Boston. . . . The people of Boston are ready, and we are united. We are united today; we will be united behind the US bid; and we will be united in 2024."[45]

It was an important sentiment to share with the USOC, but it didn't express the reality back home. The week before, the bid committee's continued refusal to share even basic details of the bid had motivated a vote by the Cambridge city council to actively oppose the Boston 2024 bid. Cambridge was Boston's neighbor across the Charles River, the home of Harvard University and MIT, and the proposed home of some Boston 2024 events. Young, ambitious city councilors Nadeem Mazen and Leland Cheung had led the charge there, with Mazen appearing in a No Boston Olympics web video and Cheung personally writing an email to USOC officials sharing the news that the council had opposed the bid.

Reports from USOC sources later would reveal that of all four US cities under consideration, public polling showed that Boston had the lowest levels of support and the highest levels of opposition. Support in Boston was in the 50s at best. Los Angeles, by contrast, had multiple polls that showed support in the high 70s. Contrary to Walsh's words, Boston was far from united in support of Boston 2024's bid.[46]

As Walsh delivered his hopeful remarks inside, No Boston Olympics stuck to its responsive media strategy on the sidewalk outside Electronic Arts headquarters. The group hired people from Craigslist and the "gig" website Task Rabbit to create what it called a "pop-up billboard" outside the meeting. The large, black-and-white sign, printed at a local FedEx, said simply "No Boston Olympics" and included the group's website URL. The stunt would be mentioned in national stories about the bid process as the USOC neared a decision. It cost No Boston Olympics a grand total of $400—by far the group's single largest expenditure to date.

Boston was destined to be America's bid.

MAYOR MARTY WALSH, USOC/BOSTON 2024 PRESS CONFERENCE, JANUARY 9, 2015

THREE

JANUARY 2015

On Monday, January 5, 2015, the USOC announced that January 8 would be the day its board of directors would finally crown either Washington, D.C., San Francisco, Los Angeles, or Boston as "the United States' bid." The board would convene in a conference room at the mammoth Denver International Airport, an eighty-minute drive up Interstate 25 from the USOC's longtime headquarters in Colorado Springs. Denver International was one of the country's busiest airports. It offered direct, nonstop flights to all four of the prospective cities. That meant that Olympic officials could hop on a plane as soon as a decision was made and arrive with plenty of time to attend a morning press conference with the victorious boosters.

January 8, 2015, also happened to be the date of governor-elect Baker's inauguration. To No Boston Olympics' leaders, this could be a signal that their work had paid off and that Boston 2024 already had been ruled out: surely the USOC knew better than to upstage the new governor on his big day. Even a rudimentary analysis of Massachusetts's political landscape would conclude that Baker's support would be a *sine qua non* for a successful Boston bid. Boston was New England's most prominent city, but it was still far too small demographically, geographically, and economically to host the Games on its own. With a population of 650,000 packed into just forty-eight square miles, Boston was only the twenty-fourth most populous municipality in the United States, smaller than Memphis or El Paso. The city's budget in fiscal 2015 was a mere $2.7 billion, a fraction of what hosting the Olympics would cost. (By contrast, the Commonwealth of Massachusetts's fiscal 2015 budget totaled more than $36 billion.) Most "Bostonians" don't actually live in Boston, but in one of the dozens of cities and towns that surround Boston proper, places like Cambridge (population 105,000), Somerville (population 78,000), and Brookline (population 59,000), all of which had been rumored as potential hosts for some of the myriad Olympic events.

To compensate for such a fractured municipal landscape, the state government has always played an outsized and singular role in regional affairs and large projects—from the development of eastern Massachusetts's regional water system, beginning in the 1890s, to the construction of the Big Dig in the 1990s. This state-level influence included responsibility for the funding and operations of the MBTA and all of the region's highways. This infrastructure was central to Boston 2024's logistical plans and a cornerstone of its sales pitch, both to the USOC and to the public at large. Boston's mayor might be the one to sign the bid documents, but Massachusetts's governor would also play a vital role. Upstaging the fiscally conservative, no-nonsense Baker by awarding the bid to Boston on the very same day that he would be sworn into office certainly would seem to be awkward timing for taking that relationship to the next level.

There were also signs that Boston 2024's bid was still in play. For one, Fish had not backed down from his statement that his bid had a 75 percent chance of winning at the USOC level. The boosters had done little to temper expectations. But the most prominent signal was a decision by IOC president Thomas Bach to submit an op-ed to the *Boston Globe* that ran on January 5. The piece explained the IOC's Agenda 2020 reforms to the *Globe*'s hundreds of thousands of Massachusetts readers and promised that improvements would be made in the bidding process that would ensure better outcomes for host cities.[1] Bach could have sent his piece almost anywhere—*USA Today*, the *New York Times*, the *Wall Street Journal*. A regional paper in any of the potential host cities gladly would have published the piece. Why choose the newspaper-of-record in Boston? Was Bach's op-ed a playful hint from the IOC's leadership to the USOC that Boston was the IOC's preferred choice? That was the conclusion arrived at by Olympic journalist Alan Abrahamson, writing a few days after the USOC decision: "What [the USOC] needed was a wink and a nod . . . from the International Olympic Committee. . . . [It] got that last week when IOC president Thomas Bach wrote an op-ed in the *Boston Globe* two days before the USOC picked its city for the 2024 Summer Games."[2] (While Abrahamson's conjecture was plausible, one wonders why

Bach could not simply have called Probst on the phone to give Boston the nod. Perhaps instead it was the USOC communicating through Bach, hoping that the piece could prime Boston's residents for the long slog ahead.) Knowing a decision by the USOC was imminent, Kerr and Dempsey happened to have submitted to the *Globe* an op-ed of their own—it ran just below Bach's piece and concluded, "Bostonians should cross their fingers and hope that the USOC sends the US bid elsewhere."[3]

As January 8 dawned, crossing their fingers was about the best No Boston Olympics could do. Because, ultimately, the decision came down not to Bostonians or to the *Globe* op-ed page, or even to Bach, but instead to the USOC's fifteen board members. Eleven members of the board of directors received a full vote: Robbie Bach (no relation to Thomas), Bob Bowlsby, John Hendricks, Bill Marolt, Mary McCagg, Dave Ogrean, Whitney Ping, Jim Benson, Ursula Burns, Nina Kemppel, and Susanne Lyons. According to USOC rules, the four board members who were members of the IOC were eligible to cast only a quarter of a vote: chairman Larry Probst, Anita DeFrantz, Angela Ruggiero, and Jim Easton. (According to the USOC's concise meeting minutes, CEO Scott Blackmun participated in the meeting but it isn't clear whether he received a vote.)[4] Many of these voting members had connections to Boston. Ruggiero, Ogrean, and Lyons had all been educated along the Charles River. Benson lived in Boston and had close ties to Boston's business community. McCagg was a Harvard graduate who still lived in Cambridge. Kemppel had earned a BA and MBA at Dartmouth, just a few hours north of Boston. Ping was from the West Coast and a Stanford grad, but she worked for Bain Capital, where Boston 2024 vice-chairman Steve Pagliuca was a powerful figure. This dense web of business and personal connections pre-disposed a majority of the board to take seriously Boston 2024's underdog bid—even if, as reported later, USOC staff favored the bid from Los Angeles. In fact, some of these members were communicating directly with Boston's bid committee in the months leading up to the vote. (That communication may have contributed to Fish's confidence in Boston's chances.) Bach's op-ed might have been all they needed to finally be persuaded that Boston 2024's bid was the USOC's best choice.

Back in Boston, No Boston Olympics' leaders believed they had done enough to convince the USOC to go elsewhere. It was clear that their opposition had made an impact. As the national media speculated on the USOC's decision that week, No Boston Olympics was regularly noted as an effective and engaged opposition group. Opposition had been almost nonexistent in the other bid cities. But Dempsey, Gossett, and Kerr couldn't rid themselves of doubt. Bach's op-ed made them especially anxious. It was ultimately a guessing game. On the afternoon of January 8—decision day—No Boston Olympics drafted two statements to supporters: the first announcing that the USOC had chosen Boston 2024's bid, the second announcing that the board had chosen another city. Optimistically, Dempsey loaded the latter into No Boston Olympics' email delivery system and waited to hit "Send."

Mayor Marty Walsh was sitting in his office at city hall, clutching his cellphone. The call from Colorado could come at any moment. It finally buzzed just before 6:30 p.m. Probst and Blackmun were on the other end, delivering the news Walsh had desperately wanted to hear, the call he would later say Boston was "destined" to receive. The USOC board had chosen Boston 2024. Walsh turned to Koh and said, "We got the Olympics." Probst and Blackmun then called Fish, who broke the news to the team at Boston 2024 headquarters, just minutes before the USOC's Twitter account shared the news with tens of millions of people around the world.[5]

Publicly, Probst and Blackmun expressed joy and excitement at the decision. Privately, they must have felt conflicting emotions as they dialed Walsh's number. They had wanted the board to pick Los Angeles. As Casey Wasserman, bid leader in Los Angeles later told the Los Angeles city council, "And at the end of [the 2014 vetting and diligence] process it was both the staff, the chairman, and the CEO's recommendation to have LA be the city for the USOC."[6] But Probst and Blackmun had deferred to the board, who had voted for Boston by the narrowest of margins. Boston 2024 had beaten LA 2024 by just half a vote.

Knowing the decision would arrive on Thursday, No Boston Olympics had asked a small political-consulting firm that had been involved in Connolly's mayoral campaign to lend the group its space near the State House for the evening. On the seventh floor of 6 Beacon Street, above two of Beacon Hill's favorite watering holes, Dempsey, Gossett, and Kerr were joined by a handful of fellow volunteers who had assisted the organization over the preceding months. They waited with a mix of anxiety, curiosity, and excitement—refreshing webpages, checking Twitter, and trading text messages with supporters and members of the media. Aaron Leibowitz, a recent Tufts University graduate and an aspiring journalist who had been volunteering for No Boston Olympics since November, was the first person in the organization's makeshift war room to see the USOC's tweet. "Fuck. It's Boston," he exclaimed.

The No Boston Olympics team sprang into action. The first task was to send an email to its list of supporters and media contacts—the draft Dempsey had hoped wouldn't have to be sent. Next was to field incoming phone calls from reporters and to respond to email inquiries from outlets looking for additional information and comment. Then, to coordinate logistics with news crews that wanted comment on camera that evening. Next, to arrange a series of radio and TV interviews for the following day. It was a frantic scene. At least for a few moments, the adrenaline and accompanying exhilaration overwhelmed the underlying dread. Defeating the bid had felt within the group's grasp. Looking ahead, it now felt like a hopelessly naïve fantasy. No Boston Olympics already had been outgunned and outmatched by Boston 2024's local boosters over the past fourteen months. Now that Boston 2024 was "the United States' bid," the scales would only tilt further, as national interests began to bolster Boston's boosters with resources and support. Even President Obama and the First Lady had sent their formal congratulations to Boston 2024 in the minutes following the decision.[7] No Boston Olympics had less than $5,000 in the bank, no full-time staff, and only a loose affiliation of volunteers. How could the opponents hope to compete with Boston 2024's juggernaut?

As revealed by the deluge of media requests in the wake of the USOC's decision, the Boston 2024 debate had entered an entirely new level of prominence, dramatically increasing the attention on both Boston 2024 and the bid's opponents. Overnight, the bid would become the dominant civic debate in Massachusetts, and No Boston Olympics was now the most prominent group on one side. This was No Boston Olympics' opportunity. More than a thousand people signed up to join No Boston Olympics' email list in the seventy-two hours after the USOC's decision, doubling the list's size.

The reality was that most people in Massachusetts hadn't been paying much attention to the bid or the debate surrounding it. Around the state, the USOC's decision was greeted with a mix of shock, surprise, skepticism, curiosity, and pride. Could the USOC *really* have picked Boston to potentially host the *Olympics*? How did this happen without more public debate or a vote by the city council or state legislature? What was in the bid documents that had convinced the USOC that Boston 2024's bid was better than that of Los Angeles or San Francisco? Might Bostonians get to experience the dream of an Olympic event right in their own back yard? Was this Boston's chance to shine on an international stage? What did this mean for taxpayers?

The next morning's jubilant press conference at the Boston Convention and Exhibition Center was Boston 2024's opportunity to begin to answer some of these questions. Mayor Walsh, USOC chairman Probst, and Boston 2024 chairman Fish each delivered prepared remarks, emphasizing the strength of the bid, its alignment with the IOC's goals and Agenda 2020 reforms, and their excitement at the opportunity to work together in the coming years. Governor Baker rearranged his first day's schedule to speak at the event, though he was more circumspect, saying, carefully, "Boston was selected by the USOC to be this country's representative in a global competition. . . . There will be significant opportunities for all of us to engage in a very robust and thorough debate about what we can bring to this opportunity."[8] It wasn't exactly a ringing endorsement, but Baker's participation in the press conference at least gave the appearance that Massachusetts's political leadership was united behind the bid. (The headline of a *Boston Globe* report by political analyst Jim O'Sullivan printed the following week asked, "Why is there no political opposition to the Olympic bid?"[9]) It was a triumphant moment for Boston 2024's boosters—they had cleared an enormous hurdle, and would now compete against the likes of Paris, Rome, and other cities submitting bids for the 2024 Games.

The boosters knew they had to at least pay lip service to criticisms about the lack of public input into the bidding process. Mayor Walsh pledged that Boston 2024 would be "the most transparent" Olympic bid in history and announced that the city of Boston would hold nine public meetings in 2015—one each month in nine different neighborhoods throughout the city. But despite these gestures, Boston 2024 maintained the position it had held in December: that it was under no obligation to share the bid documents it had submitted to the USOC. Defending this decision the week following the USOC's announcement, O'Connell said in an interview with WGBH's Adam Reilly on January 14 that "the documents are at this point not where we are in the iterations moving forward of where the bid's going."[10] That is, the bid documents were already outdated and thus, irrelevant. O'Connell challenged the idea that they should even be called a "bid," instead insisting they were only a "proof of concept"—a term of art Boston 2024's team would use frequently to assuage fears that key decisions were being made without public input. Boston 2024 made only one small concession to persistent media requests to see the documents: credentialed media members, under the watchful eye of Boston 2024 employees, would have the opportunity to view—but not make copies of—a redacted version of the documents for a short period on the day that the group held its next press conference. It was hard to see how this approach matched Walsh's promise that the bid would be the "most transparent" in Olympic history.

The boosters also reiterated their position that no referendum was necessary, with Walsh clearly stating at the January 9 press conference that he opposed the idea. For the boosters, submitting a bid to the IOC was not a question of "if" but "how." O'Connell told WGBH's Reilly: "There will be a lot of comments that will lead us to modify the bid as it goes forward . . . but the momentum for the effort moving forward is pretty strong right now." He was pressed by Reilly, who asked, "There's no way that the public could weigh in and say 'we don't want these Games'? . . . The outcome has been decided?" O'Connell responded, "I think it's a question of putting the best bid forward that we can as the City of Boston . . . I've sensed overwhelming support in the city for pursuing this effort."[11] Translation for those watching at home: the bid was happening whether voters liked it or not.

No Boston Olympics' cochairs were devastated by the USOC's decision. A week before, they felt they had done enough to persuade the USOC to choose another city. Now a Boston 2024 Olympics felt almost inevitable. But the group's leaders knew they needed to show they weren't giving up, despite the long odds. They decided to go on the offensive and to hold their first public meeting the week following the USOC's announcement, before Boston 2024 could hold public meetings of its own. No Boston Olympics spent $700 to rent the main sanctuary of a church in the Back Bay—it would be the group's single largest expenditure of its entire twenty-one-month campaign. Dempsey invited Professor Zimbalist to speak at the meeting, figuring he would help draw a crowd and lend intellectual heft to the group's presentation. No Boston Olympics leaders thought they might get fifty or seventy-five people to show up.

For media members who had attended Boston 2024's triumphant press conference at the modern, spacious Convention Center, the No Boston Olympics meeting must have provided quite a contrast. Boston 2024 had shown off a stage full of elected officials who were enthusiastically supporting the bid. Not a single elected leader even attended No Boston Olympics' meeting. Boston 2024 had utilized state-of-the-art audiovisual equipment. When the doors opened at the church in the Back Bay, the media found Dempsey still fumbling with a borrowed digital projector that eventually would display the group's homemade PowerPoint presentation. He got it working only minutes before the meeting was supposed to start.

Still, the January 14 event seemed to make an impact as reports on social media filtered out that the group had drawn a large crowd—more than double No Boston Olympics' initial expectations. Just a few hours before the start of No Boston Olympics' meeting, O'Connell had reiterated Boston 2024's position to WGBH—that the bid documents would not be made public. But only minutes after the conclusion of the No Boston Olympics meeting, Boston 2024 announced that it had reversed its position. The bid documents would now be made public. The boosters said they would withhold only "a limited amount of proprietary information that the USOC has asked us not to release because they believe it will put Boston and the United States at a competitive disadvantage," according to a statement by Boston 2024's executive vice president, Erin Murphy.[12] The bid—or at least most of it—would now be public. No Boston Olympics had established an important proof point: sufficient public pressure could force a change in Boston 2024's tactics.

Another encouraging development for No Boston Olympics was city councilor Michelle Wu's brave decision to write an op-ed, published January 16, that questioned the wisdom of pursuing an Olympic Games.[13] Wu became the first elected official representing the City of Boston to ask tough questions about the bid. She called for Boston 2024 to immediately release the complete, unredacted, and uncaveated, version of the documents it had submitted to the USOC. Wu also suggested a public vote in every community that was to host an Olympic venue—meaning that voters in Boston, Cambridge, Brookline, Lowell, and other communities would have a chance to weigh in. The ambitious, smart, and savvy Wu was making a principled stand in the face of significant pressure to go along with other elected leaders supporting the bid. If No Boston Olympics could encourage more activism from civic leaders like Wu, it might be able to broaden its impact.

Even as the bid was made public, questions remained about what sections of the documents would be held back and whether what was being made public would provide a complete picture of Boston 2024's planning efforts. A typical reaction was conveyed by David Bryant, of the Boston suburb Dedham, whose letter to the *Boston Globe* appeared on January 18, ten days after the USOC's decision:

> What particularly troubles me about this Olympics bid is the undemocratic
> process. How did a self-appointed group of businessmen and politicians
> get to represent "Boston" to the US Olympic Committee? What gave them
> that authority? Did the Boston City Council or Massachusetts Legislature
> vote? Was there a referendum and I missed it? Now the powers that be are
> looking for our support in what they promise will be a transparent process.
> It is already not transparent, and this is another case of seeking forgiveness,
> not permission.[14]

Like Mr. Bryant, many Massachusetts residents felt ambushed by the USOC's decision. A large number hadn't even been aware that Boston 2024 had submitted a bid in December. Others had dismissed the effort as whimsical, convinced that the USOC would pick another city that was better suited to the event. Overnight, a Boston Olympics had gone from a seeming impossibility to what now felt like an inevitability. At a minimum, the city was locked into an international bidding process that could last until September 2017. And that process was controlled by Boston 2024, the USOC, and the International Olympic Committee—not the residents who would be affected and might be picking up the bill if the Games came to town. The boosters' initial reluctance to share the bid only increased residents' skepticism and anxiety. Still, most people, like Mr. Bryant, didn't totally rule out the idea of supporting the Games. Indeed, polling indicated a majority of residents in *Greater Boston* supported the bid. Less than two weeks after the usoc announcement and the jubilant morning press conference at the Convention Center, public radio station wbur would release the results of its first poll on the subject; it found that 51 percent supported the bid, while just 33 percent opposed it.[15]

On January 21, Boston 2024 released to the public the "complete" bid documents that it had submitted to the United States Olympic Committee on December 1 (with that important caveat that some information had been kept private for competitive reasons). On local television news and in the pages of newspapers, the media shared Boston 2024's artfully crafted images of fireworks exploding over a new Olympic stadium, with Boston's beautiful, gleaming skyline in the background—the image that a billion or more television viewers around the world would see the evening of the opening ceremonies in the summer of 2024.[16] Even to bid opponents it was an inspiring scene of which any Bostonian would be proud. A Boston Olympics had inherent appeal.

The plans were unveiled at the Boston Convention and Exhibition Center to a packed room of citizens and media members. Dempsey attended on behalf of No Boston Olympics. There he ran into Evan Falchuk, who had run for governor as a third-party candidate in 2014. Falchuk and No Boston Olympics were natural allies. On the campaign trail, Falchuk had been the only candidate to oppose the bid outright. (Runner-up Martha Coakley, whose top political consultants, Northwind Strategies, were the very same people Boston 2024 had hired to advise their bid, had said "Go for the gold" when asked about Boston 2024. Coakley's campaign spokesperson, Bonnie McGilpin, would later become spokesperson for Mayor Walsh.)[17] On January 16, Falchuk had announced that he and his political party, known as the United Independent Party, would explore the idea of collecting signatures to place a question on the 2016 ballot barring public funds from being used to support the Olympic Games. Falchuk and Dempsey decided to sit together in the front row, within the line of sight of the boosters who would be speaking at the podium.

As images of a vibrant, thriving Boston in the year 2024 graced the large projection screen, Boston 2024 turned over the microphone to a series of civic and athletic stars. Fish and O'Connell spoke. Reverend Jeffrey Brown, a well-known African-American pastor who had been instrumental in the reduction of street violence in the early 1990s known as the "Boston Miracle," talked about how sports could provide hope to inner-city youth. Rúben Sança, an Olympic runner for Cape Verde who had grown up in Massachusetts, talked about how the state had helped him achieve his Olympic dreams. Sança's hometown now had the once-in-a-lifetime opportunity to host the world's best athletes. Manfredi spoke eloquently about how Boston 2024's plans for Widett Circle, home of a future Olympic stadium, would help reknit Boston's booming South Boston and South End neighborhoods, currently divided by a no-man's-land of railroad tracks, highways, and rundown warehouses. It was an impressive performance, one that connected with Bostonians on an emotional level. Boston 2024 was presenting a compelling vision for a bolder, stronger Boston.

The boosters were on a roll. They were up eighteen points in opinion polls even before the release of the attractive, glossy images of renewed neighborhoods and vibrant Olympic celebrations and they had the resources and political and civic backing to widen that lead. They enjoyed the full support of the USOC. While questions remained about just how the details of the bid would come together, they had two years to iron out any issues before they had to submit their bid to the International Olympic Committee. Unbeknownst to anyone in the audience, the meeting was to be Boston 2024's high-water mark.

Boston 2024's striking and inspiring presentation had been paired with the release of a collection of bidding documents—the ones that had been kept from the media and public for months. A press corps of mostly young, hungry journalists, including Lauren Dezenski of the *Dorchester Reporter*, Adam Reilly of WGBH, Adam Vaccaro of boston.com, Hayden Bird of *BostInno*, Kyle Clauss of *Boston Magazine*, Catherine Carlock, Greg Ryan, and Craig Douglas of the *Boston Business Journal*, Chris Faraone and Emily Hopkins of *DigBoston*, John Ruch of the *JP Gazette*, Garrett Quinn of *MassLive* (and later of *Boston Magazine*), Jack Encarnacao and Matt Stout of the *Boston Herald*, and Michael Levenson of the *Boston Globe*, were eager to delve into the documents and break some news. Boston 2024 soon would be forced to move beyond the glossy images and scripted press conferences and to defend the particulars and details of the bid it had submitted to the USOC with Mayor Walsh's blessing.

The first embarrassing bombshell was language in the City of Boston's contract with the USOC (the joinder agreement) that seemed to prohibit city employees from publicly or privately disparaging the Games, and, in fact, required city employees to say positive things about the Olympics and the bid. The key language was the following:

> The City, including its employees, officers and representatives, shall not make, publish, or communicate to any Person, or communicate in any public forum, any comments or statements (written or oral) that reflect unfavorably upon, denigrate or disparage, or are detrimental to the reputation or statute of, the IOC, the IPC, the USOC, the IOC Bid, the Bid Committee or the Olympic or Paralympic movement. The City, including its employees, officers and representatives, shall each promote the Bid Committee, the USOC, the IOC Bid, US Olympic and Paralympic Athletes and hopefuls and the Olympic and Paralympic movement in a positive manner.[18]

Observers reacted to this language, which came to be known as the "gag order," with shock and anger. Bostonians are proud inheritors of the birthplace of the American Revolution. They cherish free speech, which isn't so much seen as a constitutional right as a birthright. It all comes naturally to citizens of a region that was dissenting fifty years before the Bill of Rights was ratified.

Mayor Walsh, who had signed the document, explained away the language as "boilerplate" and pledged to have it rewritten. Nondisparagement clauses are common in legal contracts between two private parties. But, for good reason, they are rarely seen in government contracts—they are certainly not boilerplate. Any possible interpretation of the mayor's decision to sign the document reflected poorly on the city's decision-making process. One interpretation was that city hall had not paid very close attention to the details of the contract—despite it being one of the most important it would sign in years. Another possible interpretation was that city hall had understood the language, but had chosen to agree to the USOC's offensive demands for fear that rejecting them would push the USOC into the arms of a more compliant bidding group in Los Angeles or San Francisco. Here, again, the Boosters' Dilemma was at play. The high-profile revelation, which made national headlines, only exacerbated the feeling held by some residents that the bid was being shoved down their throats. It certainly seemed to be consistent with the boosters' approach to that point. After all, neither Boston 2024 nor the City of Boston had held a single public meeting about the bid until after the USOC's decision (despite those earlier promises to the contrary). And Mayor Walsh and other bid boosters still opposed a public vote outright, with his spokesperson writing, "Mayor Walsh is not in support of a referendum on the Olympics."[19] (This despite the January WBUR poll revealing that 75 percent of *Greater Boston* residents wished to weigh in on the ballot.) Even if Mayor Walsh was now insisting that the "gag order" be rewritten, the original language raised legitimate questions about the city's oversight of the bid process to date.

Next, the media turned its attention to Boston 2024's proposed venue locations. The most controversial of all was the boosters' proposal to host beach volleyball on one of New England's most revered public spaces: the Boston Common. Set aside in 1634 and now hailed as the oldest public park in the United States, in many ways the Boston Common is the figurative heart of the entire New England region. According to the Friends of the Public Gardens, a well-established and deep-pocketed advocacy group that supports the common and the neighboring gardens, Boston 2024's plan for beach volleyball required the takeover of three-fourths of the common for private use in the months leading up to, during, and after the Games. Even worse, building a temporary volleyball stadium on the common's southwest corner, as proposed by Boston 2024, meant the destruction of at least fifty trees that were more than seventy-five years old. This was sacrilege. How could Boston 2024 have conceived of the idea of disrupting such a hallowed space?[20]

The answer could be found 3,270 miles away, in the backyard of Buckingham Palace. London's 2012 Games had featured a temporary beach volleyball venue at the Horse Guards Parade, a dramatic, historic parade ground immediately next to the queen's residence. With its mix of fast-paced action and skimpy uniforms against a buttoned-up Buckingham backdrop, the event had become one of the Games' hottest tickets. But even more importantly, the outdoor, roofless, temporary venue had made for compelling television. And after all, television ratings have become by far the most important measuring stick of a successful Games. Los Angeles's 1984 Games have been praised for their financial surplus, but it was their television ratings that were most impressive. The Games had been timed perfectly for maximizing ratings, sandwiched in the weeks between the 1984 Democratic and Republican Presidential Nominating Conventions, so as not to compete for viewers. The opening ceremonies began at 5:00 p.m. Pacific Time in temperatures above 90 degrees. That wasn't ideal for attendees, but it meant the ceremonies could be aired in prime time for East Coast viewers. Roughly 24 percent of US households tuned into the opening ceremonies—more than double the number that had watched the ceremonies in Montreal eight years earlier. ABC claimed that more than two billion people worldwide watched the 1984 opening ceremonies. About nine hundred million watched London's opening ceremonies in 2012 and up to two billion watched Usain Bolt win a gold medal in the 100 meters. So Olympic bidding groups are under immense pressure to find television-friendly venues, especially for popular events such as beach volleyball. The International Olympic Committee, and the television networks that are its most significant source of funding, would have salivated at the opportunity to recreate in Boston what London had invented in 2012—a scene that could keep the eyes of hundreds of millions of viewers from around the world glued to their screens.[21]

Boston 2024's decision to put beach volleyball on Boston Common went to the core of Boston's appeal to the IOC. The city's striking skyline and historic neighborhoods made a stunning setting for live television. The beach volleyball venue in the common—the heart of the city—would be a shiny gem in the bid's made-for-television crown.

Boston's location on the East Coast also may have been a determining factor in the USOC's choice of Boston over Los Angeles. When it comes to live television events, the Eastern time zone is the most valuable in the world—commanding viewers not only across the United States (roughly half of the US population lives within Eastern time), but also in Western Europe. Daytime events that occur on the East Coast fall squarely into European prime-time television viewing. The Pacific time zone, at nine hours separated from most of Western Europe and another nine hours from markets in Asia, is far less advantaged.

The importance of developing a bid that produced compelling television was reinforced by the bird's-eye perspective taken by most of Boston 2024's glossy renderings of the Games. The reaction it conjured from Bostonians was not "It will be cool to be in that stadium," but rather, "It will be cool to watch that on television." And that made sense—at most, perhaps 30,000 or so Bostonians would actually get to attend the opening ceremonies in person—fewer than attend a typical Red Sox game. Hatched behind closed doors without public input, perfected to meet the needs of a television audience (not to address the needs of the neighboring community, which cherished access to its park and the shade of its elegant, mature trees), Boston 2024's proposal to put beach volleyball on historic Boston Common landed in the public sphere with a thud.

A third damaging revelation was that the bid documents included major inaccuracies about the region's public transportation system. Whether naïve errors or intentional misrepresentations, these inaccuracies called into question what until then had been one of the boosters' more successful selling points to the public—that the Olympic bid could be a catalyst for major improvements to the MBTA.

It turned out that some transportation projects that the boosters had described to the USOC as already-funded "planned investments" were, in fact, little more than conceptual designs, with no funding identified. Boston 2024's long list of planned improvements didn't come close to matching the reality of the state's meager transportation funding picture. Some of the projects listed in the documents, such as improvements to a notoriously congested Dorchester rotary known as Kosciuszko Circle and upgrades at the JFK/UMass MBTA station, hadn't even been included in one of the legislature's bond bills—an obligatory and initial first step in securing state funding. Boston 2024 had told the USOC that these projects were funded. In fact, they weren't even in the pipeline. Even if they were projects that had merit, forcing them through the funding pipeline now would come at the expense of other worthy projects across the state, unless new funding sources were identified.

A fourth revelation was that some owners of property slated to be taken over for Olympic venues and facilities had not been contacted prior to the inclusion of their property in the bid documents—despite claims in the bid documents that Boston 2024 was "working closely with the owners to reach a mutually beneficial agreement." Lauren Dezenski, an ambitious young journalist at the *Dorchester Reporter*, and Bill Forry, the *Reporter*'s longtime publisher and editor, were the first to bring these issues to light. It had been a logical story for the *Reporter* to pursue—the newspaper's offices happened to be located in a building that was slated to be demolished and replaced by the 170-acre Athlete's Village, according to the bid documents. Forry and Dezenski had simply called their landlord and asked if the company had been told that, according to Boston 2024's plans, the building would not exist in ten years. It turned out the answer was no.[22]

Boston 2024 also claimed that its proposal to turn over the Olympic village to UMass-Boston at the conclusion of the Games fit with that public university's master plan to transition from a mostly commuter school into a residential campus. UMass-Boston chancellor Keith Motley had been part of Boston 2024's delegation to the USOC meeting at Electronic Arts in December, so the USOC had little reason to doubt the boosters' claims. But UMass-Boston's master plan, developed over many years with significant community input, had called for adding only two thousand beds for students by 2024. Boston 2024's plan called for housing that would serve six thousand students—three times the number in the school's master plan. Financing for the buildings would be backed by student residence fees, meaning the public university was ultimately responsible for its construction. To Boston 2024's opponents, it was a perfect example of both how a host community's public priorities could be warped by Olympic planning, and how indirect public subsidies would be needed to pay for the IOC's extensive requirements.

The release of Boston 2024's bid documents also provided an opportunity for bid opponents and the media to analyze Boston 2024's proposed budget in greater detail.[23] Like many bidding committees around the world, Boston 2024's boosters broke down their overall budget into four buckets: (1) the OCOG (Organizing Committee for the Olympic Games), or the operating budget for the Games; (2) the non-OCOG, or development budget for Games' venues and facilities that would have some permanent use; (3) the public infrastructure budget; and (4) the security budget. All told, the four budgets would total at least $14.3 billion according to Boston 2024's estimates (before any cost overruns or expansions in scope)—squarely in the middle of No Boston Olympics' earlier cost estimate of $10 to 20 billion. In theory, buckets 1 and 2 would be paid for privately (a combination of Olympics revenues and funding from private developers) and, according to the documents released in January, would balance perfectly, with revenue exactly matching costs. These buckets would require a guarantee that taxpayers would step in if budget deficits did occur. Budgets 3 and 4 would be funded with public monies—they would be the direct responsibility of taxpayers. Below is a breakdown of the four budgets.

1. THE OCOG BUDGET. The OCOG budget is meant to fund the operations of the Games themselves, including everything from the torch relay, to the opening and closing ceremonies, to event staff, to IOC executive hospitality, to athlete services. Because they typically do not include major construction or anything else that is "left behind" after the Games, it is relatively easy for host committees to keep this budget in balance. When boosters point to Olympic "profits," as Bach claimed for Sochi, they typically are referring only to this operating budget. Boston 2024's OCOG revenues were to be derived from corporate sponsorships, a modest share of the IOC's international television contracts, ticketing, licensing, and an array "other" revenue for which the boosters did not provide much detail. On the cost side of the ledger, the OCOG covered games operations, transportation, support service, technology, joint-venture costs, workforce, and other costs. Because the International Olympic Committee has indicated that spending on "temporary" venues is an acceptable use of OCOG funds, Boston 2024 included the costs of significant facilities in this bucket. This was a novel approach, but also one that increased the likelihood that the OCOG would face appreciable cost overruns. The OCOG budget included a sixty-thousand-seat Olympic stadium, an aquatics center, and a main tennis stadium. All of these would be torn down or dismantled after the Games. Boston 2024's OCOG budget totaled $4.7 billion.

2. THE NON-OCOG BUDGET. Boston 2024's non-OCOG budget for permanent facilities totaled $3.4 billion. On the revenue side, the bid ominously

listed only "Public Private Partnerships"—contributions from unidentified universities and private developers who would own the permanent venues and facilities after the Games left town (in fact, the only potential partner identified in Boston 2024's bid was UMass-Boston, a public university supported by taxpayers). Included in this bucket was the Olympic village—estimated at $2.5 billion, by far the most expensive construction project associated with the bid. The non-OCOG budget also included $200 million for acquisition of land for the main Olympic stadium at Widett Circle—an unlovely parcel of land in South Boston surrounded by highways, bypasses, frontage roads, and train yards (which Boston 2024 had dubbed Midtown), $500 million for the one-million-square-foot media center, and $200 million for the permanent Olympic sporting venues it would construct: a velodrome, canoe course, BMX course, pentathlon stadium, and handball arena.

3. PUBLIC INFRASTRUCTURE. In its December submission to the United States Olympic Committee, Boston 2024 included a long list of purportedly publicly funded transportation infrastructure projects that it called "Planned Transportation Infrastructure." The boosters claimed that all of these projects were funded, required no additional tax dollars, and would be completed by 2024. This impressive list would have reassured the USOC that Olympic visitors would be the beneficiaries of billions of dollars of new infrastructure spending that would transform the city and make it infinitely easier to get around. As it turned out, many of these projects still lacked funding, and would never be built unless new revenue sources were identified. Neither the federal government nor the IOC provides funding for transportation projects associated with Olympic Games, meaning funding for any new projects would have to come from the state and local level. Boston 2024 projected these costs at $5.2 billion, all public dollars.

4. SECURITY. Boston 2024's organizers never provided significant detail on the security budget, which they claimed would be paid for by the federal government. The documents submitted to the USOC estimated security costs totaling at least $1 billion. This was a lowball estimate—the actual costs were likely to be much more—probably north of $2 billion. London

spent $1.6 billion on security for the 2012 Games and Rio is estimated to have spent $2.2 billion in 2016.

This initial budget was riddled with inconsistencies, incompleteness, unrealistic assumptions, misrepresentations, and wishful thinking. Despite proposing smaller and less elaborate facilities than in London 2012, Boston 2024 expected to best London's ticket sales by better than 15 percent (in constant prices). The bid identified no private sector companies or private universities that were expressing an interest in building the non-OCOG sporting venues, the media center, or the Olympic village. Given that the private developers of the proposed Olympic villages in both Vancouver 2010 and London 2012 pulled out and stuck the public sector with the obligation to fund the construction, the absence of private sector interest was potentially a serious and costly problem.

Most of the investments listed in the Public Infrastructure bucket lacked funding. A glittering "Olympic Boulevard" and walkway that Boston 2024 proposed to connect "Midtown" with Fort Point Channel and downtown Boston would not be possible unless a new home was found for the city's central post office—a potentially massive expense that was not included in the initial budget.

For months, Boston 2024 had promised that an insurance package would cover the public against cost overruns. Chicago's 2016 bid had done the same. Boosters there included tens of millions of dollars in insurance premium payments as part of their budget. But premium payments were nowhere to be found in Boston 2024's budget, despite Boston's boosters saying they would take Chicago's insurance model "to the next level."[24]

Many of the venues to be built had no location identified and, in order to honor a pledge not to build white elephants (which have been a major embarrassment to the IOC in places such as Athens and Beijing), many of them were to be dismantled after the Games. Boston 2024's boosters waived away these concerns by saying the December bid was just a "proof of concept" and that future iterations would iron out any details. But the release of the documents had demonstrated that the plans developed without public input had troubling flaws.

On January 24, 2015, Boston 2024 named Rich Davey as its new CEO, replacing Dan O'Connell, who had led the day-to-day operations of the bid since 2013, when Fish had first taken the reins. A former secretary of transportation for Governor Deval Patrick, the affable Davey was a well-known figure in Massachusetts political and business circles. A native of Randolph, south of Boston, and a graduate of Boston College High School (a stone's throw from the proposed Olympic village), Davey had experienced a quick rise to Governor Patrick's cabinet. He had served as the general manager of the private entity that operated the MBTA's commuter-rail system, then as the general manager of the MBTA itself for less than two years, before being promoted to be Governor Patrick's secretary of transportation—all before turning thirty-nine years of age. Davey had flourished in these roles. As a public official, Davey had led public hearings for transit fare increases, faced withering questions from legislators at budget hearings, and held his own in the face of high-stakes media scrums. He had a well-deserved reputation for being comfortable with the media and managing tough public settings—skills that Boston 2024 desperately needed. Davey was also an expert on Massachusetts's transportation system, a rhetorical linchpin of the bid. In many ways, Boston 2024 could not have picked a better leader to assuage the concerns of a skeptical public while refining a bid that fit with Boston's present realities and future goals. Fish certainly seemed to think so, saying in the press release announcing the hire that Davey had a reputation for "smart, innovative leadership and management of large and complex transportation systems and projects [that would be] indispensable as [Boston 2024] enters this next stage of our efforts."[25]

Davey and No Boston Olympics' Dempsey had worked together in the Patrick administration, were friendly, and had many acquaintances in common. It wasn't a coincidence, then, that when Davey announced in October 2014 that he would be stepping down as Governor Patrick's secretary of transportation, No Boston Olympics had tweeted this: "You heard it here first: [Davey's] next job is running @Boston2024. Already lined up, according to our sources."[26] In truth, the tweet had been a bit of a bluff. No Boston Olympics hadn't actually heard the job was lined up—but Dempsey had heard that Davey was considering it. Subsequent Public Records Law requests revealed that Davey had met with Boston 2024's representatives on multiple occasions while he was secretary, even as he expressed some skepticism of the wisdom of the bid.[27] Within hours of Davey's official hiring, Dempsey sent his former colleague a congratulatory text message. The two agreed to meet for a drink to discuss the bid.

No Boston Olympics' Dempsey and Boston 2024's Davey would keep in occasional contact throughout Davey's time at the helm of the organization, mostly exchanging text messages and phone calls. Davey, Dempsey, and Gossett met a handful of times formally, at Boston 2024's offices, and informally, at a bar in Gossett's and Davey's Back Bay neighborhood. The two sides of Boston's Olympic debate would remain cordial and friendly.

But not everyone was so warm to No Boston Olympics' leaders. In the wake of the USOC's decision, the group was facing pressure to drop its opposition. Gossett, with her ties to the legislature and strong relationships with some of Walsh's staff in city hall, was being told that she was now persona non grata at social gatherings organized by members of Walsh's team. The board members at Kerr's political organization, Democrats for Education Reform, were telling him to keep a low profile—a near impossibility as one of the cochairs of No Boston Olympics. A friend of Dempsey's with deep political ties in city hall told him that they shouldn't be seen together on the street. No Boston Olympics' leaders were being ostracized by both the political establishment and the business community.

FOUR

FEBRUARY 2015

Boston 2024 was a perfect storm for Boston's media. The story had a little bit of everything: sports, politics, urban planning and development, transportation projects, downtown power brokers, star athletes, and scrappy underdogs, all wrapped into a massive proposal that had billions of dollars at stake. Barrooms and barbershops across the city were abuzz with chatter and speculation about whether Boston could pull off the games, how much residents could get for renting out their homes to Olympic visitors, what secret deals had been struck by insiders, and how, exactly and inevitably, taxpayers would get screwed. February would add to this irresistible mix another eternal New England conversation topic: the weather.

February 2015 eventually landed in the record books as the snowiest month in Boston's history. Since record keeping began in the late nineteenth century, no single month had delivered more than 44 inches of snow. In February 2015, Mother Nature dumped 64.8 inches of snow on the region. The month would make a hefty down payment on what ended as the snowiest year on record—with more than 108 inches falling before the end of March. All across eastern Massachusetts, roofs collapsed, ice dams flooded homes, pipes froze, and streets became impassable. The brutal winter left nothing in New England unscathed—and Boston 2024 was no exception.[1]

But the month actually got off to an auspicious start for Massachusetts, with the hometown New England Patriots making a dramatic goal line stand in the Super Bowl, as rookie cornerback Malcolm Butler picked off a pass by Seahawks quarterback Russell Wilson to end what had seemed like an inexorable comeback for Seattle. The Patriots were Super Bowl champions for the fourth time in the twenty-first century. So as the snow began to fall, Bostonians were in high spirits. International Olympic Committee chairman Thomas Bach was probably in high spirits, too. He had escaped the Swiss winter to see the Super Bowl for himself in warm and sunny Glendale, Arizona. His host was NBC, the football game's broadcaster, as well as the IOC's broadcast partner in the United States. Bach had also stopped off in New York to meet with former President Bill Clinton, and visited the USOC's headquarters in Colorado Springs. There he dined with John Fish and former Massachusetts Governor Deval Patrick who, no doubt, had reminded Bach that the same state that had produced the Super Bowl champions was also one that wanted to host his Olympic Games in 2024. But if Bach had enjoyed the thrilling game, he could not have been happy with the news that came from Boston the following day.[2]

On February 2, the day after the Super Bowl, Boston city councilor Josh Zakim threw Boston 2024 a sidewinder. Zakim filed a legislative order that, if approved, would place four nonbinding, Olympic-related questions on the municipal ballot in November 2015. The first asked simply, "Should Boston host the 2024 Summer Olympic & Paralympic Games?" That was straightforward enough. But the next three questions had been artfully crafted to expose some of the important tensions in an Olympic bid. The second question asked, "If Boston were to host the 2024 Olympics, should the city commit any public money to support the Games?" The third asked, "If Boston were to host the 2024 Olympics, should the city make any financial guarantees to cover cost overruns for the Games?" These questions were destined to fail in a municipal referendum—public polling had made it clear that voters didn't want their tax dollars spent on the Games and that they didn't want to bear the risks of cost overruns.

Councilor Zakim's fourth question inquired, "If Boston were to host the 2024 Olympics, should the city use its power of eminent domain to take private land on behalf of the Games?" Zakim had noticed that Boston 2024's bid documents had contemplated the creation of an Olympic quasi-public authority vested with powers of eminent domain. Atlanta had used a similar authority in the lead-up to 1996, initiating hundreds of eminent domain proceedings to clear out existing owners and users to make room for Olympic venues and the Olympic Park.[3] But Boston's citizenry was leery of using eminent domain, especially when the goal was the type of large-scale urban renewal proposed by Boston 2024. This question was also unlikely to pass.

Zakim's filing didn't guarantee that the questions would appear on the ballot in November. In fact, they had to wend through a complicated process before they did. First, they would need to be reported out of a special committee that the city council president, Bill Linehan, had formed to handle the Boston 2024 bid. Then, they would need the support of a majority of Boston's thirteen city councilors, many of whom were strong supporters of the bid and allies of the mayor. Finally, they would need to be approved by Mayor Walsh, the bid's most enthusiastic political supporter and one who had said he opposed a referendum on the Olympic bid.

Even if the chances remained slim that they would ever make it to the ballot, Zakim's thoughtful questions gave hope to No Boston Olympics and other Olympic opponents. They opened a plausible, if unlikely, path to defeating the bid before the end of the year. Zakim was old friends with Dempsey, and Gossett was a constituent, but he hadn't coordinated with them when formulating the referendum language. In fact, Zakim smartly kept his distance from the group—he never once spoke with Dempsey, Gossett, or Kerr about Boston 2024. (However, Zakim and his chief of staff did meet and discuss these questions with Zimbalist.) He remained publicly neutral on the bid throughout the process, positioning himself as a credible, open-minded contributor to the civic debate.

On February 5, the City of Boston announced that Mayor Walsh's close confidant, Joe Rull, was leaving city hall to become chief administrative officer at Boston 2024. Rull had a remarkable personal story. His father wasn't around when Rull was growing up and his mother died when he was just seven years old, leaving Rull and five siblings to fend for themselves. Rull had persevered through these difficult circumstances. He was street smart and driven. *Globe* columnist Adrian Walker sang Rull's praises in a column that followed the announcement of his departure from city hall for the $175,000-per-year post at Boston 2024, calling him "one of the hardest-working staff members of city hall for the past two administrations."[4]

Rull was fiercely loyal to Walsh, and the Mayor pitched Rull's move as an opportunity for his administration to have eyes and ears at Boston 2024. "Having Joe in that position is a tremendous opportunity for the City of

Boston," the mayor said.[5] Rull was indisputably an asset to the bidding committee, further cementing its strong relationship with Walsh, the boosters' most important political supporter. But the hire raised legitimate questions about where city hall ended and where Boston 2024 began.

Some of Boston's state legislators were concerned about how closely city hall and Boston 2024 were tied. Two state representatives, Michael Moran of Brighton and Aaron Michlewitz of the North End, had served alongside Marty Walsh when he had been in the legislature, but each had a cool relationship with the mayor. After Walsh had jumped into the mayoral race in 2013, they had encouraged a different candidate to run.[6]

Moran and Michlewitz also had close ties with Gossett, who had worked for State Representative Paul Donato, a popular legislator in the Massachusetts House of Representatives. Gossett and the two Boston representatives occasionally shared a drink at a bar near the State House. Gossett helped persuade Moran to organize an audience for No Boston Olympics before "the Boston delegation," the state senators and representatives who represented different parts of the city of Boston. On Monday, January 26, Gossett, Dempsey, and Kerr visited the state house and shared a PowerPoint presentation that included a dissection of Boston 2024's budget. Moran later told the state house media that the meeting was "eye-opening."

A few weeks later, Moran and Michlewitz filed a bill that challenged the notion that Boston 2024 had nearly unanimous support in the halls of the state house. The bill proposed the creation of a state commission as a bid watchdog, forcing the boosters to open up their books and share records of all public and private spending on the bid. Moran explained the bill to reporter Jim O'Sullivan at the *Globe*, "At this point, I'm not for [Boston 2024], I'm not against [Boston 2024], I think we just need to take a real hard look at what this means from where we sit in state government and the fiduciary responsibility we have to the taxpayers."[7] Reached by O'Sullivan before the bill had even been filed with the State House clerk, Walsh responded in a way that revealed that he interpreted the legislation as a personal attack. "I don't need legislation to explain to me how important it is to have transparency," he said. "If we need legislation to have transparency, then we should just forgo the bid altogether." It was a prickly response, one that seemed out of touch with how many citizens were feeling about a project that had the potential to be the next Big Dig if it didn't have proper oversight. Mayor Walsh was making the case that *he* was the bid's watchdog, but the only public actions he had taken to date had served to strengthen the bid, not rein it in. His chief of staff's live-in girlfriend remained on Boston 2024's payroll. The mayor's confidante, Rull, was now on its payroll, too. Moran and Michlewitz's bill reminded residents that other than the mayor, no elected leader was really charged with ensuring that Boston 2024 was acting in the best interests of the city and state. That was a lot of faith to place in a new mayor, especially one who seemed to be backing the megaproject without reservation.

February also ushered in the exposure of some distance between the statements Boston 2024 had made about its support from universities and the reality of those commitments. The bid documents had indicated that Boston 2024 would work with "college and university partners . . . whose established fundraising programs have created endowments that are among the largest in the country, including Harvard University's $32 billion endowment and MIT's $11 billion endowment."[8] The embodiment of that potential partnership was Boston 2024 vice-chairman Steve Pagliuca, who headed up the bid's fundraising and was also the chair of the Harvard Business School Fund, charged with raising funds from alumni and other donors around the world for the business school.[9] The bid documents had listed Harvard as the home for aquatics, fencing, field hockey, tennis, and water polo—all part of an Olympic "University Cluster" with Boston University and MIT located along the Charles River.

But in an interview published on February 11 in the *Harvard Crimson*, Harvard College's esteemed student newspaper, Harvard University president Drew G. Faust said that the school would not help the Boston 2024 Olympic bid with fundraising. "We will not make any compromises in resources that would be allocated to our academic mission and of our institutional program," Faust said. Faust also denied having seen Boston 2024's bid documents before they were submitted to the USOC. Boston 2024 had pitched the bid as the "University Games," but the city's most influential university seemed to be indicating that it had made few commitments to support the effort, and that the bid had overstated the university's support.[10]

But it wasn't Harvard, the country's oldest institution of higher learning, that was grabbing headlines and shaking confidence in Boston's Olympic plans. Instead, it was the country's oldest subway. Bostonians have a complicated, tumultuous, and passionate relationship with the region's large, quasi-public transit agency, legally called the Massachusetts Bay Transportation Authority but known to everyone as the MBTA, or simply the "T." The T is one of the region's iconic institutions, as integral to the city's character and self-image as are the Boston Red Sox, the Museum of Fine Arts, or Massachusetts General Hospital. The Kingston Trio even made famous a song about the T: "Charlie on the MTA." The T is both loved—for its ability to shepherd people to work or to a game at Fenway Park or TD Garden—and loathed—for its frequent breakdowns, aging stations, and often lackluster customer-service practices. Like much of the nation's public infrastructure, the system has languished from decades of underfunding, neglect, and mismanagement. Still, it has remained one of the largest and most popular public transportation agencies in the country, serving 1.2 million trips on a typical workday. Fully a third of all workers in the city of Boston commute by transit, one of the highest percentages anywhere in the country.[11]

Even before Boston's snowiest winter in history would expose the T as a transportation system hanging by a thread, there was general consensus among policymakers, advocates, and the downtown business establishment that the MBTA needed significant attention and renewal. As the United States urbanized, millennials and empty nesters were eschewing car-ownership and choosing to live in cities that had good public transit. Massachusetts's economic future seemed to rely on "fixing the T," yet the agency was largely stuck in place. The T was caught between competing demands—on the one hand, to expand to new neighborhoods, and, on the other, to spend its limited resources fixing the system that already existed. Governor Deval Patrick had successfully delivered more resources to the T and made customer-service improvements under Davey's leadership, but he had also been frustrated by legislative reluctance to go further with new revenue sources. The system had also been set back by voters, who had approved a referendum in November 2014 that eliminated a provision indexing the state's gas tax to the rate of inflation, further sapping the state's transportation revenues. It was a sign of the state's schizophrenia—everyone wanted the T to work better, but the political conditions were not ripe to solve the problem.

Boston 2024 had positioned its bid as an opportunity to finally address the MBTA's shortcomings. But over the course of its more than two years of existence, Boston 2024 never presented a plan that, when held up to scrutiny, could credibly ensure the improvements to the MBTA for which so many clamored. On February 4, state representative Bill Straus, the cochairman of the state legislature's transportation committee, joined Massachusetts media personality Jim Braude on New England Cable News. He told Braude that he had added up the transportation projects listed in Boston 2024's bid and that they had totaled over $13 billion, more than double the $5.2 billion estimate that Boston 2024 had used in the bid. Braude had hosted Rich Davey on his show just the day before, and Davey, the former transportation secretary, had told Braude that all the projects that were needed were already funded. Straus challenged that claim. It was a clear discrepancy, and Straus, not Davey, was right. There was simply no money to pay for the long list of transportation goodies that Boston 2024 told the USOC would be in place for Olympic visitors by the summer of 2024.

The boosters' inability, or unwillingness, to articulate a clear plan would prove especially damaging to their interests as the MBTA's service ground to a halt under multiple feet of snow. The complete breakdown of the system, one relied upon by hundreds of thousands of workers and businesses, could have been an opportunity to gain support for the bid. In a time of crisis, riders might have looked to the Olympic boosters as the saviors of a system badly in need of attention and new funding. But Boston 2024 had made an early strategic decision that it would tell the public that the Games would not require additional public funding beyond that already committed. And it wasn't proposing to dedicate private resources to address the T's woes. That meant that even as Boston 2024 called itself a "catalyst" for transportation improvements, it didn't support new revenue sources that might actually fund those improvements. The boosters weren't seeking to grow the pie of transportation revenues; they were just looking to cut a bigger slice for the projects that they deemed were a priority.

Faced with mountains of snow, the MBTA shut down service on Monday,

February 9 at 7 p.m.—forcing some workers to head home early and stranding others at their jobs. The T would remain closed on Tuesday, February 10, the first time in decades that the system had shut down for a full day of service. The next day, MBTA general manager Beverly Scott, a holdover from the Patrick administration, resigned in a dramatic press conference, leaving responsibility for the system squarely in the hands of the Baker administration. The MBTA would close again all day on Sunday, February 15. *Greater Boston*'s public transportation system—a supposed strength of the Boston bid—was in disarray. Radio talk shows and Internet comment sections were flooded with residents who wanted to know: "If Boston can't handle the snow, how could it handle an Olympics?"

Just a few weeks before, Boston 2024 chairman Fish had lauded the transportation expertise of his new hire, Davey. But now the transportation bureaucracy that Davey had led just three months before was falling apart. Davey had stepped down well before the first snowflake had fallen, but, as *Boston Globe* columnist Joan Vennochi put it later that spring, "Davey's close ties to T troubles are an extra bit of bad karma for Boston 2024."[12] The number of residents who bought in to Boston 2024's initial pitch that the Games would be a catalyst for transportation improvements began to dwindle. Instead, more and more residents were questioning why Boston's wealthy boosters—who weren't exactly the type to take public transportation—were focusing on a frivolous event such as the Olympics when Massachusetts clearly had more pressing priorities.

No Boston Olympics was well positioned to exploit Boston 2024's mishandling of transportation in the bid documents and in its public messaging. Dempsey, who had been an assistant secretary of transportation in the Patrick administration, was familiar with all of the (unfunded) projects of which Boston 2024 had boasted to the USOC. Indeed, one of Dempsey's initial misgivings about the bid had been that Boston 2024 would force the reordering of transportation projects to benefit the Games, at the expense of projects that were needed for day-to-day operations or long-term planning. Dempsey had lived in greater Boston his entire life and had never owned an automobile. Like many daily T riders, he desperately wanted to see improvements, but he believed that Boston 2024 only made those improvements less likely, not more so, as the boosters claimed.

Stranded at home on February 10, like hundreds of thousands of other MBTA commuters, Dempsey sat on his couch and added a page to No Boston Olympics' website that asked: "Would Boston 2024 Fix the T?" The page informed readers that if the Games came to town, the MBTA would not receive any additional funding from the IOC or the federal government. It also reminded readers that Boston 2024 didn't support raising new revenue to improve the system. The boosters had no intention of fixing the system— and they could, in fact, make things worse, as priorities were reordered to address the needs of the Games. The explanation became one of the most popular pages on No Boston Olympics website, receiving thousands of views and hundreds of Facebook likes.[13]

The new content was representative of No Boston Olympics' broader communications strategy. The approach had a few key components. First, the organization responded rapidly. Dempsey, Kerr, and Gossett only occasionally saw each other in person, but were in near-constant email contact and could make decisions quickly. It look less than a day to develop and post the "Would Boston 2024 Fix the T?" page, so the content was fresh and timely. By contrast, before Boston 2024 could issue a statement, it often needed approval from its management, its communications staff, its political consultants, the mayor's office, and the United States Olympic Committee, all of which had different perspectives and objectives. Second, No Boston Olympics produced factual information that reinforced simple talking points, like "Boston 2024 isn't proposing to spend a single dollar of its budget on transportation improvements," or "Boston 2024 requires building the three most expensive Olympic venues." Third, No Boston Olympics used a broad range of social media tools that made it easy to share the information it produced. The organization was most active on Twitter and Facebook, platforms where the group's content and talking points were shared far and wide by supporters and without any cost to the grassroots organization.

Almost without exception, members of Boston's press were active and engaged on Twitter, and Olympic opponents dominated the platform. Here, No Boston Olympics was just one voice in a chorus. No Boston 2024's Jacks and Cohn were prolific tweeters (a later *Globe* story noted that on the day the reporter interviewed him, Cohn had sent a hundred tweets before 11:00 a.m.), and they were joined by a small army of like-minded residents who entered the fray. One prolific Tweeter, Chip Goines, told the *Globe*: "Some people tweet about their cats. I tweet about my indignation about the Olympics."[14] Goines claimed to have sent more than eight thousand tweets about Boston 2024. As the debate moved forward, bid opponents found that conversations on Twitter often could drive broader conversations in the media. For example, both the *Boston Globe* and the *Boston Herald* reported that "#PullTheBid" had become a trending Twitter hashtag in the Boston area. These stories strengthened a growing perception that Olympic opponents represented the many, while the bid's boosters represented the elite few.

But it would be a mistake to conclude that the actions of these citizen activists were limited to social media, as Boston 2024 had once claimed in its bid documents. Goines was a regular attendee at public meetings. He often brought with him a large homemade sign that was sometimes used as a backdrop by television cameras and photojournalists. Goines even created and distributed bumper stickers and t-shirts that proclaimed his opposition to the Games. Another activist was Joel Fleming, a Harvard-trained lawyer who made meaningful contributions to the so-called Twittersphere. But, like Cohn, Fleming also spent hours drafting and submitting Public Records Law requests that helped illuminate how city hall and officials in other public bodies were interacting with and responding to Boston 2024.

In contrast to Olympic opponents' success on social media, Boston 2024's efforts were often hapless. In one instance, Boston 2024 tweeted an online article with a list of "10 Best Olympic Movies." But the boosters' social media team hadn't noticed that one of the movies was 1938's *Olympia*, a film by Leni Riefenstahl, a filmmaker with ties to Adolf Hitler, which was widely viewed as Nazi propaganda. Reaction on social media skewered Boston 2024. In another instance, Boston 2024 tweeted a posting on the popular Universal Hub blog about how Boston 2024 would be a "catalyst" for getting the city's children to start eating their vegetables. Boston 2024's social media team hadn't comprehended that the post was meant as satire.[15]

The city of Boston was scheduled to hold its first public meeting on the bid on Tuesday, January 27, but a snowstorm—just the first of so many that winter—forced a move to February 5. No Boston Olympics knew the meeting would be a critical test of the strengths of both sides of the debate, one that had the potential to set the tone for the other eight city of Boston meetings that would follow. The group emailed its growing list of supporters and encouraged them to (1) arrive early, so as not to be crowded out by Boston 2024 supporters, (2) wear clothing that showed off their pride in Boston, and (3) speak about how Boston would be better off without Boston 2024. On another bitterly cold night, with lows of 7 degrees Fahrenheit, more than three hundred residents packed into a room at Suffolk Law School, a building across the street from the Old Granary Burial Ground, the final resting place of three signers of the Declaration of Independence.

As the meeting's start time neared, the atmosphere in the room was tense. Bid proponents and opponents mingled nervously in the seating area, as media members and city officials carved out spaces to stand on the sides of the room. No Boston Olympics volunteer and Somerville resident Claire Blechman led an effort to distribute signs the organization had printed for attendees, based off a template shared with the group by No Games Chicago. They read "Better Transit / No Olympic Games" "Better Schools / No Olympic Games" "Better Housing / No Olympic Games" and, simply, "No Boston Olympics." As Boston 2024's panelists entered the room to kick off the meeting, dozens of bid opponents throughout the room held up their signs, taking a cue from Dempsey, who was sitting near the front. It was a dramatic moment, one captured by the Associated Press's Charles Krupa, among other media photographers. The resulting image portrayed a sea of regular citizens proudly declaring their opposition to the bid. Boston 2024's boosters hadn't distributed signs of their own. So even though the room held plenty of Boston 2024 supporters, the image of the event that appeared in the *Globe* and media outlets around the region—and around the world—gave the impression of nearly unanimous opposition. It would become one of the defining images of the battle over Boston 2024.

January's bid bombshells and early-February's transportation failings had had an impact on Boston 2024's support. On February 19, WBUR's new poll showed that, for the first time, more Bostonians—46 percent—opposed the Games than supported them—44 percent. Kerr emailed his cochairs at 12:23 a.m., just minutes after the poll was released, using the parlance of a political pollster (or financial analyst): "Boston 2024 is underwater!"

FIVE

MARCH 2015

Boston 2024's bid had been buffeted by the winter storms and media tempests of January and February 2015. The month of March proved just as unforgiving. First, Boston 2024 would be rocked by the public release, at the urging of Mayor Walsh, of the salaries and compensation rates of its employees and consultants. Then, in an effort to reverse declining poll numbers, Boston 2024's chairman would agree to support a public referendum on the bid, officially subjecting it to the will of voters. Finally, credible reports would emerge that the United States Olympic Committee had quietly reached out to Los Angeles officials about pulling the bid from Boston and returning it to the City of Angels. These three unforeseen, deeply damaging waves would leave the bid listing, struggling to right itself as March came to end.

But as March began, Mayor Walsh was reemphasizing his full-throated support of Boston 2024 in a signature speech before one of the city's most respected civic institutions. Founded in 1932, the Boston Municipal Research Bureau was an "independent, member-supported, non-partisan research organization" with a small staff but a big presence.[1] Since its origins in the Great Depression, the bureau's mission has been to analyze the city's budget and fiscal policies, exposing threats to the city's financial well-being and its ability to provide basic services, especially public education. Each year, the mayor of Boston delivers a policy-focused speech to the bureau's members and guests. It is one of the mayor's most-watched speeches, second only to the annual State of the City address in January. Mayor Walsh chose to use this platform for a speech that *Boston Globe* Olympic beat reporter Mark Arsenault would call Walsh's "strongest and most passionate case [yet] for Boston's pursuit of the 2024 Olympic Games." The mayor brushed aside any notion that his commitment to the bid had wavered in the face of declining poll numbers. "Make no mistake, we are in this to win it: to bring the Olympic Games to Boston, along with the immense global investment and community benefits that come with it," he told the audience.[2]

Mayor Walsh's intense support of Boston 2024 did not come without significant risk, and it must have provoked concern from some of his more veteran political advisors. With the bid struggling, Walsh needed to promote it at every opportunity. His use of the high-profile Research Bureau speech to emphasize the benefits of the bid made sense. But if Walsh came off as an uncritical, undiscerning booster, he would look as if he were deserting his obligation as mayor to protect taxpayers from financial risk. As *Boston Globe* columnist Yvonne Abraham, a frequent Walsh critic, put it, "You can't be both cheerleader and watchdog."[3] The Boosters' Dilemma had Walsh performing a high-wire act.

And as the mayor and his advisors looked ahead, the timing of the Olympic process presented some troubling political obstacles. Even a year into his first term, it was no secret that Walsh wanted to run for reelection. That meant he would face voters on November 7, 2017—just weeks after the International Olympic Committee would pick its 2024 host at a meeting in Lima, Peru. Whether the IOC picked Boston 2024, or passed it over for another city's bid, the timing created great uncertainty and insecurity for Walsh's reelection prospects. Growing disapproval of the bid, and the mayor's reluctance to support a plebiscite on the issue, were the perfect opportunity for a potential mayoral challenger. Even a mediocre opponent could effectively turn the mayoral election into a referendum on the Boston 2024 bid. If support for Boston 2024 didn't improve, the bid would become a credible threat to Mayor Walsh's reelection prospects. Walsh understood how important the bid had become to his political future, and he turned to two trusted aides to help him increase support for the bid with Boston's voters. In early March, Boston 2024 announced that it had hired CK Strategies, a political-consulting firm with two employees: Walsh's senior campaign strategist, Chris Keohan, and Walsh's former press secretary, Kate Norton. With Rull, Keohan, and Norton all at Boston 2024, the bidding committee was becoming a proxy for Walsh's political operation.[4]

While Boston 2024 was hiring Walsh-campaign alumni, No Boston

Olympics was quietly adding some experts of its own. A handful of media and communications veterans pledged their support to No Boston Olympics and regularly advised the group, but asked to remain anonymous, not wanting to risk their current or future careers in the city. But others with strong ties in the political and business worlds were willing to associate themselves publicly with the Olympic opponents. On March 22, an email from Ray Howell, president of Howell Communications, arrived in the group's inbox. Howell, an erstwhile journalist, had been press secretary for Bill Weld when Weld had been an underdog candidate for the Republican nomination for governor in the 1990 election. Weld had upset the Republican favorite, Steven Pierce, and then the heavily favored Democrat, John Silber, to win the governor's office. Weld became the first Republican governor since Republican Frank Sargent lost the job to Mike Dukakis in 1974. Howell had joined the administration as Governor Weld's press secretary and communications director, then managed Weld's campaign for reelection in 1994. Weld trounced his Democratic opponent, Mark Roosevelt, in that race, winning a majority of votes in all but six of Massachusetts's 351 cities and towns. After leaving government, Howell had transitioned successfully into the world of corporate communications. He represented and advised such worldwide brands and local institutions as Microsoft, Waste Management, GlaxoSmithKline, Partners HealthCare (the parent of Massachusetts General Hospital), the University of Massachusetts, and the New England Sports Network (NESN).

For their first meeting, Howell invited Dempsey to lunch at Oceanaire, whose dining room in a converted bank on Boston's Court Street, within sight of city hall, was frequented by the city's power brokers. Howell wanted to help No Boston Olympics—he thought the bid looked disastrous for Massachusetts taxpayers, and he liked the idea of aiding another underdog campaign. He agreed to be a pro bono advisor to the group on an ongoing basis.

As chance would have it, Governor Bill Weld, Howell's former boss, was also having lunch at Oceanaire that afternoon. After they finished eating, Howell brought Dempsey over for an introduction. "So you're the guy keeping John Fish's political consultants busy!" the former governor good-naturedly joked with Dempsey. Weld, a Harvard College and Harvard

Law School grad known for his wit, must have recognized the irony—his colleagues at the white-shoe law firm Mintz Levin were among those advising Boston 2024. It was an affirming moment for No Boston Olympics—Howell's willingness to be seen with the group's leadership and to make the introduction to Weld were signs that the group was gaining legitimacy and credibility.

While Boston 2024 had neglected to hold public meetings before the USOC decision, it was trying to make up for lost time by both hosting and participating in a series of community meetings around the state. In addition to the nine meetings hosted by the city of Boston, Boston 2024 held meetings of its own, which it called Citizens Advisory Group meetings. The boosters held these meetings in Cambridge, Lowell, Dartmouth, and other places that were expected to host Olympic events or venues. Boston 2024 also participated in events hosted by others, including an eventful meeting that took place in Franklin Park.

Franklin Park is Boston's largest open space, a Frederick Law Olmsted–designed gem that sits among the Boston neighborhoods of Mattapan, Jamaica Plain, Roxbury, and Dorchester. The park is home to a zoo, playing fields, a public golf course, roads, bridle paths, and walkways. Its meadows and rugged wooded areas are tucked in the midst of the city—not unlike Olmsted's better-known Central Park and Prospect Park in New York City.

Boston's Olympic boosters wanted to use the park in the summer of 2024 for equestrian events and the modern pentathlon, both of which required large open spaces for their competitions. The plan meant giving up parts of the park to a private use for up to a year, what the *Dorchester Reporter*'s Dezenski called "a virtual takeover."[5] But in exchange, the boosters were promising long-term improvements to a vital and underfunded community resource, including an upgrade to White Stadium, the 1940s-era concrete structure that was the park's centerpiece.

The Franklin Park Coalition, a small nonprofit dedicated to serving as a voice for the diverse community that surrounds and uses the park, became the de facto convening authority for discussion about the Games' potential impact on Franklin Park. On Thursday, March 5, the coalition invited Boston 2024 to present its plans at a public meeting at the park's public golf course clubhouse. Reports from the meeting by Dezenski and others described a mixed reaction by community voices—some reflected optimism that the Games could shine a spotlight on the needs of the 130-year-old park, while others were aghast that Boston 2024 had signed up their neighborhoods for weeks of disruption without first asking for input from residents. Others were troubled that Boston 2024 proposed to turn more of Olmsted's cherished green space over to concrete for a new Olympic swimming pool and other facilities. The reactions were quintessentially Bostonian: diverse, fiercely proud, skeptical of promises from outsiders, but also willing to make short-term sacrifices if it meant improvements for future generations. Whereas Boston 2024's plan for Boston Common had been a nonstarter, its plan for Franklin Park had some promise. Though they had mishandled the rollout, the boosters had reason to believe they could win over many of the skeptics in the months and years ahead.[6]

As a curious side note to her reporting on the coalition's public meeting, Dezenski reported that former governor Deval Patrick had attended the meeting and sat in the back of the room. It was one of the former governor's first public appearances since leaving office two months earlier. Despite his prominence, Patrick went unacknowledged during the meeting, and made no public remarks or statements.

The reason for his attendance became clear the following day, when Governor Patrick released a statement announcing that he had joined Boston 2024 as a part-time "global ambassador." The former governor would represent the bid as a delegate at IOC meetings and other events around the world, lobbying the IOC's ninety-plus members to vote for Boston over competing bids from Paris, Rome, and elsewhere. *Boston Magazine* writer Erick Trickey later would report that Patrick's hiring was done at the urging of the USOC, whose leadership thought the genteel former governor would prove to be an amiable and effective face for the bid. Patrick admitted that he would be paid for his advocacy of Boston 2024, but when pressed by reporters, he refused to reveal how much he would receive in his new role.

Patrick had signed the resolution creating the Feasibility Commission on Halloween, 2013. At Boston 2024, Patrick joined a bevy of those who had worked on his campaigns or in his administration. Patrick's former secretary of economic development, Dan O'Connell, had been Boston 2024's first CEO. He had been replaced by Davey, who had been Patrick's secretary of transportation. Boston 2024's vice president for engagement, Nikko Mendoza, had been Patrick's director of operations. The bid's chief political strategist, Doug Rubin, also had been Patrick's top campaign strategist in 2006 and 2010 (and Coakley's in 2014). Mo Cowan, an advisor of the bid who worked at Weld's law firm, Mintz Levin, had been Patrick's chief of staff. Patrick had appointed Cowan to the United States Senate when John Kerry resigned to become secretary of state. John Walsh, hired to run Boston 2024's grassroots outreach, had been Patrick's first campaign manager.

Even bid supporters like *Globe* columnist Shirley Leung recognized that the optics of so many Patrick administration alumni joining Boston 2024 were not good. "The trouble is that Mount Olympus looks an awful like the Patrick administration in exile," she wrote. "It feels like Boston 2024 has become a shadow government, working the system to put on a multibillion-dollar event that could transform the city and the region for decades to come. And just like that, without even a special election, we now have three seats of power in this town: Beacon Hill, City Hall, and Mount Olympus." Even worse for the boosters, Leung also reported that Patrick's hiring had come as a surprise to Baker and Walsh—the bid committee had impolitely hired Patrick without giving advance notice to the governor or the mayor.[7]

Patrick's hiring deepened the perception that Boston 2024 was an insider's game. And the risk of a further erosion of public trust was not lost on Mayor Walsh. Patrick's refusal to disclose his salary was yet another contradiction to Walsh's promise that Boston 2024 would be "the most transparent" bid in Olympic history.

Mayor Walsh finally had found the right time to play watchdog. In response to the Patrick announcement, he asked Boston 2024 to make public all salary and compensation information for the bid's employees and consultants, "as a testament to the transparency and openness of this process."[8] Walsh must have known that the disclosure would hurt public support for his signature project. But the mayor probably felt he had no choice—the salary information was just too titillating not to be leaked eventually, by someone. Better for Walsh to get credit for forcing its disclosure than to be blamed later for helping keep it secret.

Boston 2024's salary and compensation disclosures were stunning. The bid committee's payroll included both the top Democratic *and* Republican political strategists in the state. Boston 2024 had loaded up on consultants from both sides of the aisle, with Governor Baker's key campaign advisor, Will Keyser, paired with a stable of Democratic advisors from Governor Patrick's administration. And it wasn't just a bipartisan team of outside political and communication consultants who were being well compensated for their work with Boston 2024. The bidding committee was paying politically connected employees hundreds of thousands a year in salaries. Almost everyone working on the bid was getting paid handsomely. Davey, the CEO, was being paid $300,000 a year, a number that had been disclosed previously but hadn't attracted much attention. Erin Murphy, executive vice president, was receiving $215,000 a year. In all, six of Boston 2024's ten employees were getting more than $100,000 per year. Even the Reverend Jeffrey Brown, who had talked eloquently about how the Olympics might help reduce inner-city violence, was getting paid $5,000 a month to appear at community events. But by far the most damaging revelation was the amount of Governor Patrick's compensation: he would be paid $7,500 *per day* (plus expenses) when working as a global ambassador for Boston 2024. The amount left mouths agape and tongues wagging. And it stuck in people's heads—it was an easy number to remember, and an easy number with which to do some simple comparative calculations. For example, for seven days of work, Patrick would take home more than most Massachusetts workers earned in an entire year.

That $7,500-per-day figure featured prominently on the front page of the next day's *Boston Herald* and would be repeated hundreds of times on talk radio and television programs in the coming weeks and months. The hiring of Patrick, a Democrat who was a close friend and vocal supporter of President Barack Obama, would also help erode support for Boston 2024 by Republican voters in *Greater Boston*. In January and February polling, Republicans had supported the Games more strongly than Democrats: January's WBUR poll, for example, had Republican support for the bid at 58 percent, while Democrats supported it at just 52 percent. After the news of Patrick's hiring, WBUR's March poll had Republican support at a paltry 14 percent—a dramatic drop of 44 percentage points in just two months! (Democratic support declined by only 11 percentage points over that same time period.)

Boston 2024's Consultants as Revealed in Q1 Progress Report

NAME	ANNUALIZED PROJECTED CONSULTING	TYPE OF SPENDING	NOTES
Interpublic Group	$1,300,000	Marketing and communication	Includes spending on Weber Shandwick, a longtime Olympic bid consultant.
Teneo Sports	$1,000,000– $1,250,000	Bid presentation services	Longtime Olympic bid consultants.
Elkus Manfredi Architects	$800,328	Architecture	Also donated additional services.
Broadstone Group, LLC	$556,672	Sports event consulting	Owned by Doug Arnot, a USOC consultant.
CBT	$496,588	Urban design and architecture	Focused on Olympic Village.
USOC	$461,200	Staff support	Pursuant to the bid city agreement, Boston 2024 reimbursed the cost and expenses of certain USOC staff subject to a cap of $3,000,000 over the multi-year term of the agreement.
JTA	$250,000– $500,000	Sports communications	Lead bid consultants for Sochi 2014.
SCR & Associates, LLC	$249,600	Fundraising	Republican political fundraiser.
WilsonOwensOwens	$195,311	Sports and event design	Consultants to London 2012.
Keyser Public Strategies	$180,000	Political consulting	Chief strategist for Governor Baker's 2014 campaign.
Northwind Strategies	$180,000	Political consulting	Chief strategists for Governor Patrick's 2006 and 2010 campaigns.

Company	Amount	Service	Notes
VHB		Engineering	
Insource Services, Inc.	$160,990	HR, finance, IT	
Populous	$156,618	Architecture	Stadium designers.
Nelson Mullins Riley & Scarborough LLP	$145,720	Legal	
Walsh Strategies	$120,000	Political consulting	Campaign manager of Governor Patrick's 2006 campaign.
William F. Coyne, Jr., Esq. P.C.	$120,000	Lobbying	
CK Strategies	$120,000	Political consulting	Chief strategist of Mayor Walsh's 2013 campaign.
Dumontjanks	$110,000	Urban planning and design	
Kiley & Company	$74,500	Polling	
Smith Sullivan & Brown PC	$68,800	Accounting and tax consulting	
Rev. Jeffrey L. Brown	$60,000	Community support	Leader in Boston's African-American community.
Swiftkurrent	$60,000	Political consulting	TV ad creator for Governor Baker's 2014 campaign.
Archipelago Strategies Group, Inc.	$54,420	Marketing and communications	Advisor to Mayor Walsh's 2013 campaign.
Environmental Systems Research Institute, Inc.	$26,000	Planning services	
Corey Dinopoulos	$14,740	Design and social media	Cofounder of Boston 2024 with Eric Reddy.
Molly Arnio	$1,300	Design	
ASL Interpreting	$660	Interpreting	
Total	**$7,083,447–$7,583,447**		

Boston 2024 had wanted to avoid being seen as a partisan, political effort, but the hiring of Governor Patrick reinforced the notion that raw politics would be needed to win support—both from the public at home in Massachusetts, and from the voting members of the International Olympic Committee. "There is nothing more political than an Olympic bid," the *Boston Globe* quoted Daniel Durbin, director of the University of Southern California's Annenberg Institute of Sports, Media, and Society, as saying in response to the news of Boston 2024's salary disclosures. Durbin elaborated: "You need as many influential, coercive personalities as you can get." In fact, some believed that, notwithstanding a job description that indicated that he would be lobbying the IOC, Patrick actually was hired primarily to lobby President Obama, whose support could prove crucial in convincing the IOC to award the Games to the United States.[9]

While President Obama might have sent his congratulations to Boston 2024 after the USOC's selection, he was no fan of the International Olympic Committee. Early in his presidency, in the fall of 2009, the president had flown to Copenhagen to address IOC members in person in support of Chicago's bid for the 2016 Olympics. In doing so, Obama became the first US president to lobby the IOC directly. Despite those efforts, Chicago had been eliminated in the first round of voting, losing out to Tokyo, Madrid, and the eventual winner—Rio de Janeiro. It had been an embarrassing defeat for President Obama—the IOC hadn't just rejected the US bid, it had rejected the president's adopted hometown and done so only moments after the president had addressed the assembled IOC members. It would take some mending of bridges to get President Obama to back another American bid forcefully—and Patrick, a longtime friend and ally of the president, was the right person for the job.

But as valuable as Patrick might have been to Boston 2024, the salary needed to hire him proved far more costly to the organization than $7,500 per day. Disclosure of the compensation amounts caused public support to plummet. WBUR's March poll, conducted a week after the salaries were front-page news, found that just 36 percent of *Greater Boston* residents supported the Boston 2024 bid. The poll found that 52 percent now opposed the bid, the first time opposition had crossed the 50 percent threshold. It was a new low for an effort that now had seen sharp declines in support over two consecutive months.[10] The bid's support would never recover.

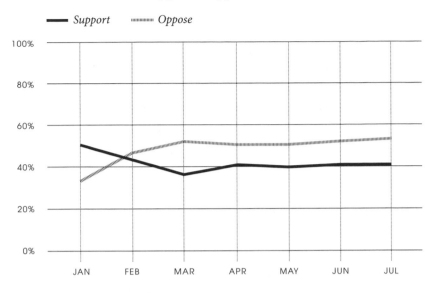

Greater Boston Support / Opposition for Boston 2024

—— *Support*   ⸽⸽⸽⸽⸽⸽ *Oppose*

Public support for Boston 2024 dropped in early 2015 and then leveled off at around 40 percent. No Boston Olympics. Based on statistics from WBUR/MassINC Polling data

No Boston Olympics' three cochairs were meeting over lunch at a restaurant in Boston's financial district when news of Patrick's salary information went public. "We've got to draw a contrast with that," Kerr said emphatically to his cochairs. No Boston Olympics quickly emailed its supporters with a list of the salaries for its own employees and consultants: "In the spirit of transparency, No Boston Olympics is today releasing its own compensation information: Co-Chair Chris Dempsey: $0, Co-Chair Kelley Gossett: $0, Co-Chair Liam Kerr: $0, Retained Consultants: $0 (there are none), Full-Time Staff: $0 (there are none)." It *was* quite a contrast. The narrative was becoming clear: No Boston Olympics was a band of scrappy volunteers challenging some of the city's wealthiest individuals and the well-compensated political consultants whom they employed. Boston 2024's opponents had seized the mantle of David in a battle with Goliath.

The disclosure of Boston 2024's financial information spurred by Boston 2024's hiring of Patrick was an enormous benefit for No Boston Olympics, but it also created some complications for the bid's opponents. Up to that point, No Boston Olympics had declined to release the names or amounts of its own donors. *Boston Globe* beat reporter Mark Arsenault, perhaps tipped off by one of Boston 2024's media consultants, noticed the inconsistency. Arsenault, in turn, called Dempsey to ask whether No Boston Olympics would release the names of the organization's donors. Arsenault wanted to know who was paying for David's slingshot.

No Boston Olympics faced a strategic choice. As a 501(c)(4), the group was under no legal obligation to share the amount it had raised or the names of those who had contributed. On the one hand, if it chose not to release that information, it would look hypocritical as it called for more transparency from Boston 2024. On the other hand, releasing the names of its donors and the amounts they had given would expose just how out-gunned the bid opponents were—by mid-March, the group had raised less than $15,000 from a total of about 150 contributors. Releasing donor names might reinforce the David vs. Goliath narrative, which played in No Boston Olympics' favor, but it also might also scare off prospective contributors who agreed with No Boston Olympics' position but didn't want to be seen as challenging Boston 2024's powerful boosters. The decision weighed heavily on Dempsey, Gossett, and Kerr—each of whom could see both sides of the issue. Ultimately, the group decided not to release donor names or amounts in March, a position it promised to reconsider continually. Instead, No Boston Olympics shared with Arsenault its average contribution size: $100.97.

Despite the hits the bid had taken, political pundits like WGBH's Adam Reilly, a keen follower of Boston politics, still called No Boston Olympics' fight "pretty much unwinnable." Reilly caught up with Dempsey and Gossett after Dempsey's testimony at a Boston city council meeting on March 6. Reilly had noticed that Dempsey had struck a compromising tone in his testimony—even calling the idea of the Olympics in Boston "inherently cool." "It's not inconsistent to oppose the bid while also working to make the bid better," Dempsey told Reilly. "It's possible that the bid becomes so much better, that it's a bid we can get behind." Reilly provided on-target analysis: "I got the sense talking to the two of them that they are trying to figure out this balancing act. They can't be too strident in their opposition because they want a seat at the table . . . at the same time, they have this habit of mind from [before the USOC decision] when they wanted to kill this thing altogether."[11] Just as Mayor Walsh was trying to walk the line between cheerleader and watchdog, No Boston Olympics' leaders were trying to oppose the bid without appearing like obstructionists.

While No Boston Olympics didn't exactly have a "seat at the table," it did have open lines of communication with Boston 2024 and the Walsh administration. Dempsey, Kerr, and Gossett met with Mayor Walsh at his office in City Hall a handful of times in early 2015, and Koh occasionally traded text messages or emails with No Boston Olympics' cochairs throughout the process. No Boston Olympics also made visits to Boston 2024 headquarters in the city's Seaport District to meet with Fish, Davey, and other Boston 2024 staff.

In late March, Dempsey told *Globe* columnist Joanna Weiss that No Boston Olympics could potentially "vacate" its opposition should Boston 2024 agree to certain conditions the opponents had outlined.[12] Dempsey's friend Davey, Boston 2024's CEO, had even begun publicly calling No Boston Olympics by the name "Maybe Boston Olympics," saying that it was his job to get Dempsey, Gossett, and Kerr to agree that the bid was in the best interests of Boston's future. In his testimony before the city council, Dempsey had laid out three specific conditions that No Boston Olympics felt might make the bid more responsible. The first was to reject the International Olympic Committee's customary request for a taxpayer guarantee. The second was to divert Olympic funds that normally would flow to the USOC to an escrow account. The funds would stay in escrow until *after* the Games and would only be handed over to the USOC if Boston 2024 had met its promises of not needing public funding. Finally, No Boston Olympics asked for the creation of a genuinely independent watchdog that would monitor and assess the bid's impacts on taxpayers and public resources, along the lines of what Representatives Moran and Michlewitz had proposed in their legislation.

No Boston Olympics had chosen these conditions carefully: the group asked not for changes in *outcomes*, but for changes in *incentives*. Promises about outcomes, whether they were improvements to city neighborhoods or no use of public funding, would have been easy for Boston 2024 to make, yet difficult for No Boston Olympics to enforce. Changing incentives, however, might actually influence if and how the bid moved forward. For example, eliminating the taxpayer guarantee would force both Boston 2024 and the International Olympic Committee to conduct more thorough due diligence on the bid, forcing both parties to sharpen their pencils. If the taxpayer guarantee remained in place, the IOC had little reason to reject a financially responsible bid. The request also allowed No Boston Olympics to remind observers that Los Angeles had rejected the taxpayer guarantee in 1984. The opponents' argument became pretty simple: Boston should be asking the IOC for the same deal that Los Angeles got. This was a particularly effective message because Boston 2024 often cited the Los Angeles games as a financial success and a model for other US bids.

Likewise, No Boston Olympics' second condition—an escrow account that would hold USOC marketing funds in Boston until after the Games left town—would alter the USOC's incentives. With this condition in place, USOC leaders in Colorado Springs would have to ensure that Boston 2024 wasn't overpromising, or they would risk losing the windfall marketing dollars that accompanied Games on US soil. No Boston Olympics was hopeful that the idea of an escrow account would appeal especially to Boston 2024's local political supporters, such as Walsh, who might see it as an insurance mechanism; the funds could be used after the Games to safeguard improvements to parks, venues, and infrastructure that Boston 2024 had promised.

The release of these conditions rattled some of No Boston Olympics' grassroots supporters, who questioned Dempsey, Gossett, and Kerr's commitment to their cause. But it ultimately strengthened No Boston Olympics' position. When asked, as they often were, "Would *anything* make you drop your opposition?" the organization's leaders could respond with some easily digestible talking points that were both rationale and public spirited. The opponents didn't come across as naysayers or NIMBYs; they were reasonable citizens fighting for a better future for their city.

But there was another reason for No Boston Olympics to be "Maybe Boston Olympics." The three cochairs weren't confident that they could afford, personally or professionally, to continue their advocacy. Gossett had been let go from her job at a charitable foundation funded by a well-known Boston family—with some evidence that pressure from Boston 2024's boosters had played a role in her dismissal. Dempsey's last day at the management consulting firm Bain & Company would be March 20 (a date he had negotiated before the USOC's decision in January, when Dempsey had still been hopeful the USOC would choose a different city). No Boston Olympics hadn't raised enough money to pay the two cochairs, but Gossett and Dempsey found themselves too busy fighting the bid to take on new jobs. They were each now dipping into personal savings to continue their efforts. Kerr had a young family and a full-time job with Democrats for Education Reform. No Boston Olympics' leaders wanted to fight on to the finish, whenever that might be, but they also had to be realistic about what was achievable when they were being outspent by boosters by more than 1,000 to 1. If Boston 2024 met their three conditions, Dempsey, Gossett, and Kerr would have to consider dropping their opposition to the bid and moving on with their lives.

As No Boston Olympics struggled to shore up its organizational foundation, Boston 2024 continued to flex its muscle with Boston's prominent institutions. One of these was the Boston Foundation, which was positioned squarely in the boosters' corner. The foundation is one of the city's oldest philanthropic foundations, tracing its roots back to 1915, when it primarily responded to the needs of Boston's poor immigrants and laborers. By 2015, the foundation had transformed from these philanthropic roots to take a more activist approach, turning itself into a powerful political and institutional presence in *Greater Boston*. The foundation was no longer just a charity—it now made noteworthy contributions to a number of Boston's civic debates and helped push major pieces of legislation and public sector reform, especially in the areas of housing, education, and health care.

Later public records requests revealed how closely tied the foundation was to Boston 2024. As early as August 2014, when Boston's selection by the USOC still seemed very much in doubt, the Boston Foundation had reached out to the Donahue Institute at the University of Massachusetts about commissioning a study on the potential impact of the Games. This had led to a meeting in September 2014 with Boston 2024's Fish and O'Connell and Donahue Institute researchers at the Boston Foundation's offices in Boston's Back Bay. By October of 2015, with funding from the Boston Foundation, UMass was under contract and the Donahue Institute's researchers were given special access to Boston 2024's bid documents—the very same documents that Boston 2024 was, at that time, refusing to share with the media or the public. The foundation then convened several additional meetings between its hired consultants and Boston 2024's senior team—all behind closed doors.[13]

In the midst of its research, the Donahue Institute emailed Zimbalist to request a meeting regarding their impact study. The email did not mention who had commissioned or was paying for the study. Zimbalist responded that he would be willing to meet with the researchers if he was assured that their effort was independent. He asked for information on whether the institute was under contract and, if so, by whom and how much it was being paid. The institute never responded to Zimbalist's query.

By mid-February, the institute's research was complete and Boston 2024 was provided access to the results—a month before they would be shared publicly.[14] In conjunction with Boston 2024's communications team, the decision was made to share the report first with the *Boston Globe*. Exclusive access for the *Globe* ensured a front-page headline on March 18, 2015, declaring that the Games would "bring billions" to the region. "A Boston Olympics in 2024 would pump billions of new dollars into the Massachusetts economy, potentially creating 4,000 construction jobs annually for six years and tens of thousands of temporary jobs the year of the event, according to a new analysis of Boston's Olympic bid by researchers at the UMass Donahue Institute," the *Globe*'s Arsenault led off, only noting later that there were "caution flags" scattered throughout the report.[15] The *Globe* called the report "independent"—but had it been? The study had been commissioned and funded by an organization that was sympathetic to the bid. It had been completed in close collaboration with the boosters and released only after Boston 2024's staff had first had a chance to review the report.

It would have been fair for No Boston Olympics to reject the Donahue Institute's findings outright, but instead bid opponents embraced parts of the report. It *had* highlighted some weaknesses in Boston 2024's bid, especially the need for a taxpayer guarantee that put public funds at risk. The institute acknowledged that the concept of insurance against cost overruns was "fairly novel." Dempsey told the *Boston Business Journal*, "We are glad that respected organizations like the Boston Foundation are starting to talk more about some of the risk."[16] And even if the economic numbers presented by the Donahue Institute were to be believed, the positive economic impact on the Massachusetts economy was relatively limited. As

No Boston Olympics pointed out, even these rosy projections indicated an economic impact of less than 1 percent of the state's output over the 2018 to 2024 time period when most construction and activity would occur. Most important, the report made it clear that benefits accrued only to certain sectors of the economy, while other key Massachusetts industries were left out. The forty-page report used the word "construction" over one hundred times. It did not use the words "health care" or "education"—both pillars of the Massachusetts economy—even once.[17]

But the Donahue Institute's study had much deeper problems, as Zimbalist pointed out in an op-ed in the *Boston Globe* on March 20.[18] The report accepted the basic assumptions of Boston 2024 in order to make its projections, to wit: all operating costs would be covered by revenue from the Games, all non-OCOG construction costs would be covered privately, and the federal government would pick up 100 percent of the security costs (optimistically forecast at only $1 billion). The report proceeded to use an inappropriate input-output methodology and to ignore the scholarly literature on the subject of mega-events like the Olympics.

Consider a few examples. The Boston 2024 bid showed operating costs and revenues at $4.7 billion. To get to this figure, Boston 2024 invoked $1 billion in "additional" or "other" revenue, the sources of which were not revealed. Boston 2024 also assumed it would take in $1.15 billion in ticket sales. London had an eighty-thousand-seat Olympic stadium, replete with luxury boxes and other revenue-generating accoutrements. Boston 2024 was promising a temporary, spartan, sixty-thousand-seat stadium. London generated only $990 million in ticket sales. How would Boston top that by more than 16 percent? Rather than challenge these numbers, the Donahue Report simply accepted Boston 2024's projections.

The Donahue report likewise assumed an unrealistic number for net new spending spawned by the hosting experience and, then, based on its IMPLAN model, multiplied the number by 1.9 to derive its estimated output contribution from the Olympics.

IMPLAN is an input-output model that depicts the relationships among the economy's branches. It is based on fixed ratios between inputs and outputs and uses highly aggregated data. This model is inappropriate for estimating the economic impact of mega-events.[19] The sheer volume of construction around mega-events leads to the use of companies and workers from outside the hosting region, leading to much larger leakages out of the local economy and unrealistically high multipliers, among other problems.

Most macroeconomic models of the entire US economy have multipliers of 1.2 or below. Since the Boston economy is only a small fraction of the US economy, it is not feasible that it would have a multiplier that is higher than the national multiplier, let alone more than 50 percent larger than the entire US economy. Yet that is what the report's results depended on. The Donahue Institute's report was added to a long list of booster-commissioned, booster-friendly economic impact reports that dramatically overstate the expected economic impact of the Olympic Games.

No Boston Olympics was ramping up its efforts to draw attention to the bid's costs and risks. Dempsey and Gossett found a welcome reception with former lieutenant governor Tim Murray, with whom they had worked at the state house. Murray was a fierce advocate for central Massachusetts and had become the president and CEO of the Worcester regional chamber of commerce, the most important business group in Massachusetts's second most populous city. Murray invited Dempsey and Gossett to share No Boston Olympics' presentation with the chamber's policy committee, just one week after Boston 2024 made its pitch to the same group. The visit put No Boston Olympics on the front page of the *Worcester Telegram & Gazette*, the county's largest newspaper. *Worcester Magazine* described No Boston Olympics appearance as a "stat-heavy presentation"—and contrasted the grassroots organization with its deep-pocketed opponents: "Even though Dempsey and Gossett drew on statistics and empirical evidence with astonishing effectiveness—many in the room thanked them for their work afterward—they face an uphill battle."[20] The Worcester area was still smarting over the Big Dig—especially because many continued to pay tolls on the Massachusetts Turnpike that were used to pay for Big Dig debt. Stories about wealthy insiders pushing another megaproject on Beacon Hill helped reinforce suspicions that residents of central Massachusetts would be paying for something that mostly benefited Boston.

On March 21, the day after WBUR's poll showed statewide support at just 36 percent, Mayor Walsh retrenched. An unnamed Walsh aide told the *Boston*

Herald, "Mayor Walsh has hit the reset button on the Olympic effort given that this is his city and he has the most to lose politically."[21] But even as he acknowledged its shortcomings, Boston's mayor still defended the bid, blaming the drop in support on "distractions" and claiming that residents were only "getting one side of the story."[22]

It was true that the bid was getting hammered by No Boston Olympics, No Boston 2024, and skeptical columnists and pundits. But if Boston 2024 wasn't getting its message out, it only had itself to blame. For example, bid CEO Rich Davey had asked to make a monthly appearance on Jim Braude and Margery Eagan's popular daytime talk show on WGBH radio. Davey appeared one time, by phone, then canceled future visits as the bid began to face increased scrutiny. On another occasion, Braude invited Boston 2024 and No Boston Olympics to debate on his television program—but only the bid's opponents showed up.

Commonwealth Magazine editor Michael Jonas summed up the mayor's uncomfortable situation: "[Walsh] went all-in. While Gov. Charlie Baker and legislative leaders continue to kick the tires and raise questions about a Boston Olympics, Walsh alone at this point is the political leader with his neck on the line."[23] What could the mayor and Boston 2024's boosters do to reset public opinion? The Boosters' Dilemma meant that Boston 2024 had few good options.

Walsh and Boston 2024 chose a bold gesture that was sure to improve public perception, even if it risked stoking the ire of the IOC and USOC: they finally agreed to a plebiscite. On March 24, John Fish announced at a breakfast address that he and Boston 2024 would support a public referendum to decide whether to move forward as the US bid city. The referendum would have to win majority support at both the state and city level—that is, it would need to be approved by "50 percent + 1" of voters in both Massachusetts and in the city of Boston. Just weeks earlier, Boston 2024, the USOC, and the mayor of Boston had all insisted that no referendum was necessary. Now, they would have to run a gauntlet of city and state electorates. It was a dramatic and risky move, one that could not have pleased the International Olympic Committee, which earlier had stated expressly to the USOC that it did not want a public vote on a US Olympic bid.

Indeed, to close observers of the USOC and IOC, the decision might have been fatal. On March 20, Olympic writer Alan Abrahamson wrote that the Boston bid had a communications problem, but even with just 36 percent support, it could be salvaged, writing, "a pause and a deep breath . . . there's a long way to go."[24] The referendum seemed to change things. Just ten days after telling boosters to take a deep breath, Abrahamson wrote a new post with a different recommendation to the USOC: "Boston 2024 is doomed: be done with it."[25]

But to observers in Boston, less familiar with the IOC and more attuned to Massachusetts voters, the announcement seemed to buy some time for Boston 2024 while also playing to its strengths. Any vote wouldn't occur until November 2016 at the earliest—so Boston 2024 had nineteen months to put together a sophisticated campaign that would swing support back above 50 percent. And if anyone knew how to win an election, it was Boston 2024's talented stable of campaign operatives and communications gurus, especially if they were aided by the unlimited campaign funds that legally could be spent on a ballot campaign.

Unlike Abrahamson, Mayor Walsh certainly wasn't giving up on the bid—if anything, he saw a need to assert more control over the situation. A referendum was an opportunity to compete on the ground that Walsh knew best—electoral politics. Walsh activated his political network, instructing his campaign team to send an email to "Team Walsh," a list of political supporters and activists who had helped campaign for the mayor in 2013. Keohan and Norton, Walsh's former campaign staff who were now Boston 2024's consultants, convened this group at a union hall in Walsh's home neighborhood of Dorchester, where Walsh had won some precincts over rival Connolly with dominant margins of more than 87 percent support. At that meeting, Keohan described the grassroots campaign that would be needed in Boston's neighborhoods: "We'll be able to go [to] the Little League fields. We'll be able to go [to] the Pop Warner fields. We'll be able to go to the ice skating rinks. We'll be able to talk to kids that actually aspire to be in the Olympics. We're going to organize at Rotary Clubs. We're going to organize at VFWs. We're going to organize wherever anyone will allow us to speak, because there is nothing secret here. We want to hear the feedback from every community we possibly can, in order to build the best bid."[26]

Keohan was describing the type of neighborhood-by-neighborhood, door-by-door campaign for which Boston is famous—and which Team Walsh was uniquely positioned to win, even if they had to dig out of a deep hole.

Across town on that same day, the state house's "Big Three"—Governor Baker, Senate president Stan Rosenberg, and House speaker Bob DeLeo—announced that the state would spend up to $250,000 to hire an independent consultant that would evaluate Boston 2024's next iteration of the bid, which was coming to be known as Bid 2.0 and would be released at some point that summer. While the fiscally conservative Baker seemed loath to spend public dollars on the bid, he justified the expense against the risk. "I think in this particular instance spending a couple of hundred thousand dollars on something that could cost the Commonwealth as much as two billion dollars, I think that's money well spent," Baker said.[27]

The Big Three were both hiring expertise and buying time. They weren't ready to weigh in with their opinion on the bid, but had to show they were thinking about it. Increasingly, as the highest-profile story of the first half of 2015, Boston 2024 was becoming an issue on which every elected official in Massachusetts had to have prepared talking points—if not a firm opinion. On March 30, in an interview with WBUR, United States Senator Elizabeth Warren said she was "really concerned" about the Boston 2024 effort. "I want to see much better information—you won't be surprised about this—about how they're going to pay for it."[28] Warren's voice had immense credibility with her engaged, progressive, and working-class base that comprised a significant and vocal share of the Massachusetts voting population. The deal that the IOC was offering to Boston residents—in which a private party profits, while the public bears the risk when things go wrong, was not unfamiliar to Warren. It was the same "too big to fail" bargain that Warren had railed against in 2008, that had helped elect her as a US senator in 2012, and that hard turned her into a darling of the left. "Washington works for those who hire armies of lobbyists," she had once said. Perhaps to Senator Warren, Boston 2024, with its long lists of politically connected consultants and lobbyists seeking a taxpayer guarantee from public officials, didn't look too much different from a Wall Street bank.[29]

John Fish was the only person in Massachusetts who could have shepherded Boston 2024's bid to the national stage. He was fiercely committed to seeing it succeed. Fish had personally contributed as much as $2 million to fund Boston 2024—he was easily the bid's largest donor. In January, at the bid's high-water mark, he had stepped down from his role as chairman of the *Greater Boston* chamber of commerce to focus more time on the bid.[30] But the bid's declining public support and questionable strategic choices were eroding John Fish's ability to lead the organization. His control of the bidding committee was looking increasingly shaky. Fish had always been a controversial face of the organization. He was the owner of the state's largest construction company, and the construction industry clearly would benefit from hosting. Fish's decision to recuse Suffolk Construction from bidding on Olympic projects did little to diminish perceptions that a successful bid would provide Fish with a financial windfall. Beyond the question of whether Fish stood to benefit from the Games, the businessman's blunt style simply had not translated well to the public arena.

In late March, *Globe* columnist Joan Vennochi published a devastating column that started: "If you really want the Olympics to come to Boston, you must be asking yourself: How do you solve a problem like John Fish?" Vennochi went on to paraphrase anonymously one of Boston 2024's consultants (presumably one who was getting paid $5,000 per month or more by Boston 2024), comparing Fish to "a man who has been nudged from the roof of a 20-story building, but has yet to accept his fate." Vennochi cited an anecdote from a Boston 2024 meeting with the *Globe* editorial board. When questioned about the potential effect of Boston 2024 on Franklin Park, Fish said, "You need to have your head examined" if you didn't understand the benefits that Boston 2024 would deliver for the park.[31] Fish's competitive drive and intensity had helped him amass immense power in the city's boardrooms, but he was struggling to adapt those attributes to the messy, democratic environment where a much broader and more diverse range of people and interests needed to be accommodated.

On the last day of March, the *Wall Street Journal's* Matthew Futterman, a longtime sports and Olympic reporter with deep sources at the USOC, reported that "people familiar with the [USOC's] plans" had told him that Boston's bid would be dropped if public support didn't improve. The USOC denied these claims. But Futterman cited two people close to the discussions who indicated that the USOC, or its representatives, had held discussions with leaders of the defunct Los Angeles and San Francisco bids. Separately, during the same week, Zimbalist had attended a meeting in Washington, D.C., where a long-standing member of the USOC had told him that the Boston bid could be dropped.

The news was tremendously encouraging for Boston's Olympic opponents. The IOC required the USOC to submit its country's bid officially by September 15. Futterman's report ignited hope that Boston 2024 might not last until the end of the summer. Dempsey and Gossett were acutely aware that they were drawing down personal savings to work on No Boston Olympics full time. This was not a sustainable long-term arrangement—but they might be able to make it work until September. Thus, by the end of March, the door was cracked open for a graceful exit by the USOC into the safe and welcoming arms of southern California.

SIX

APRIL 2015

Boston's boosters were relieved to move on from a tough March, but April didn't seem to start any better for them. In an early morning speech to the CEO Breakfast Forum, hosted by Northeastern University at Boston's Four Seasons Hotel, John Fish, in a concession to transparency, said that he would open up Boston 2024's books so that the public could see how the bid was being run. That was supposed to be the news. And it was the story that most media, including the *Boston Globe*, went with.[1]

But Fish also offered these words to the crowd of businesspeople: "What bothers me a lot is the decline of pride, of patriotism, and love for our country." The remarks seemed to link low support for the Boston 2024 bid to a lack of patriotism. It was not at all clear that Fish intended to draw this connection, but some reporters covering the event pounced on his words. Channel 5, Boston's most-watched local news station, ran a report saying that Fish had questioned the patriotism of Olympic opponents. The report was later pulled from Channel 5's website, but it survived on YouTube and quickly entered the Boston 2024 storyline—with Fish's words bouncing around social media and getting replayed on morning talk radio shows. Even WEEI radio's Gary Tanguay, a staunch bid supporter, called the organizers "buffoons" and said Fish's remarks "were like nails on the chalkboard." He noted that the controversy—like Fish's interview with the *Herald* in October 2014—only improved the standing of opponents. The patriotic ones were the scrappy volunteers standing up to a proposal that enjoyed the nearly unanimous support of Boston's business and political elite. Whether or not the interpretation of Fish's words was fair, the narrative stuck. Fish's position as chairman of the bid had already been in jeopardy. Now it was untenable. The man who had brought Boston 2024 to life would never make another public appearance in Boston on behalf of the bid.

Meanwhile, Mayor Walsh was reportedly "furious" with the *Wall Street Journal*'s report that the USOC was talking with other cities.[2] Frustrated with how little control he truly had over the process, he told Boston's WBZ News that he would create within city hall an "Office of Olympic Accountability"—and that he would ask Boston 2024 to fund the costs of the office, which might reach $750,000.[3] Walsh was again playing watchdog. The mayor's staff told No Boston Olympics that the opponents could count on the new office to have real teeth and to strictly monitor Boston 2024's plans and proposed spending.

But by the time the office actually got up and running in late April, Walsh had changed the name to the Office of Olympic *Planning*—no longer a watchdog, it now seemed to be responsible for helping develop an Olympic plan that fit with city hall's agenda. "The office will work collaboratively with Boston 2024 and the United States Olympic Committee," a city hall press release said. This watered-down approach came as a surprise to No Boston Olympics, which had been given assurances that the new office was going to be focused on protecting taxpayers. The group told boston.com's Vaccaro, "The city's watchdog needs to be truly independent. It should be a distinct and separate entity entirely, not one wrapped into the planning function. When the two [planning and oversight] are in the same office, neither function will excel." Walsh had reversed course. It was the Boosters' Dilemma in action again. The mayor repeatedly had stated that no taxpayer dollars would be spent on the bid, so he couldn't afford to use city funds to pay for a watchdog. Instead, he had to turn to the boosters for funding. The boosters were willing to fund the office to keep Walsh happy, but they had balked at the idea that they needed to be held "Accountable"—so instead of a watchdog, city hall got an Office of Olympic "Planning."

Boston 2024 continued to follow the Olympic-booster playbook to build support for the bid at home. Part of that was inviting and welcoming Olympic advocates from prior host cities to boast about the benefits that the Olympics had delivered to their city. The bid's most notable guest was the eccentric London mayor Boris Johnson, who visited Boston in February of 2015. The mayor's visit was tightly coordinated with Boston 2024. When Johnson sat down for an exclusive interview with the *Boston Globe*, the conversation was monitored by a Boston 2024 representative. (When asked for comment from the *Globe*, No Boston Olympics offered this response to

Johnson's boosterism: "Boston's citizens have a proud history of standing up to elites in London telling them how to do things—we're not sure why Boris thinks this time will be any different."[4]) Johnson was scheduled to participate in a "fireside chat" with John Fish and the Walsh administration's chief of economic development, John Barros. The event was open to the public, but had to be canceled when one of February's major snowstorms hit that day. Johnson had to settle for a snowy walking tour of downtown Boston.[5]

Boston 2024's willingness to overlook troubling budget realities was a behavior Johnson and other London boosters knew well. London 2012's initial budget submitted to the IOC was GBP 2.6 billion. After the bid was won, bid authorities revised the budget upward to GBP 9.3 billion. When the reported costs actually came in at GBP 8.7 billion, London's Olympic organizers claimed the bid was "under budget." UK sports minister Hugh Robertson called the results a "testament to the sound financial management of all involved," despite the fact that the costs were more than three times initial estimates.[6]

Another key part of the Olympic-booster playbook is associating popular sports figures with the bid, hoping to convince the public that the Games are a once-in-a-lifetime opportunity to experience athletic greatness in their own backyard. On April 22, Boston 2024 made what the *Boston Globe* called a "star-studded" set of additions to its board of directors. The new members included some of the best-known names in Boston sports, including Celtics legend Larry Bird, Red Sox slugger David Ortiz, and Boston Marathon winner Meb Keflezighi.[7] Although these figures were broadly loved by Massachusetts residents, the announcement may have been counterproductive. By April, No Boston Olympics, No Boston 2024, and other bid opponents had helped persuade many Bostonians that Boston 2024 was much more than a sporting event—it was a public policy matter worthy of thoughtful analysis. David Ortiz and Larry Bird weren't going to help with that.

Rather than more sports stars, Boston 2024 needed new political and managerial leadership. No Boston Olympics' leaders were haunted by the notion that Boston 2024 might bring in a new chairman, chief executive, or management team that could instantly reset the public's perception of the bid. The leading candidate was perhaps former Massachusetts governor Mitt Romney, who was still seen by Bay State voters as a competent manager, even if many disagreed with positions he had taken as a presidential candidate in 2008 and 2012. Romney was credited by some with "rescuing" the Salt Lake City's 2002 Winter Olympics after a bribery scandal and budget overruns had threatened to permanently tarnish the Games and their host city. Romney had rescued Salt Lake City's Olympic bid (with the help of $1.5 billion of taxpayer support);[8] he might be able to do the same for Boston 2024. Although it was never reported, it is probable that the USOC's Probst and Blackmun reached out to Romney to test his interest in returning to Massachusetts to lead Boston's bid. But the former governor had many reasons to turn down these overtures. Romney had taken control of the Salt Lake organizing committee less than two years before the opening ceremonies. The Salt Lake Games were happening one way or another—and Romney knew if he got the bid on track, he could bask in the glow of seventeen days of fawning Olympic coverage.

Boston 2024 was still more than two years away from the IOC auction's final gavel—so the bid could still end in an embarrassing defeat to rival cities such as Paris or Rome. And even if Boston were selected, it would be another seven years of risky construction and execution before the opening ceremonies. Whereas leading Salt Lake City 2002 had been a political launching pad, leading Boston 2024 had the potential to be an awkward bookend to Romney's career. A second Olympic act just didn't hold much appeal to the grandfather of twenty-three, especially given the risks to his reputation. It wasn't that Romney didn't have the energy or ambition for the job—just months before, in January, Romney had toyed with taking a final, serious run at the presidency, deciding only in late January that rival Jeb Bush's fundraising and strength with mainstream Republicans was too strong for him to overcome. (Little did he know.) Romney never swooped in to rescue the bid. If anything, his ties to the bid loosened over time. In November 2013, the *Boston Globe* had reported that Romney was a "key adviser" to the fledgling bid. And in February 2015, *Globe* reporter Beth Healy wrote a piece about Romney's central role on the committee, with Fish describing him as a "quiet but influential behind-the-scenes player." But by May, Romney was evading any association with the bid. "[Boston

2024 is] a great group and I wish them well," he told the *Boston Herald* before ducking in to a speaking event in New Hampshire.[9]

Romney was not going to be Boston 2024's savior, but there were others who might be interested in giving it a shot. One prospect was Red Sox president and CEO Larry Lucchino, a well-known and respected figure in Boston's business, political, and sports communities. Lucchino's business acumen had helped overhaul the Red Sox organization. He had overseen a team that saved Fenway Park with $300 million of private funds and had produced three World Series Championships in ten years, breaking the infamous Curse of the Bambino. On April 24, a front-page story in the *Boston Globe* (owned by Lucchino's boss at the Red Sox, John Henry), reported that Lucchino had already engaged in discussions with John Fish and Mayor Walsh to take a senior role at the bid committee. The *Globe* said that bringing Lucchino on board, "would signal a dramatic reboot for an Olympic campaign that got off to a difficult start."[10] It was exactly the type of reboot that No Boston Olympics feared.

Exploring a role with Boston 2024 made a lot of sense for Lucchino. It wasn't yet public knowledge, but Lucchino already knew that his time as Red Sox CEO was drawing to a close. The opportunity to run another large sports-related organization in Boston had to be attractive to the energetic and talented executive. Lucchino had led successful efforts to build new stadiums in Baltimore and San Diego, as well as the equally successful venture to impressively modernize Fenway Park. This was exactly the type of skill set that Boston 2024 required. Indeed, Lucchino is known as the chief architect of baseball's strategic shift to move from cookie-cutter stadiums in the suburbs to retro-designed facilities in downtown areas close to the central business district. The strategy produced a financial windfall for baseball, and, eventually, for many basketball and hockey franchises as well. As *Globe* reporter Arsenault wrote, "His presence could lend the bid new gravitas and provide a public face with a proven legacy at the top levels of professional sports."[11] Four days later, *Globe* columnist Leung wrote an open letter to Lucchino in the *Globe*, comparing a potential Lucchino leadership role to Red Sox pitcher Curt Schilling's stepping in to pitch Game 6 of the ALCS in 2004—the famous "bloody sock" game.

But Lucchino had a professional relationship with Professor Zimbalist that went back many years, and had reached out to him the day after the first story appeared in the *Globe*. Lucchino had listened to the pro–Boston 2024 pitch from Mayor Walsh, Fish, and Boston business icon Jack Connors. Now he needed to hear the other side. In an hour-long conversation, Zimbalist helped persuade Lucchino that taking the reins at Boston 2024 would be a perilous choice. The numbers just wouldn't work—and Lucchino would be left with responsibility for a project that almost inevitably would spiral out of control. Lucchino, like Romney, determined that leading Boston 2024 would risk an embarrassing end to his career—not the triumphant capstone for which he might be hoping.

By coincidence, Lucchino had invited Zimbalist and a few guests to join him in the Red Sox owners' suite on April 29. As Sox starter Rick Porcello pitched the team to a 4 to 1 win over the Blue Jays, Dempsey and Zimbalist chatted with Lucchino and the gracious Linda Pizzuti Henry, wife of *Boston Globe* and Red Sox owner John Henry. Linda Henry was a native of nearby Lynnfield, and a proud Bostonian unafraid to think ambitiously about the city's future. She had been inclined to support the Boston 2024 bid. Dempsey and Zimbalist made the case to her that the city she loved would be better off passing on the Olympic opportunity.

The next day, April 30, Lucchino joined popular WEEI radio morning show *Dennis and Callahan*. He was circumspect about taking on the job at Boston 2024. "I am flattered to be asked to play some role in it, and we'll see how that plays out," he said. "I've got a bunch of existing commitments that I've got to examine and then re-examine to see if there is a role that I can play."[12] Lucchino was searching for a graceful exit. Because the job offer had already been publicly reported, turning it down outright would be an embarrassing public rebuke to the mayor's signature project. Lucchino and the Red Sox needed to stay in Mayor Walsh's good graces. So instead of stepping in to lead the effort, Lucchino decided in early May that he would take a position as a "senior advisor" to the bid. Other than helping host "Olympic Day" at Fenway Park on June 23, when 175 children and athletes formed human Olympic rings in center field, Lucchino would have very few public associations with the bid after the announcement of his role in mid-May. Lucchino would step down from his role as Red Sox CEO at the end of the 2015 season, but he continued to work as a high-level team advisor as he took on a major commitment as the CEO of the Red Sox Triple A affiliate, the Pawtucket Red Sox.

When *Boston Magazine*'s annual "Power Issue" hit newsstands on April 28, the rankings surprised some pundits. John Fish was still at the top, ahead of Governor Baker, Mayor Walsh, *Globe* owner John Henry, and Senator Elizabeth Warren. His face was one of a handful that graced the cover with a simple headline: "I run this town." Even if Fish's Olympic troubles had threatened his power, he still ranked as Boston's top dog. But even Fish now understood that the bid could not be successful if he remained its public face. The reins would have to be passed to someone with a less controversial profile.

No Boston Olympics cochairs Liam Kerr, Chris Dempsey, and Kelley Gossett.
Andy Laub/Boston.com

Professor Andrew Zimbalist speaks at the first No Boston Olympics organizing meeting in January 2015. Steven Senne/Associated Press

Mayor Marty Walsh speaking at a Boston 2024 event in October 2014. Steven Senne/Associated Press

Kelley Gossett at Widett Circle, planned home of Boston 2024's Olympic stadium. No Boston Olympics

A rendering of Widett Circle during the Boston 2024 Olympics. Boston 2024

Residents hold signs at the first public meeting on Boston 2024 in February 2015. Charles Krupa/Associated Press

Residents hold signs before the community meeting in Jamaica Plain,
June 30, 2015. No Boston Olympics

Boston 2024 chairman Steve Pagliuca, USOC board member Dan Doctoroff, Chris Dempsey, and Andrew Zimbalist at the *Globe*/Fox 25 debate, July 23, 2015
Keith Bedford/*Boston Globe*

Speaker of the House Bob DeLeo, Senate president Stan Rosenberg, Governor Charlie Baker, and Lieutenant Governor Karyn Polito talk to the media about the demise of Boston 2024. Ted Fitzgerald/*Boston Herald* via Associated Press

SEVEN

MAY 2015

With Fish's leadership no longer viable, and Romney and Lucchino demur-
ring, Boston 2024 vice-chairman Steve Pagliuca stepped up as the bid's new
chairman (Fish took the title of vice-chairman). Pagliuca, who described
himself as a "frumpy, boring accountant," would take on the role of putting
a less polarizing public face on Boston 2024, while shoring up its financial
underpinnings. In some ways, Pagliuca was an ideal fit for the job that Boston 2024 needed done. Affectionately known to his friends and colleagues
as "Pags," Pagliuca was approachable, self-deprecating, and gregarious. He
had been an early employee of the Boston-based private-equity firm Bain
Capital, where he still had a leadership role as managing director. Pagliuca's success at the firm had helped him build a net worth of hundreds of
millions of dollars. He had an office on the forty-first floor of the Henry
Cobb–designed 200 Clarendon, the tallest building in New England, which
locals still lovingly referred to as the John Hancock Building. Befitting a
man with sweeping views of most of eastern Massachusetts, Pagliuca had
gradually shifted his focus away from private-equity investing and toward
other pursuits. In 2003, Pagliuca had purchased an ownership share of the
Boston Celtics. He was often seen courtside. The team had won a championship in 2008, the first for the storied franchise in more than twenty years.

Pagliuca also had an interest in politics. He had run for United States
Senate in 2009, in a special election held after the death of Senator Ted
Kennedy. Up against experienced politicians in Martha Coakley and Congressman Mike Capuano, and the social entrepreneur Alan Khazei, Pagliuca
had come in a disappointing last place in the Democratic primary. He spent
more than $7.75 million of his own money to win just 80,248 votes—at $104
per vote, that campaign held the ignominious mark as the statewide cam-

paign with the highest cost per vote in Massachusetts history. But Pagliuca's disappointing performance in that election was more a function of his political inexperience and naïveté than it was a reflection of his likability and character. Fish, in his worst moments, had been perceived as a self-serving construction magnate eager to pad his wealth and solidify his influence. Pagliuca seemed much less threatening. At worst, he was a bored rich guy who was eager to get off the sidelines and try his hand at civic affairs. Some might question Pagliuca's wisdom, but few would question his motives.

For Pagliuca, Boston 2024 may have presented a tantalizing opportunity for a second, redemptive act in Massachusetts politics. In that, he had a role model in his friend and former business partner Mitt Romney. Pagliuca had watched Romney triumphantly enter the 2002 opening ceremonies in Salt Lake City. "Mitt's walking with kings," Pagliuca had mused at the time.[1] Like Pagliuca, Romney had failed in his first run at political office, losing to Ted Kennedy in 1994 in a campaign for the US Senate. The Salt Lake City Games had revived Romney's political career; he had pivoted on the notoriety to launch another statewide campaign in Massachusetts, this time for governor. Just nine months after the Salt Lake City closing ceremonies, Romney would win Massachusetts's corner office. For Romney, competent management of the Olympics had been a path to political success. It might be the same for his friend Pagliuca.

Indeed, Pagliuca's Bain Capital was known for its corporate turnarounds—which was exactly what Boston 2024 needed. So as Pagliuca assumed the helm of the beleaguered bid, the talking points were no different from the ones Bain Capital might share just after it had purchased a controlling stake in a failing company: "Yes, Boston 2024 had struggled. But the fundamentals behind the idea were strong, and new leadership, direction, and expertise could get things back on track."

One problem with this narrative was that Pagliuca wasn't new to Boston 2024. Back in January 2014, Pagliuca had been listed in Boston 2024's articles of incorporation as one of just five directors (the others were Fish, O'Connell, Bentley University president Gloria Larson, and New England Patriots owner Bob Kraft). Pagliuca had backed the bid throughout 2014, advocating for it in television appearances and writing an op-ed in Boston's *Banker & Tradesman* magazine that hailed the bid that had been submitted to the USOC as "A Boon for Beantown" and a "well thought-out plan."[2] As reported by *Boston Globe* reporter Shira Springer, Pagliuca had been ensconced at Boston 2024's headquarters the night of the USOC decision in January, wearing his Celtics championship ring for good luck. Pagliuca was hardly swooping in from the outside to clean up the mess—he'd been an integral part of the effort from its earliest days.

But even if he wasn't new to Boston 2024, Pagliuca was effective at communicating a fresh, humbler approach. In addition to talking about the bid's benefits, Boston 2024 was now willing to acknowledge that the bid had risks. As Pagliuca put it to the *Boston Globe*: "The crux of this is getting an objective, fact-based [plan] out there for all constituencies so they can see the potential benefits and risks."[3] Thus Pagliuca's pitch to Bostonians resembled one he might make to an investment committee at Bain Capital: any investment has risks, but, in this case, the risks were far outweighed by the potential for a lucrative return.

But to compare Boston 2024 to one of Bain Capital's leveraged buyouts was a dramatic oversimplification. In a Bain deal, an investment pool is sprinkled around to a half-dozen investments or more. If any single investment flounders, the potential losses are limited to whatever amount was invested in that particular deal. For Boston 2024, Pagliuca was asking Boston taxpayers to sign a financial guarantee to cover losses if the costs of the investment doubled, tripled, or quadrupled—a condition to which an investor in one of Bain Capital's funds would never agree.

Boston 2024 also announced the addition of new heavy hitters to bolster Pagliuca's leadership. Lucchino and former advertising executive Jack Connors were made unpaid senior advisers to the bid committee. Peter Roby, the athletic director at Northeastern University, became another vice-chairman. But the new additions weren't steeped in the day-to-day details of the bid and weren't being asked to make substantive contributions to the organization. When the well-liked Roby joined Jim Braude on WGBH's *Greater Boston* show, he acknowledged that the bid's communications efforts had been lackluster, grading them as a "C+ or B-."[4] But Roby had difficulty stating his own reasons for supporting the bid, falling back on the same tired talking points that had earned Boston 2024 its mediocre report card. It would be Roby's sole media appearance on behalf of the bid.

Jack Connors, the revered and respected Boston businessman and philanthropist, found himself in a similar position as Roby. Connors had run Boston advertising firm Hill Holiday and for sixteen years had been the chairman of Partners HealthCare, a hospital network that included Massachusetts General Hospital and Brigham and Women's Hospital that was one of the largest employers in the state. In the summer of 2014, Connors had offered only lukewarm support for the bid, saying, "You know I think it's a healthy exercise . . . I think it's pretty exciting. Pretty healthy. I told John [Fish] I wouldn't be playing a role . . . I think it's a good way to keep the mind and body exercised for a while. I don't see anything bad coming out of it."[5] A year later, when Connors appeared on Braude's *Greater Boston* on July 7, 2015, his support seemed similarly lukewarm—even though he was now officially part of the committee. He only half-heartedly defended the bid, saying, "It's now really in the hands of the electeds. The mayor and the governor will decide whether this is right . . . they'll make the right decision . . . This is not critical to our economy, but it's a good idea that deserves a conversation. And that's what's going on right now."[6] It wasn't exactly a hard sell from a man who had built one of the country's great advertising firms.

The task of articulating a clear case for the Games was also proving challenging for Boston 2024's supporters in the media. *Boston Globe* business columnist Shirley Leung had established herself early on as the bid's most vocal and prominent media booster, penning a series of columns that urged Bostonians to embrace Boston 2024's vision. She joined Roby on the May 26 episode of Braude's *Greater Boston* and called Boston 2024 "a great idea."[7] But even more than four months after the release of Boston 2024's bid documents, Leung's grasp of the bid details seemed tenuous. "I mean we're talking [about building] two venues, really. The temporary stadium and the athletic village. And I think everything else is already built," she said. But, of course, Boston 2024's bid required the construction of much more than that, including a velodrome, an aquatics center, and a media and press center. These were not insignificant items—London 2012's Olympic Committee had spent well over $1 billion on these facilities.[8]

Leung did have one thing right in her interview with Braude. "To me the secret weapon is Charlie Baker . . . he's the insurance policy," she said, "If people believe what Charlie Baker believes in the plan . . . people will

	LONDON 2012 Bid Estimate	LONDON 2012 Actual Cost	Percentage Overrun	BOSTON 2024 June 2015 Bid Documents
Olympic Stadium	$423 million ⟶	$1.1 billion	162%	$176 million for a "temporary" stadium at Widett Circle
Aquatics Center	$113 million ⟶	$404 million	256%	$70 million for a "temporary" venue at a still undetermined location
Velodrome	$30 million ⟶	$158 million	427%	$64 million for a "temporary" venue at a still undetermined location

> London 2012 spent more than $1.6b on venues that Boston 2024 estimates will cost only $310m.

For simplicity, figures in British pounds converted to dollars at 1 GBP to 1.5 USD.
Actual exchange rate in construction period was more than 1.6 USD to 1 GBP.

5

A table from No Boston Olympics' standard presentation, highlighting some of Boston 2024's expensive venue requirements. No Boston Olympics

come around to it." Despite being a Republican in a largely Democratic state, Baker was one of the most popular governors in the country. An April poll pegged his approval rating at 70 percent.[9] Baker had cultivated a reputation as an executive driven by dispassionate policy analysis, not ideology or political expedience. Governor Baker had the power to kill Boston 2024 outright or to give it new life.

Zimbalist happened to have met with Baker earlier in the year, as each waited in the green room of Braude's *Greater Boston* interview program. Baker had displayed an open-minded curiosity about Zimbalist's critique at the time. But while the administration had met with Boston 2024 on a number of occasions, it hadn't met with bid opponents. In early May, Gossett reached out to a friend who worked in Governor Baker's office, asking to connect with the governor's team to discuss the bid. Within a few days, No Boston Olympics was invited to meet with Governor Baker's chief of staff, Steve Kadish, who had been appointed by Baker to take the lead on the administration's response to Boston 2024, as well as Baker's chief legal counsel, Lon Povich. The brainy and genial duo seemed receptive to No Boston Olympics' detailed, analytic PowerPoint presentation. It was an encouraging entrée to Baker's team. The next day, Dempsey circled back by the governor's office to drop off a thank-you note and a copy of Zimbalist's book *Circus Maximus: The Economic Gamble behind Hosting the Olympics and the World Cup* for Kadish to read.

Kadish's assistant called Dempsey a few hours later. Dempsey answered, expecting only perhaps a recognition that the book had been received (unbeknownst to Dempsey, Kadish already owned it, and had shared it with others on his team). When he learned the true purpose of the call, Dempsey was floored. Kadish wanted No Boston Olympics to make a presentation to Governor Baker at an upcoming cabinet meeting. Arranging a meeting with No Boston Olympics was a deft political stroke for Baker. It demonstrated a clear willingness to hear both sides of the Olympic debate and positioned the governor squarely and safely in the middle of a high-profile topic that had divided voters throughout the state.

But in meeting with Baker and his cabinet on May 15, No Boston Olympics' leaders were immediately aware that the governor's interest in meeting with bid opponents was about much more than political positioning. Baker and his team were rolling up their sleeves and getting deeply engaged in the details of the International Olympic Committee's process and Boston 2024's bid. No Boston Olympics' presentation, developed largely by Dempsey, the former management consultant, was stylistically a good fit for Governor Baker, who had earned an MBA from Kellogg and had spent years in the business world. The presentation's first slide made clear the costs and risks to state government of Boston's Olympic bid: (1) the bid required either explicit or implicit approval of the IOC's taxpayer guarantee for cost overruns or revenue shortfalls; (2) the Olympics would be a statewide agenda-setter, regardless of other public priorities; and (3) state leaders would bear responsibility for Boston 2024's actions, without having control over those actions. The data-heavy PowerPoint slides then dissected Boston 2024's budget while debunking Olympic myths, including the myth that previous Games hosted in the United States had been profitable. While the cerebral Baker and his team mostly asked questions and stated few opinions, Dempsey, Gossett, and Kerr left the meeting confident that the governor intended to assess the bid objectively. For No Boston Olympics, it felt like an enormous win.

Baker wanted to assert more authority over the bid process, even as he maintained his independence from the organizing committee itself. He told the *Boston Globe* that the public needed to have ample time to assess the proposal before the USOC submitted Boston's name to the IOC on September 15, calling for Boston 2024 to share an updated version of its bid by "probably late May or early June."[10] Suddenly, Boston 2024 couldn't get away with another "proof of concept"—Bid 2.0 needed to be a thorough, detailed plan. And it needed to be delivered within a matter of weeks, not at some ambiguous point in the distant future. The governor had ratcheted up the pressure on the bid committee.

The governor was playing it down the middle, but Boston 2024 still had its staunch political supporters. One was Boston city councilor Bill Linehan. It would be hard to mistake Linehan for anything other than a proud son of South Boston. The councilor spoke with a Boston accent, was fond of donning a scally cap, and had a fierce pride for the famous working-class neighborhood he represented. Two decades earlier, Linehan had helped bring the IAAF World Cross-Country Championships to Franklin Park. In 2015, Linehan was the president of the Boston City Council, an elected body of thirteen members that often took a visible role in the city's public policy debates, even if it held relatively little formal power in the city's strong-mayor system. To help improve Boston 2024's profile and to provide a welcoming platform for the boosters to make their case to a skeptical public, Linehan created within the city council a special committee for the 2024 Olympics. He appointed himself as the committee's chair, with broad powers to set meeting schedules and agendas.

But the hearings didn't go quite as Linehan had hoped. The first meeting, in March, had provided an opportunity for No Boston Olympics to testify, putting the organization on equal footing with Boston 2024. In June, at the hearing meant to address budget issues, Boston 2024's Davey said he was unable to share updated budget documents until the full Bid 2.0 document was released the following week—leaving city councilors such as Olympic skeptic Tito Jackson slack-jawed.

But the most damaging hearing for Linehan's special committee occurred on May 18, when IOC and USOC board member Angela Ruggiero was invited to testify. Ruggiero was a Harvard graduate and a winner of four medals in Olympic ice hockey—one of the most celebrated women in the sport's history. As a member of both the IOC and USOC, Ruggiero had a unique perspective on Boston 2024 and its international prospects. Linehan invited Ruggiero specifically to discuss Agenda 2020, the IOC's nominal efforts to reform the bidding process in the wake of costly Games in Beijing, London, and Sochi. Ruggiero contributed two hours of largely competent, uneventful testimony—but just a few sentences that she uttered were what made headlines. While answering a question about the USOC's bid process, Ruggiero somewhat naively admitted that the IOC wasn't fully committed to the Boston bid. "There's no guarantee Boston will be the [bid] city in September," she said.[11] After three months of anonymous rumors that the USOC might switch to Los Angeles—all denied by USOC spokespeople—Ruggiero's testimony was the first public admission by a USOC representative that the Boston bid was in doubt. Boston's media seized on the remark. In just a few short months, the bid had gone from inevitable to very much in jeopardy.

No Boston Olympics continued to focus on building its base of grassroots support. On May 18, the same day as Ruggiero's testimony, the group held another organizing meeting, where again more than one hundred people showed up to hear from the group's leaders and learn how they could help the effort. No Boston Olympics' special guest that night was city councilor Ayanna Pressley, who voiced her concerns with the bid, even as she didn't take a firm stance on either side of the debate. The appearance by the popular, savvy, and high-profile Pressley presented quite a contrast to No Boston Olympics' January organizing meeting, when not a single elected official had attended. No Boston Olympics armed its supporters with facts, walking them through "10 Things to Know about Boston 2024," and sharing a presentation similar to the one that Dempsey, Gossett, and Kerr had provided Governor Baker. No Boston Olympics also focused on making it easy for its supporters to take action, providing online tools so that its supporters could sign a petition, contact their city councilors, or make a contribution to the organization.

It that was apparent from observing the attendees that there was no such thing as a "typical" No Boston Olympics supporter. Some were citizens who had been active in civic issues in the past—others, like Mike Casella from Boston's Brighton neighborhood, were inspired by the group to get off the political sidelines for the first time. The middle-aged Casella even built a heavy-duty homemade yard sign that he installed in his front lawn—the first political sign ever to grace his property, he told No Boston Olympics' leaders. Many No Boston Olympics supporters were progressives and liberals. But many others were conservatives. Early in their efforts, No Boston Olympics received the endorsement of Citizens for Limited Taxation (CLT), an iconic, conservative citizens' organization that had fought for lower taxes and against government waste in Massachusetts for more than forty years. Chip Faulkner, CLT's assistant director, attended the No Boston Olympics organizing meeting. The Boston 2024 bid became a punching bag for popular conservative talk-show host Howie Carr, who hosted Dempsey and other bid opponents. Dempsey, a lifelong Democrat who had been policy director for Democratic congressman Joe Kennedy III, had even been invited to speak at a meeting of the arch-conservative *Greater Boston Tea Party*. The crowd of activists there playfully booed as he confessed his Democratic allegiances.

While the battle for grassroots support raged on at home, the Boosters' Dilemma meant that Boston 2024 still needed to focus on wooing the International Olympic Committee. On May 27, Boston 2024's representatives traveled to the IOC's headquarters in Lausanne to meet with Olympic staff—its official visit as part of the "invitation phase" of the bidding process.

As fate would have it, May 27 was the very day that the United States Justice Department and Swiss authorities had chosen to arrest and indict FIFA officials in Zurich for accepting bribes in awarding of the 2018 and 2022 World Cups to Russia and Qatar, among other transgressions. The timing could not have been worse for Boston's Olympic boosters. While Boston 2024 officials were meeting behind closed doors with one unelected, secretive, and monolithic Swiss-based world sports organization, the justice department was arresting and hauling away members of another. (The feds made sure the media got good photographs to splash on websites and newspapers around the globe.) Given FIFA's geographic breadth, the news of the arrests made headlines in every country—but it was received uniquely in Boston, where citizens were weighing whether they could entrust their city's future to another unregulated, international sports monopoly.

The next day, May 28, Brookline's town meeting, the suburban town's legislative branch, voted 70 percent to 30 percent to support a resolution opposing Boston 2024's bid, joining neighboring Cambridge as the second municipality to go on record against the bid. No Boston Olympics' Dempsey and other Brookline residents had spoken on behalf of the resolution, while a handful opposed it. Boston 2024 chose not to send its staff—perhaps because its senior team was wooing the IOC in Europe. The best the boosters could do was print out a letter and place it at the entrance of the meeting hall. Most of the copies went untouched.

One final blow at the end of May was the result of clever public records requests submitted by *Boston Magazine* reporter Kyle Clauss and the staff at the *Boston Business Journal*. Both outlets had realized that because the Donahue Institute, the research team hired by the Boston Foundation to develop the pro–Boston 2024 study, was a public institution, any documents or communications they had received from Boston 2024 were subject to the state's public records law. Clauss arrived at work one day to find a manila envelope with a compact disc inside. It was labeled simply "Bid Book."

The documents saved onto the disc were versions of the December 1 bid—but they were more complete than what Boston 2024 had shared with the public in January. While they were still missing some sections that Boston 2024 had never provided the Donahue Institute, these new versions revealed a few new facts about the boosters' bid:

1. The boosters planned to use a public authority to purchase land for the Olympic stadium. The authority would use tax increment financing (TIF) to fund the purchase of the land—the public authority would issue the bonds that would be paid back by increases in real estate taxes. Those bonds put taxpayers at risk should Boston 2024's planned development not come to fruition on the expected scale or timeline.

2. Boston 2024 planned to utilize an expanded Boston Convention and Exhibition Center to host smaller Olympic events like judo and table tennis. In December, the boosters had told the USOC that the center was "currently undergoing" this $1 billion expansion. But the work hadn't yet broken ground. Governor Baker had placed a hold on that planned expansion in April and had given no indication that the expansion would proceed.

3. The boosters had told the USOC that the New Boston Food Market, a cooperative of food wholesalers that owned much of the land at Widett

Circle, was "for sale." This contradicted public statements that the market's owners had made.

The release of these documents exposed Boston 2024's penchant for stating one thing behind closed doors to the USOC and an entirely different thing to the public. This, ultimately, was how the boosters had attempted to neutralize or navigate the Boosters' Dilemma: rather than choose between the demands of the USOC and the demands of the public, the boosters would just tell each side what it wanted to hear. No Boston Olympics called the revelation "the smoking gun"—a phrase suggested to them by Ray Howell, and one that was quickly picked up by the *New York Times* and many of the local media covering the story.

The first comment posted on Clauss's online article breaking the story was emblematic of the broader public response to these revelations:

> These people are unbelievable. Boston 2024 doesn't just want to sell the Olympics in Boston, they want to shove it down our throats. Everything about this bid is so disingenuous. Every public utterance. I wish Walsh wasn't so deep into this—I like the guy but this whole thing is turning me off. And I wasn't necessarily against it in the beginning.[12]

The release of the documents further eroded public trust and heightened skepticism of the boosters' motives, intentions, and tactics. As June approached, Boston 2024 was reeling.

EIGHT

JUNE 2015

The state house's "Big Three"—Charlie Baker, Stan Rosenberg, and Bob DeLeo—announced on June 1 that they had selected the Brattle Group as the outside consultant to analyze Boston 2024's bid. A week later, No Boston Olympics' leaders were back in the governor's office, meeting with Brattle's economists to share their concerns about the bid. Encouragingly, they found Brattle's team, led by PhDs Coleman Bazelon, Steve Herscovici, and Pallavi Seth, to be open to, and inquisitive about, the opponents' concerns. It was also encouraging that the entire team at the Brattle Group was reading Zimbalist's *Circus Maximus*. Baker had stuck to his promise and his brand, hiring a group that would take a dispassionate view of the pros and cons of the bid.

In early June, much to his shock and amusement, Zimbalist received a call from bid leader Steve Pagliuca in his office. Pagliuca began the call by telling Zimbalist that he had just finished reading *Circus Maximus* and found it very interesting. Pagliuca explained his view that *Circus Maximus* provided a roadmap about how to do the Olympics the right way. Accordingly, Pagliuca told Zimbalist that he wanted him to work for Boston 2024. Zimbalist thanked him for the kind words and the invitation, but explained that it would be impossible for him to work on behalf of the group because he did not believe hosting would be good for the Boston or Massachusetts economies, and that, moreover, billions of dollars of public money would be spent with little to show for it. Pagliuca was undeterred and repeated his invitation several times during a phone conversation that lasted more than thirty minutes, insisting that a new plan (Bid 2.0) would be much different and more fiscally responsible than the early one submitted to the USOC in December. Zimbalist told Pagliuca that he would be willing to read over the new plan and make comments, but he would only do so as an interested citizen, not as a member of Boston 2024.

Zimbalist had spent much of his time since January giving public talks in *Greater Boston* and elsewhere in Massachusetts on Boston 2024's bid. This included appearances before the Massachusetts state senate, the Boston finance commission, and the Boston NAACP, at UMass-Boston, and at a citizen's forum in Jamaica Plain. He also participated in regular radio and television interviews, spoke with state legislators and city council members, fielded calls from journalists, contributed op-eds to the *Boston Globe*, and wrote an article for *Harvard Magazine*. Since Zimbalist's most recent book, *Circus Maximus*, mostly told the story of the substantial odds against hosting an economically sensible Olympics and World Cup, it seemed that Pagliuca's true purpose was not to seek intellectual guidance, but rather to co-opt a leading critical voice.

Boston 2024 was also unable to co-opt another critical voice, that of Evan Falchuk, the former gubernatorial candidate and leader of the small but vocal United Independent Party. Falchuk had committed his party to lead a statewide effort to place on the ballot a question that would bar public funds from being used on Boston 2024. It had proven to be an effective organizing tool for the party, which needed to add voters to its rolls in order to retain legal status as a "major party" alongside Democrats and Republicans. On June 23, the liberal-leaning Falchuk announced that the United Independent Party would team up with a conservative coalition known as Tank the Gas Tax, the group that had worked successfully to eliminate the indexing of the gas tax to inflation. It was yet another example of how opposition to Boston 2024 was uniting allies across the political spectrum. The announcement increased the likelihood that *multiple* questions about an Olympic bid would appear on the ballet in 2016, when Boston 2024 had committed to including a question of its own. (Zakim's questions also remained a possibility for a municipal ballot in 2015.) Falchuk's efforts complicated Boston 2024's path forward.

That path was also complicated by financial challenges—the boosters' fundraising machine was sputtering. The boosters had originally projected to raise and spend $75 million between the organization's inception and the IOC's vote in September 2017. Roughly $65 million of that would be raised and spent after the USOC's decision. That meant the organization needed to raise more than $8 million per quarter. But in the first quarter of 2015, Boston 2024 announced that it had raised just $3.9 million in cash and in-kind contributions, far below its required pace. As public opinion soured, it was becoming harder and harder for Boston 2024 to raise funds from the wealthy individuals and large corporations that had fueled it in 2014.[1] One reporter with close ties to Boston's business community telephoned Dempsey to see if he could confirm rumors that Boston 2024 was delaying payments to vendors. The cash crunch put even more pressure on Boston 2024 to produce a "2.0" bid that could get the organization back on track.

It didn't help that international Olympic journalists were reporting that the IOC had *already* given up on Boston 2024's bid. On June 18, Alan Abrahamson published a story developed after conversations with IOC members at a visit to IOC headquarters in Lausanne. "Move. They had their opportunity. They fucked it around," he quoted one influential IOC member as saying. "The sooner the better. It has to be now," said another, as he formed an imaginary pistol with his hand, held it to his head, and pulled the trigger.[2] Winning over the IOC was Boston 2024's ultimate goal, so the quotes had to be discouraging. But if Boston 2024 wanted another chance to repair its image with IOC members, first it would have to make progress in the political battle at home. Boston's Olympic opponents had forced the boosters to fight a two-front war.

Because the city of Boston's budget was too small to take on the immense financial burden of hosting the Olympics, and because the bid would now be put to a statewide vote, Boston 2024 knew it needed to build support in communities around Massachusetts—not just in Boston. The most effective tool at its disposal was to promise that regions outside Boston would play host to Olympic events, even if this idea was in conflict with the bid's original pitch—that the Games would be "walkable," and that the city of Boston would be the Olympic park. Less prosperous regions of the state were clamoring for events. Moreover, they would be unlikely to support a Games that left them out of the economic windfall the boosters claimed would accompany the event. So as June rolled on, Boston 2024 made a series of announcements about venues in different parts of the state. New Bedford, the historic whaling port that was now a working-class fishing community, was awarded sailing. Worcester, thirty-five miles west of Boston, was given team handball. Lowell, home of state senator Donoghue, was confirmed as the host of rowing and boxing. (The public would have to pay for the removal of a bridge and potentially for the construction of a dam on Lowell's Merrimack River, but no cost estimates for this work were ever included in the Boston 2024 bid. Boston's iconic Charles River, home to one of rowing's highest-profile regattas, the Head of the Charles, was deemed unfit for Olympic standards.) Holyoke, the birthplace of volleyball and home to the Volleyball Hall of Fame, and Springfield, the birthplace of basketball and home to the Basketball Hall of Fame, each ninety miles west of Boston, were promised a share of preliminary rounds in each sport.

One of Boston 2024's more controversial venues, the beach volleyball stadium on Boston Common, was moved to remote Squantum Point in the city of Quincy, where a state park offered dramatic views of the city of Boston across Dorchester Bay. Logistically, it was a difficult location. The point was part of a peninsula that had few access roads. The event would require the construction of a pier to shuttle visitors by ferry from downtown Boston. Why would Boston 2024 pick such a difficult spot for one of the most popular Olympic events? Why not pick an existing sporting facility? Why not one of the colleges or universities that the boosters were regularly referencing as potential hosts? The answer, again, was television. Those dramatic views of Boston's skyline from Squantum Point might not have been as compelling as Boston Common, but they were still pretty good, even if they would only work in one direction: immediately to the south of the proposed temporary stadium was an ugly, unadorned, two-story industrial building. Boston 2024's graphic artists chose to leave out that unpleasant structure in the renderings produced to promote the new location.

A more auspicious venue change from Bid 1.0 to Bid 2.0 was the proposal to move tennis from Harvard University's campus to Dorchester's Harambee Park. Located along Blue Hill Avenue in the heart of a tough but proud neighborhood, the park was home to the Sportsmen's Tennis and Enrichment Center, which happened to be the oldest African-American-founded and -led tennis club in the United States. The center was an oasis of learning and youth development in a community where growing up is not always easy. The center's executive director, Toni Wiley, was an eloquent advocate for the organization's work, and became a persuasive media surrogate for Boston 2024. The image of inner-city youth playing tennis appealed to a broad swath of residents across the state: The next Serena Williams or Arthur Ashe might just come from Boston, and Boston 2024 could help make that possible. If Boston 2024 was going to leave any positive legacy, a dramatically updated and improved tennis facility in Dorchester would be it.

But despite these glimmers of hope, Mayor Walsh and his team were becoming more and more worried about the bid's stagnant public support and its potential to threaten the mayor's reelection prospects. The bid's troubles were causing journalists to ask tough questions about the mayor's judgment and stewardship over the complex project. Walsh had become so flustered by the process that he had difficulty providing a clear answer when asked if he had read the bid before signing off on it.

In December 2014, Walsh had told WGBH, "I have read the bid." But on Monday, June 8, 2015, Walsh to WGBH, "No . . . It was many, many pages. Our legal counsel looked at it." Pressed for a clarification by the *Boston Globe*, Walsh's team issued this statement: "Mayor Walsh was familiar with the concept plan proposed by Boston 2024 to the United States Olympic Committee in December 2014. The City of Boston's legal department was briefed on the specifics and advised the mayor accordingly." In December, the mayor had said that he had read the bid. Now it seemed that Walsh was saying his legal team had "been briefed" on the content, but hadn't actually read it themselves.[3]

It was an embarrassing situation for the Walsh administration. But in this case, the mayor may have been choosing embarrassment over a far worse outcome: having to release the full, unredacted bid documents that had been submitted in December. The chapters shared with the Donahue Institute had been released, but other chapters still remained secret. If the city admitted it had been in possession of the bid, by law, Bid 1.0 would be a public document, subject to public records law requests. After the mayor's remarks to WBGH in June, *Boston Magazine* reporter Kyle Clauss made just such a request to city hall. The city's response to Clauss's request was telling:

> The City of Boston's legal department engaged in discussions with Boston 2024 and its consultants in order to be briefed on the specifics that would

be included in Boston 2024's proposal to the United States Olympic Committee in December 2014 and advised the mayor accordingly. Examples of those discussions would be negotiations on the Joinder Agreement (a document that was received by the City of Boston and provided under the public records law), briefings on venue plans and securing the insurance policy to indemnify the City of Boston (also a document that was received by the City of Boston and provided under the public records law). All of these discussions would have taken place as the bid book was being prepared and finalized. The City of Boston was never in receipt of the bid book that was officially submitted to the USOC in December 2014.[4]

In hindsight, city hall must have known that the release of the full, unredacted bid documents would be a devastating blow to the bid's prospects. The Walsh administration was better off denying it ever had possession of the documents, even if this contradicted the mayor's earlier statements. As a result, city hall's official position was that the mayor had signed off on the bid documents, even though neither he nor anyone on his team at city hall had actually received or read them.

The mayor and the boosters were eager to move the conversation beyond "Bid 1.0." Boston 2024 released "Bid 2.0" on June 29, at an event at the Boston Convention Center, the same building that had hosted the triumphant press conference in January. Bid 2.0 retained the same high-level budget structure as Bid 1.0, with four major buckets: the OCOG, the non-OCOG, public infrastructure, and security. For the OCOG and non-OCOG, the boosters now provided much more detail. And unlike Bid 1.0, in which revenues and costs neatly balanced, Boston 2024's updated bid actually projected a surplus in the OCOG budget of $210 million, with $4.805 billion in revenues outpacing $4.595 billion in costs.

The boosters had also created two lengthy, glossy prospectus documents that described the two most substantial construction projects: the Olympic village, on Dorchester's Columbia Point; and the "Midtown" development, home first to the temporary Olympic stadium and then after the Games to a new, mixed-used neighborhood.

Boston 2024's Olympic village complex would create 2,950 housing units, additional housing for 2,700 students at nearby UMass-Boston and elsewhere, restaurants, art space, parking, and improved neighborhood amenities including a street grid and parkland. The prospectus included detailed information on each site's existing infrastructure—down to the diameter of water pipes in close proximity—and the future investments that would be needed. The plan would rely on a master developer, to be chosen by the city of Boston, to assemble $2.9 billion in financing. Boston 2024 was proposing a vibrant, dynamic new neighborhood on a valuable piece of land that was clearly underutilized. By almost any standard, it was a vast improvement over the site's current condition and uses, which included a derelict convention hall, parking lots, and decades-old office buildings.

Boston 2024's proposed transformation of Widett Circle was even more impressive than what it promised for Columbia Point. In place of low-slung food warehouses and above the active rail and train maintenance yards, a developer would erect a massive steel superstructure that would host the temporary Olympic stadium and other athletic facilities. Once the Games left town and the stadium was demolished, the structure would be the foundation of a new neighborhood with nearly eight million square feet of offices, residences, hotels, and shops.

The visions were appealing. But both proposals came with enormous costs and risks that ultimately would be borne by taxpayers. First, Boston 2024 was asking for deep property tax breaks—what the *Boston Globe* called "probably the largest deal of its kind in the city's history."[5] The tax breaks at Widett Circle would start at 85 percent, gradually scaling down over the next forty years. Even civic watchdogs who had remained largely quiet throughout the Boston 2024 debate, muffled by fears of affronting their funders, expressed skepticism of the wisdom and scale of Boston 2024's suggested subsidies: "It seems overly ambitious or optimistic from a developer's perspective of what the city would agree to, given their past experience," Boston Municipal Research Bureau President Sam Tyler told the *Globe*.

But it was more than just the immensity of the required tax breaks—it was also the fundamental risk of the construction itself. If private developers never materialized to begin the project, as was the case with the Olympic village for London 2012, or if they abandoned the deal halfway through, as was the case of Vancouver 2010, the city and its taxpayers would be on the hook to step in and complete the construction. Boston 2024's attempts to address these risks with insurance are discussed below.

Bid 2.0 also laid out specific public infrastructure projects that would be associated with the bid, including improvements to JFK/UMass Station, a revamp of Kosciuszko Circle by Columbia Point, and an expansion of Broadway Station in South Boston. But just as they had from the early days of the process, the boosters could not identify new transportation revenues that would pay for these projects. To pursue them would mean crowding out other projects around the state.

Just as with the release of the Bid 1.0 documents in January, Boston 2024's plan was quickly picked apart by No Boston Olympics, No Boston 2024, and members of the media. Bid 2.0 had some glaring omissions—for example, it identified no location for the velodrome, one of the most expensive Olympic venues. London had projected its velodrome to cost $32 million; it ended up costing more than $160 million. Boston 2024 had budgeted only $64 million. The aquatics center was also locationless. London's originally had been budgeted at $121 million; it had ultimately cost a staggering $430 million to build. Boston 2024 had allocated just $70 million for the structure. Nor was there a location for the 1 million-square-foot international broadcast and media center (IBC/MPC). In Bid 1.0, the IBC/MPC had been described as a permanent facility on Fort Point Channel, slated to cost $500 million; in Bid 2.0, it would be a rented facility and cost only $51 million, although no landlord or developer had been identified.

The budgets for the Olympic village and Olympic stadium were even more fanciful and financially destructive for Boston. The tax subsidies to be offered to the prospective developers at Widett Circle were estimated at $269 per square foot and at the Columbia Point Olympic village at $199 per square foot. Contrast these bloated tax subsidies with those offered by the city to the developers at Fenway Center at $4 per square foot or at Vertex Pharmaceutical at $11 per square foot. That is, the city was being asked to offer subsidies twenty or more times the subsidy size of similar development deals. Even assuming that Boston 2024 could find willing developers at these subsidy levels (and the eventual report to the governor by the Brattle Group questioned whether it could), it is uncertain whether the city council would have gone along with these incentives. If economically viable projects can

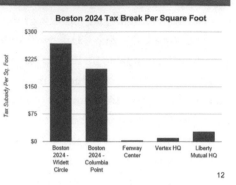

A graph from No Boston Olympics' standard presentation, highlighting Boston 2024's lucrative proposed tax incentives. No Boston Olympics

be induced with 1/20th or 1/67th the level of subsidy, why forego the tax revenue and give up some of the few remaining developable plots of real estate in the city?

The question becomes even more pressing because the Boston 2024 plan involved adding 4,000 housing units at Widett Circle and 2,700 at Columbia Point post-Olympics, but the plan had no space or financial allocation for schools, libraries, public health clinics, or police stations. Boston 2024 Bid 2.0 also relied upon quixotic cost assumptions. For instance, Boston 2024 planned to build a 20-acre-plus deck over the railyards at Widett Circle, upon which it would build the stadium. It budgeted only $10 million for the air rights to these 20 acres. Yet, based on air rights at Hudson Yards in New York City and the Fenway Center development over the Massachusetts Turnpike, the air rights were worth more than $300 million. Boston 2024 projected that the deck itself would cost only $785 million to build, but, based on the construction costs of the decks at Hudson Yards and Fenway Center, a more realistic projection would have been $1.4 billion. Further, the Widett Circle and Columbia Point projects included a 10 percent contingency fund, but projects at similar early conceptual stages more typically contain 20 to 30 percent contingency budgets.[6] Moreover, Summer Olympics cost overruns since 1980 have averaged 252 percent—a 10 percent contingency hardly seemed adequate. Boston 2024 projected transportation costs at $50 million during the Games, even though Atlanta 1996 spent $150 million (in 2016 prices) on this operating expense.[7]

The temporary Olympic stadium, now designed to hold sixty-nine thousand in Bid 2.0 (up from sixty thousand in Bid 1.0), would be the largest temporary stadium ever built and was projected to cost $175.5 million; yet, a temporary Olympic stadium that was to be constructed in the Chicago 2016 plan was budgeted at $392 million (in 2016 prices).[8] Overall, in its report for the governor's office, the Brattle Group estimated that Bid 2.0 understated likely costs of hosting the 2024 Games by $2.9 billion, before considering indirect and opportunity costs.[9]

Numerous sanguine assumptions on the revenue side of the ledger also appeared in the bid. For instance, Bid 2.0 assumed that average ticket prices for all events would be $137. Such a number might make sense for premier events. But when preliminary volleyball matches or handball games between Slovenia and Argentina are included in the mix, an average price of $137 becomes starry-eyed. One factor boosting average ticket prices was Bid 2.0's intention to hold some preliminary events in major arenas throughout the northeast corridor from Washington to Boston. Since the City of Boston was being called upon to provide a financial guarantee, the location of these events was problematic. Another assumption was that 90 percent of all available tickets would be sold. Given that Atlanta sold 85 percent of its tickets, on this score Bid 2.0 again seemed optimistic.

Boston 2024 acknowledged the cost overruns and risks of previous Olympic Games, but the boosters claimed to have developed a new model for insurance against such risks. Bid 2.0, unlike Bid 1.0, included a line item for insurance payments. These payments were estimated at $128 million and would purchase multiple, layered insurance policies that the boosters claimed would guarantee that no public dollars would be used in the end. While these proposed policies did mitigate certain risks, they did not come close to what was being asserted, which insurance experts explained. "Insurers do not cover risks that are certain to materialize, and almost every Olympics in the recent past has had major cost overruns," offered Boston College law professor Patricia McCoy. "Any suggestion that private insurance will pick that up is smoke and mirrors."[10] The basic problems are that insurance policies will not cover changes in scope and they will not insure a holder against the holder's own mismanagement.

Moreover, Boston 2024's insurance plan was conceptual. No company had signed on and no company would provide pricing quotes until more was known about the final plans and about the construction companies and general contractors.

The Brattle Group's report to Governor Baker assessed Boston 2024's proposed insurance policies as follows:

> Of course . . . not every contingency is insurable; insurance for scope creep—expansions in what is included in preparing for an Olympic Games—could be prohibitively expensive because it could increase the likelihood of scope changes. It was also too early in the bid process to evaluate the expected cost of the proposed insurance plans; the cost and terms of many of the types of insurance that Boston 2024 proposes would not have been known until a contractor was selected. The costs of such plans would have been sensitive to the details of the final Bid requirements. For example, insurance against cost overruns is very sensitive to how well costs have been estimated because every dollar of expected overruns will be included in the calculation of premiums. . . . Although details about various components of the Bid were continuously being developed by Boston 2024, sufficiently detailed information to evaluate the costs of the proposed insurance policies were still years away.[11]

Boston 2024's inability to find locations for key facilities raised further questions. Pressed by *Globe* reporter Michael Levenson about the location of the IBC/MPC, Boston 2024 CEO Richard Davey responded, "We feel like there's a solution that hasn't presented itself."[12] That comment seemed to summarize some of the ongoing challenges with the bid. Boston 2024 was trying to squeeze too many large venues into Boston's dense urban fabric. It claimed it was offering a low-cost, frugal bid, but in many cases had chosen more expensive, riskier alternatives that would reinforce its pitch as a chance to spur economic development while remaking entire neighborhoods in the city. Continuing to spread the venues around the state would make things easier, but it would further degrade the "walkable, compact Games" that had held much of the original appeal to the USOC. It would also increase the risk of white elephants, which Boston 2024 had promised wouldn't be built. An Olympic-sized velodrome in Somerville, the state's densest community, just northeast of Boston, might be viable after the Games. But it would eat up valuable land that might be used for housing or parks. It would be easier to find land in Western Massachusetts—but would an Olympic-sized velodrome there be a viable facility after the Games? Bid 2.0 left these and other questions unanswered.

NINE

JULY 2015

July started quietly, with the Independence Day holiday permitting proponents and opponents a rare opportunity to unplug from the frenzied debate.
But as others hit the beach or backyard barbecues, WBUR was back in the
field, asking residents their opinion of the bid in the wake of the changes
that Boston 2024 had incorporated into Bid 2.0. WBUR's June poll results
had offered the boosters a glimmer of hope. The survey had indicated that
while only 39 percent of Massachusetts voters supported the bid, a slim
majority would support a bid that successfully spread venues around the
state. Boston 2024's Bid 2.0 had done just that. WBUR's July poll, eagerly
anticipated by both supporters and opponents, would demonstrate whether
Boston 2024's strategy had worked.

The results, released by WBUR on the morning of Friday, July 10, were
devastating for Boston 2024. Statewide, 50 percent of residents still opposed
the bid, while just 42 percent supported it—within the margin of error of
the 39 percent support figure in the June poll.[1] After a month of unveiling
new venues and an error-free launch of an impressively detailed, yet deeply
flawed, Bid 2.0, Boston 2024 had perhaps perceived a slight breeze at its back
in June. In fact, Bid 2.0 hadn't moved the needle. The bidding committee
now found itself adrift in the summer doldrums.

The *Boston Globe*'s longtime Olympic reporter John Powers astutely
summed up Boston 2024's tenuous condition and shaky political support
in mid-July:

> The main stadium and Olympic village, the two most important and ex-
> pensive venues of any Games, will depend upon a yet-unidentified master
> developer (or two) to put up billions of dollars. Private universities will

provide stadia, arenas, dormitories and land at a price to be negotiated. The state controls everything from the Boston Convention and Exhibition Center to the mass transit system to the Charles River. The city owns Franklin Park, where the horses will run and jump, and the streets where marathoners and cyclists will run and roll. And the us Olympic Committee, which is the real bidder for the Games, can pull the plug whenever it pleases, which could be sooner rather than later.[2]

There was little doubt that Powers had conversed with his deep connections at the USOC before writing the piece. His final sentence read like a threat. Powers continued, "As Boston's quest for the 2024 Games continues to evolve and expand beyond the city limits, the bid committee's reliance upon the long-term buy-in of other parties is becoming ever more crucial and complex. What began as an intimate and walkable scheme—the non-LA alternative—now involves half a dozen counties and five of the state's six largest cities."

As the boosters had moved events outside the city of Boston, and even up and down the East Coast, the bid had become only more reliant on the support of state government. The village at UMass-Boston, improvements to the MBTA, crucial parcels at Widett Circle—they were all controlled by the Commonwealth of Massachusetts, not the mayor and the City of Boston. This meant that the bid needed full buy-in from the house of representatives and the state senate. But most important, it needed the governor. For Baker, the bid continued to present numerous risks with only limited upside. Even if construction and preparation for the Games went perfectly—an unlikely outcome—Baker would be out of office by January 2023 at the latest, more than a year before Boston 2024's opening ceremonies. The USOC's decision to award the bid to Boston 2024 without first confirming the governor's support had been a crucial error in judgment. The USOC either had not understood the importance of the governor's backing or it had assumed that Baker would inevitably get behind a proposal that at the time was supported by a majority of Massachusetts residents and had the near-unanimous backing of the region's power brokers.

The same day WBUR's devastating July poll was released, the *Boston Globe* editorial page editor Ellen Clegg invited Dempsey and Zimbalist to participate in a live, televised debate to be cosponsored by the *Globe* and FOX25, the local Fox television affiliate. Bid chairman Steve Pagliuca and USOC board member and former head of the NYC 2012 Olympic bid Dan Doctoroff already had agreed to participate on behalf of Boston 2024. This set up a showdown between two of the bid's loudest critics and two high-profile advocates. Notably, over the previous months Boston 2024 had turned down multiple invitations to debate Dempsey or Zimbalist. Now, it seemed, the situation was sufficiently grim that they needed to take the risk.[3]

The *Globe* and FOX25 were two of greater Boston's leading media outlets, but the origins of the debate had not been at the *Globe*'s headquarters on Morrissey Boulevard or at Fox's studios in suburban Dedham. Instead, they were a conversation held 2,500 miles away, in Sun Valley, Idaho. Each July, the investment bank Allen & Company hosts an annual conference now widely known as "mogul summer camp." As *Forbes* magazine describes it, the event brings together "more than 300 of the wealthiest and most powerful executives in media, finance, politics and technology."[4] In 2015, among those in attendance were Pagliuca, Doctoroff, who had been CEO of Bloomberg and now worked for Google, and John Henry, the chief owner of the Boston Red Sox as well as the owner of the *Boston Globe*. When the three met in Sun Valley, the conversation inevitably turned to Boston 2024. Henry, wearing his newspaper publisher's hat, proposed the debate—Pagliuca and Doctoroff quickly accepted. Henry then phoned Zimbalist to float the idea. Zimbalist accepted. Within hours, Henry had gotten word to Clegg, who reached out to FOX25 and to Dempsey.

Participating in a high-profile televised debate made strategic sense for Boston 2024, which needed to do anything it could to generate momentum and to try to get residents to take another look at the bid. Pagliuca, the bid's jovial leader, was a good choice as one of Boston 2024's participants. To accompany Pagliuca, Boston 2024 would have done well to have chosen someone such as Toni Wiley, the well-spoken leader of the Sportsmen's Tennis Club in Dorchester, whose nonprofit stood to be transformed by Boston 2024. Wiley's participation would have brought an appealing diversity to Boston 2024's panel, offsetting the ultrawealthy, suburban, white male Pagliuca.

Doctoroff was a disastrous choice as Pagliuca's partner on the debate stage. Like Pagliuca, Doctoroff was an ultrawealthy white male executive. But unlike Pagliuca, Doctoroff had a hard-headed and supercilious personality. Even worse, Doctoroff was a New Yorker, who could easily be portrayed as a carpetbagging outsider trying opportunistically to sell the bid to the Massachusetts public.

Doctoroff's participation in the debate was emblematic of Boston 2024's broader failings—an arrangement made in the elite circles of "mogul summer camp" had produced an outcome that would only deepen cynicism about the boosters' intentions. It was another missed opportunity for Boston 2024.

For much of 2015, city councilor Tito Jackson had maintained a skeptical—though low-profile—stance toward Boston 2024's bid. Jackson's life had had an interesting and improbable trajectory. He had spent the first two months as a newborn in the hospital—healthy but unwanted by his birth mother. Jackson eventually was adopted by Herbert and Rosa Jackson, who raised him lovingly in Boston's tough Roxbury neighborhood. As a child, Jackson participated in the METCO program, founded in 1966 to provide some of Boston's African-American students the opportunity to attend school in the region's wealthier, whiter suburban school districts. (METCO remains the longest continuously running voluntary school desegregation program in the country.) Jackson attended Brookline Public Schools—the same ones Dempsey attended—and then the University of New Hampshire (UNH), where he became the first African-American student body president of an overwhelmingly white campus. Jackson and Dempsey had met years later, back at UNH in November 2008, when they had spent four days organizing students to vote for Barack Obama. Jackson had a playful personality and natural leadership abilities that made him a potent political operator. For example, in 2008, he had returned to UNH with massive DJ speakers—creating a party atmosphere that had energized volunteers and drew attention to their get-out-the-vote efforts. Three years later, Jackson was successful in a run for Boston city council. He now represented Roxbury, the neighborhood in which he had grown up.

Frustrated by Boston 2024's refusal to share basic bid details with the city council and city of Boston residents, Jackson roared to life in July. When focused on an issue, Jackson could be a forceful advocate. He was a prominent, young, high-energy leader of the African-American community who was well known throughout the city's neighborhoods. Jackson was unafraid to challenge Boston 2024's boosters on issues of transparency.

On July 13, Councilor Jackson asked Boston 2024 to release the full, unedited, and unredacted chapters of the bid book signed off on by Mayor Walsh and submitted to the USOC on December 1, 2014. When Boston 2024 responded with a letter that acknowledged Jackson's request but still refused to share the documents, Jackson upped the ante. At a charged press conference on the steps of Boston City Hall on Monday, July 20, Jackson announced that he would be filing a subpoena order, the first step to a legal subpoena that could force Boston 2024 to share the December 1 documents. Jackson delivered a dramatic speech that made clear that he wouldn't be satisfied until the full bid was public:

> The drawing of beautiful buildings and venues has been very impressive. But the important part of the winning bid, Bid 1.0, is the financials. No intelligent business person, especially not one as savvy as those involved in this bid, would do a business deal without all available financial information. So why are you asking the citizens of Boston and the Boston City Council to go forward without complete disclosure? I am disappointed that Boston 2024, a group of individuals who no one has elected, would make financial promises, commitments, and speculations on behalf of the City of Boston, and have the audacity to tell us it is none of our business: "Look at Bid 2.0 because that is the most current." Sorry, Boston 2024, you don't get to tell our body, our city, or our constituents what to do, when to do it, and how. We are Boston.[5]

At the subsequent city council meeting on Wednesday, July 22, Jackson's order was blocked by city council president Bill Linehan, who remained a staunch Boston 2024 supporter. Even if he couldn't force immediate action from Boston 2024, Jackson's efforts put the boosters on their heels. As a private organization, they had no legal requirement to share the documents until required to do so by a judge. But Jackson was launching a political attack, not a legal one. To the public at large, the conclusion was simple:

if even a subpoena order couldn't compel the boosters to share their bid, they must really have something to hide.

Linehan's parliamentary procedure had bought Boston 2024 a few weeks of time, but its position wasn't going to improve. Just hours after the council meeting, Pagliuca and Boston 2024 made the decision to release the unedited, unredacted December 1 bid documents. These documents existed as a PDF—it should have taken no more than an hour or two to post them to Boston 2024's website, but Boston 2024 couldn't afford to release them before that Thursday's *Globe*/Fox25 debate, which would have shifted the focus of the hour-long debate back to Bid 1.0, instead of on Bid 2.0, where Boston 2024 wanted it. Boston 2024 announced that it would release the documents the following week.

The debate organizers had chosen two moderators: the feisty FOX25 newscaster Maria Stephanos and the *Boston Globe*'s more reserved Sacha Pfeiffer. (Pfeiffer had gained prominence investigating the Catholic priest abuse scandal in the early 2000s. She was played by the actress Rachel McAdams in the Academy Award–winning film *Spotlight*.) Despite the best efforts of Stephanos and Pfeiffer, the debate quickly turned into a free-for-all.

Pagliuca and Doctoroff were more aggressive, dominating the airtime in the first half of the debate, and frequently interrupting their opponents and the moderators. The airtime never balanced out, but Dempsey and Zimbalist were able to land a few punches. In particular, Zimbalist countered Doctoroff's claims that the IOC had reformed itself and was seeking "a new kind of Olympics." If that was the case, Zimbalist asked, then why not prove it by rejecting the taxpayer guarantee that had proved so troublesome to prior hosts? Neither Pagliuca nor Doctoroff had a good answer. Dempsey was most effective when contrasting his views with Doctoroff's—and by reminding viewers that Doctoroff was a New Yorker. Zimbalist helped shift the momentum further with his comment that, despite Boston 2024's repeated assertions that their financial projections were based on very conservative assumptions, the assertions rather reflected "drunken optimism." The phrase became the evening's most memorable moment.

Doctoroff had been the leader of New York City's failed bid for the 2012 Games (eventually won by London, which also beat out Paris). The NYC bid had required backing from the New York state government. New York legislators, wary of signing a blank check to the IOC, protected the state budget by putting a cap on liability of $250 million—meaning then-mayor Mike Bloomberg could sign the IOC-required financial guarantee, but that it was worth no more than $250 million. Given New York's high construction prices, that amount wouldn't even cover one-third the cost of the proposed Olympic stadium on Manhattan's West Side. Given this cap on taxpayer contributions, the IOC was probably smart to pass on New York's bid. The eventual winner, London, went more than $10 billion over budget, all of which was paid for by taxpayers in the United Kingdom.

Doctoroff had supported the legislation capping public liability in New York's bid. Now, he was asking Massachusetts taxpayers to accept unlimited liability. It was glaring hypocrisy. But Doctoroff didn't have much choice. He knew the financial guarantee was a nonnegotiable requirement from the IOC. With the exception of Los Angeles in 1984, the International Olympic Committee has never accepted a bid that caps local liability. When Mayor Daley of Chicago dealt with the IOC during the Windy City's bid for the 2016 Games, four years after the failed New York bid, the IOC made it clear that only unlimited public liability would give Chicago's bid a chance of winning. Daley previously had promised Chicago taxpayers that he would refuse to agree to the IOC's terms, but he caved at the last minute, agreeing to the IOC's standard terms and sheepishly returning to Chicago to admit to Chicago voters that he had signed the complete terms of the host city contract.

Doctoroff and Pagliuca also peddled the tired refrain of American exceptionalism. They argued that although history was littered with cities with unsuccessful Olympic hosting experiences, US cities that hosted the Games always turned a profit. In fact, with the exception of Los Angeles in 1984, US hosts have stumbled economically. There are good reasons for this, which we discuss in chapter 11.

Another point of deceit was Doctoroff's claim that the USOC was 100 percent committed to Boston. The events of the coming days, if not the earlier *Wall Street Journal* reports and statements from USOC members, put the lie to Doctoroff's misdirection. By the hour's end, Dempsey and Zimbalist felt that the debate had gone well, despite Pagliuca dominating airtime. When *Globe* columnist and staunch Boston 2024 supporter Shirley

Leung said in the post-debate analysis that she thought the opponents had won, it appeared that their hunch was on target.

During the debate, Stephanos had pressured Pagliuca to release the Bid 1.0 documents immediately, rather than waiting until the following week. Pagliuca relented. The following day—almost eight months after they had been delivered to the USOC—the complete and unredacted Bid 1.0 finally was made public. If Boston 2024's bid needed another nail in the coffin, these documents were it. Stunningly, they revealed that Boston 2024 had initially projected an OCOG *deficit* of $471 million (almost 20 percent of the city's annual budget.) The version of the documents released to the public in January simply papered over these projected losses by assuming the receipt of "Other Revenue." For months, the boosters had been assuring voters that American Olympics were always profitable, when in fact their own bid was projecting a massive loss. The full bid documents also revealed that Boston 2024 had excised from public release a section on political opposition to bid. The boosters had downplayed and dismissed the prospects of Olympic opponents, but had neglected to share that with the public.

Meanwhile, the Associated Press reported the same day that the USOC was pressuring Governor Baker to demonstrate his support for the bid. It was an ultimatum—a last chance for Boston 2024 to line up the single most critical supporter of the Games. But Baker continued to play it down the middle, refusing to provide a firm view of the bid until the Brattle Group had completed its analysis of Bid 2.0, which wouldn't happen until mid-August at the earliest. (Privately, Baker had seen a draft of the Brattle Group report and it was far from encouraging to Boston 2024.)

The writing was on the wall. Without Baker's full endorsement, the bid was dead. Over the weekend, the Walsh administration sought to limit the damage to Mayor Walsh's reputation. If the ship was going down, they needed to do what they could to get Mayor Walsh on a lifeboat. The first sign was a *Globe* report on Saturday, July 25, quoting an unnamed source "close to the process" that the USOC was *also* pressuring Walsh (not just Baker) to put his political support behind the bid. The unnamed source wanted to create the impression that Walsh, like Baker, had kept the bid at arm's length. But Walsh's support had never been in doubt, and the Associated Press report had made no mention of the USOC pressuring the mayor. It was

Baker, not Walsh, who was asked to phone in to the USOC's conference call on Monday, July 27. Saturday's *Globe* story helped Walsh, but his advisers deemed that it hadn't been sufficient. In the final hours, the mayor needed to make a public gesture of defiance to Boston 2024, or the bid would be enshrined as an embarrassing hallmark of his first term.

Mayor Walsh arranged a hasty press conference for Monday morning, just hours before the USOC was meeting to pull the bid formally. The press conference was awkward—with Walsh attempting to separate himself from the bid without actually saying that the bid was finished. Why didn't Walsh pull the bid himself? Walsh's hesitance to revoke the city of Boston's participation might have reflected a glimmer of hope that the bid might somehow still survive the USOC's conference call. But more likely, it was driven by fear of violating the joinder agreement, the document Walsh had signed with the USOC in 2014. Tucked into that agreement was an often-overlooked provision requiring a $25 million payment to the USOC if the city withdrew its bid. In 2014, the city had asked Boston 2024 to purchase an insurance policy to protect against this potential payment. But the insurance policy had specific exceptions for willful misrepresentations. Because the bid had included significant errors, the policy was essentially void. If the mayor formally withdrew his support, the City of Boston might be liable for a $25 million payment to the USOC.

Mayor Walsh couldn't afford to risk that situation. Instead, the mayor attempted a high-wire act: providing himself sufficient cover to look as if he had stood up to the USOC, without ever actually saying he wouldn't sign the host city agreement with the International Olympic Committee. His statement went like this: "If committing to signing a guarantee today is what's required to move forward, then Boston is no longer pursuing the 2024 Olympic and Paralympic Games." It was threading the needle. "The idea of hosting the Olympics I still feel today as I did three months ago . . . but I'm hearing too many other voices talking about Los Angeles," Walsh added.[6] The gambit seemed to work—in the days following, many residents credited Walsh with standing up to the USOC, even though Walsh *already* had signed the joinder agreement with the USOC that committed the city to signing the IOC's host city contract "in the form provided by the IOC"— which would have included the financial guarantee.

In the question-and-answer session following his statement, Walsh was asked about the role that opposition to the bid had played in the bid being on the brink of collapse. His response dismissed the role of No Boston Olympics, No Boston 2024, and other bid opponents: "The opposition for the most part are about ten people on Twitter and a couple people out there who are constantly [beating the drum]. . . . I don't view the 50 percent that aren't for the Olympics today, I view the ten people that are doing hundreds of thousands of tweets on Twitter." Thus, Walsh's view was essentially unchanged from his closed-door remarks to the USOC in December. Despite consistent public polling to the contrary, in Walsh's mind there still wasn't any "real opposition" to the bid.

Almost immediately, #10PeopleOnTwitter became a trending hashtag in the Boston area. Walsh's remarks managed to be both dismissive of, and empowering to, the citizens and volunteers who had waged a campaign against the powerful Boston bid. After all, if just ten people on Twitter had managed to deal a fatal blow to a bid strongly backed by the city's mayor and business elite—well, that was quite an accomplishment!

A few hours later, longtime Channel 5 political reporter Janet Wu was the first to break the news of the bid's demise, tweeting at 2:29 p.m. that a source close to the bid had told her that the USOC had voted to bring an end to the saga. Dempsey and Gossett were in Gossett's condo in the Back Bay setting up the organization's new inkjet printer when the news broke. (The parsimonious organizers finally had decided to splurge for a printer the week before, after months of visiting FedEx every time they needed to print a document.) Dempsey had installed the ink cartridges, but hadn't yet gotten the printer configured when he noticed Wu's tweet. He sent Wu a text message, asking for confirmation that she was reporting that the bid was pulled. "Yes," Wu replied. "Let's wait for the Associated Press or the *Globe*," he told Gossett. Minutes later, both outlets were reporting the news. Gossett and Dempsey hugged. They drafted a statement to supporters, drawing from the language of the email they had drafted—but never sent—the evening of the governor's inauguration and the USOC's decision on January 8.

After a quick and impromptu news conference on the steps of the State House, No Boston Olympics gathered bid opponents at the Beantown Pub on Tremont Street, two blocks from the State House and steps away from the

Suffolk University building where the city had held the first public meeting on the bid. No Boston 2024's Jonathan Cohn and Robin Jacks were among the first to join them. As supporters filtered into the room and ordered celebratory beverages, it was easy to appreciate the diverse array of people that had been brought together in opposition to the bid. As *Boston Magazine*'s Garrett Quinn pointed out in a tweet from the bar, "At @NoBosOlympics victory party there are people in 'Socialist Alternative' and 'Don't Tread On Me' shirts."[7] At least for one evening, citizens from both ends of the political spectrum could congratulate each other on a shared victory.

TEN

THE AFTERMATH

On July 28, 2015, PBS *NewsHour*, hosted by Judy Woodruff, carried a report on the demise of Boston 2024's bid. The segment included an extended give-and-take between George Hirthler, a longtime Olympic campaign strategist (later hired by the Los Angeles 2024 bid), and Zimbalist. It began with Woodruff asking Hirthler what had gone wrong with the Boston bid. Hirthler replied:

> What went wrong, Judy, was the public narrative that was pretty much controlled by Professor Zimbalist and the cohort of—his cohort of colleagues at No Boston Olympics.
>
> They kept the public conversation completely focused on the financial risks of the Games. So the public never had a chance to consider what it would be like to have athletes from 200 countries around the world living in an Olympic village in their midst. The Games would have been extremely walkable for 90 percent of the fans who came into the Boston. . . . Professor Zimbalist and Chris Dempsey and the others came in and attacked every single number and kept the public conversation completely focused on risk and fear.[1]

Woodruff interjected: "Well, I do want to move on to the larger question we raised here [on Olympic costs and benefits], but, Professor Zimbalist, let me give you an opportunity to respond." And Zimbalist obliged: "I just want to thank George for making me out to be so powerful. I don't think we had nearly that impact." Zimbalist went on to offer his own explanation of what had happened in Boston. Hirthler could only smirk.

USA Today sportswriter Christine Brennan called Boston 2024's demise "an organizational disaster," "a national debacle," and, "an embarrassment of the highest order."[2] She placed the blame squarely at the feet of the leadership of the United States Olympic Committee.

In anonymously sourced reporting and public statements that would appear in the following weeks and months, a picture began to emerge of what had happened in that Denver Airport conference room in January. Washington, D.C., and San Francisco had been ruled out quickly, the former because of the IOC's presumed reluctance to send the Games to the home of America's geopolitical policymaking, and the latter because of concerns over plans for the stadium and Olympic village. That left Boston and Los Angeles. Probst, the USOC's chairman, and Blackmun, the CEO, both expressed a preference for Los Angeles, a safer bet, because of the number of preexisting venues and the lack of any organized opposition groups. But some individual members of the board expressed a strong preference for the Boston bid. According to Casey Wasserman's remarks to the Los Angeles city council in late August, the Boston bid prevailed by half a vote—if just one of the USOC's board members had voted differently, Boston 2024 would have faded quietly into history.[3] These reports seem credible, although they are difficult to verify because the USOC does not publicly share detailed meeting minutes or the results of its votes.

In a September speech to USOC stakeholders in Colorado Springs, Blackmun acknowledged that he and Probst had preferred the Los Angeles bid and been overruled by the board, but he still took responsibility for the board's ultimate decision to accept the far-riskier Boston bid: "The question is, should we have taken the risk? In hindsight, the answer is no . . . we made a bad call."[4] While Blackmun and Probst seemed willing to fall on their swords, the board's vote for Boston 2024 calls into question both the wisdom of the USOC's selection process and its leadership. The USOC has offered mea culpas. But it has yet to acknowledge a need to reform the organization's selection process for host cities. Probst and Blackmun had been the ringmasters in a process that began when the USOC first wrote invitation letters to the mayors of thirty-five cities in the spring of 2013. The USOC's insistence on secrecy and avoidance of a more democratic process had sowed the seeds of its defeat in Boston. It wasn't just that it had made a "bad call"—the USOC organization demonstrated a clear willingness to lie and deceive. It had received a bid from Boston 2024 that showed a budget deficit, permitted Boston 2024 to disguise that deficit in the documents it released to the public, and then told the public and media that a Boston bid would be cash-flow positive.

The USOC also had failed its due diligence process. It clearly had not submitted the bid to independent, outside scrutiny. If it had, it would have revealed significant errors in Boston 2024's descriptions of the public transportation investments planned for *Greater Boston* (of course, making the bids public before the USOC's vote also would have uncovered these errors, but the USOC insisted on a secretive process).

The choice of Boston 2024 over the bid from Los Angeles also reflected how little stock the USOC's board members placed in the IOC's Agenda 2020 reforms. Rather than choosing a bid from Los Angeles, where the Olympic stadium and velodrome were already in place, the USOC's board members chose a risky, costly, grandiose bid from Boston.

Walsh's maneuverings in the final seventy-two hours, including the last-minute press conference, had managed to make him look like a champion of Boston taxpayers, at least in the eyes of some. But those following closely had a different reaction. As the *Globe*'s Yvonne Abraham wrote, "[The Monday press conference] looked like Walsh was riding in to rescue his constituents from the marauding Olympic officials who would shake them down if the costs of the 2024 Games ballooned. But eight months earlier, Walsh threw down a very large welcome mat for those same marauders. In an October letter, he gave the USOC good reason to believe he was willing to risk taxpayer money for the benefits an Olympics would bring: He committed to signing a Host City Agreement guaranteeing Boston would cover cost overruns."[5] Mayor Walsh's position was that he always intended to sign the host city agreement, but that he would only have done so if he was confident that Boston 2024's proposed insurance would protect taxpayers from any overruns. Yet he had approved a bid that didn't include any insurance premiums in its budget. Even if it had, it is difficult to see how any insurance package could ever fully protect taxpayers from the billions of dollars of liabilities that Boston 2024's bid entailed. The mayor would later say he had no regrets about pursuing the Olympic bid, but surely Boston 2024 proved to be a distraction from other important priorities on which he might have focused in his first term.

News of Boston 2024's demise came the same week that International Olympic Committee dignitaries were assembling in Kuala Lumpur to award the 2022 Winter Games. It was an embarrassing week for Thomas Bach—with the international media already focusing on the fact that every democracy had dropped out of the bidding process for the 2022 Winter Games, leaving Almaty, Kazakhstan, and snowless Beijing, China, as the only remaining candidates. Boston dropping out was added humiliation, and Bach smiled grimly through a press conference in which he fielded questions on Boston. In late January he had praised Boston's bid leaders, saying, "What we can see there is the bid leaders in Boston have taken the right approach, speaking with the people, offering information, being open for questions."[6] But now Bach placed blame for the bid's failure squarely at the feet of Boston 2024's leaders. "It was pretty confusing," he said. "Every day there was a new project coming from Boston or new people and new ideas. I really gave up following it in detail. But what we could see in a nutshell what happened there is that Boston did not deliver on promises they made to the USOC when they were selected."[7] Bach refused to acknowledge that Bostonians—like citizens in Kraków, Munich, and elsewhere—had rejected the basic deal the International Olympic Committee was offering. In his version of events, the people of Boston hadn't lived up to a commitment the mayor had made when he signed the USOC's joinder agreement. Never mind that the people of Boston weren't able to even read the text of those commitments until after it had been signed and delivered to the USOC!

In that same press conference, Bach made it crystal clear to the USOC that even with Boston 2024's demise he still expected a bid from the United States. "We had a commitment from the USOC for an Olympic candidature for 2024. We have this commitment," he said. "We're sure that USOC will deliver on this commitment and that we will have on the fifteenth of September a bid from the United States."[8] While the news briefly reignited the hopes of boosters in San Francisco and Washington, D.C., prognosticators guessed that if the USOC were to put forward a bid, it would have to come from Los Angeles. On September 1, the United States Olympic Committee made it official in a subdued announcement. Los Angeles would be the 2024 bid submitted to the International Olympic Committee.

In the dog days of August, the Baker administration, the senate president, and the speaker of the house received and released to the public the results of the analysis they had commissioned from the Brattle Group. The state's consultant found that the bid's boosters had underestimated venue costs by $970 million, and that risk for overruns ultimately would have fallen to Massachusetts taxpayers. "If the bid were still alive . . . I don't think it could have survived [the Brattle Group report]," the *Globe*'s Arsenault told WRKO radio.[9]

A spokesperson for Boston 2024, which was still winding down operations, accused the Brattle report of containing "misrepresentations" and "errors." Boston 2024 said it would be assembling a rebuttal to the Brattle Group report, but that rebuttal never materialized. Weeks later, Boston 2024 closed down its operation for good.[10]

No Boston Olympics had ended its efforts with a surplus—having spent less than $15,000 while raising more than $30,000, with an average contribution size of around $100. Its single largest contributors, the husband and wife duo of Diana and Lee Humphrey, had contributed less than $10,000. Out of hundreds of individual contributors, only ten individual contributors had given $500 or more.

Boston 2024, by contrast, had spent more than $15 million. It had outspent bid opponents by more than 1,000 to 1, and its average contribution size had been more than four hundred times that of No Boston Olympics' average. Despite the massive sum it had raised, Boston 2024 had spent beyond its means. It needed to ask some of its contractors and consultants to waive overdue and outstanding bills to close out its books. Fittingly, Boston 2024 ended as it was perhaps always destined to: with a deficit.

But while Boston 2024 was wrapping up its operations, No Boston Olympics' work wasn't yet done. Olympic-bid opponents in other cities were curious to learn from the playbook Boston's bid opponents had developed. Grassroots groups from Toronto reached out to the group as their city considered a 2024 bid (ultimately dropped when Toronto's mayor determined that public support would be difficult to win). Bid opponents in both Budapest and Rome sought advice from No Boston Olympics as they launched their efforts in their respective cities. In October, Dempsey and

Gossett visited Hamburg at the invitation of bid opponents there. Similarly, Zimbalist met with members of Toronto's city council and was invited to deliver a lecture at Hamburg's HafenCity University on the economic impact of hosting the Olympics.

Boston 2024's bid and Hamburg's shared many similarities. The comparisons start with the cities themselves. Like Boston, Hamburg is a prosperous northern port and industrial town that has transitioned successfully to a knowledge economy. In 2015, Hamburg was one of the richest cities in Germany, just as Boston was one of the richest in the United States. The economies in both cities were booming.

In a secretive process that mirrored the USOC's selection of Boston, the German Olympic Committee (DOSB) had chosen Hamburg over Berlin to represent Germany at the IOC level. In either German city the bid would be subject to a public referendum. Hamburg had higher popular approval ratings than Berlin, which made it the safer bet. But as in Boston, the more voters in Hamburg learned about the bid, the less they liked it.[11]

The plans for Hamburg's bid also shared many similarities with Boston 2024. Hamburg 2024 envisioned remaking an industrial district into a new multi-use community. The Olympic development was pitched as a way to build new housing, expand the transit system, and announce the city's arrival on the world's stage. Like Boston 2024, Hamburg's bid was ultimately an ambitious and risky proposal that required more than $10 billion in spending for the construction of new venues, a media center, and an Olympic village. Unlike Boston's boosters, Hamburg 2024's backers admitted that costs could far outweigh the revenue brought in by the Games, but argued that the expenditure would still be worth it because of the longer-term benefits—in economic development and civic pride—that hosting the Games would bring.

Polls by the DOSB in the early fall had shown 63 percent support for the bid. But at the referendum in the end of November, citizens in Hamburg voted down the bid, with 51.6 percent opposing the Games. It was another stunning and unexpected blow to the International Olympic Committee, and a particularly personal one for IOC President Thomas Bach, a German Olympian who himself had headed the DOSB previously. Once again, voters in a thriving democracy had turned down the IOC's overtures.

ELEVEN

AMERICAN UNEXCEPTIONALISM

Boston 2024's first CEO, Dan O'Connell, frequently brushed off discussions of botched Games in London, Athens, or elsewhere by invoking the claim that US Olympic hosts were immune from the syndrome of Olympic budget overruns. "Every game that's been held in the US, winter or summer—that's Salt Lake City, Los Angeles, Atlanta, Lake Placid—have been cash flow positive," O'Connell said.[1] Mayor Walsh and Boston 2024 chairs John Fish and Steve Pagliuca repeated this bromide throughout Boston 2024's two-year existence. The notion of American exceptionalism—generally intended to connote American superiority in the world—is often misleading and sometimes dangerous. When it comes to hosting the Olympics, it is just plain wrong.

Why would the United States' experience of hosting the Olympics be different from that of other cities? The underlying premise must be that the United States is more efficient and creative than hosts elsewhere. If compared to Rio or Sochi, it is perhaps a sensible claim. Indeed, less developed countries always will have more expenses because they do not have the needed transportation, communications, technological, and sporting infrastructure to support the Games. When government corruption is thrown into the mix, it is clear that US cities can do better than some others (although corruption stained the Salt Lake City Games in 2002).

But cost overruns have been a ubiquitous feature of all Summer and Winter Games, even those in Europe, Canada, Australia, Japan, and, yes, the United States. According to a 2012 study by the Said Business School at Oxford University, every instance of the Olympic Games since 1960 for which reliable financial data are available has experienced cost overruns. The average overrun for Summer Games since 1980 is 252 percent after adjusting for inflation.[2]

Of course, it is possible to have a cost overrun and still claim a positive cash flow. Even Sochi 2012 reported a positive cash flow, despite having an initial bid of $12 billion and a final cost in the range of $51 to $67 billion. The positive balance referred only to the operating budget and came from a massive financial transfer from the federal treasury to the books of the Sochi organizing committee. Other Games also have reported a positive cash flow. This usually results from the fact that the official report includes only the operating budget of the Games; it does *not* include either of the larger budgets for venues or infrastructure.

One striking exception to the pattern was the Los Angeles Games in 1984. Because Los Angeles was the only bidder that year, the positive result in Los Angeles largely reflected exceptional bargaining leverage, not the exceptionalism of the host country.[3] Los Angeles's rejection of the IOC's request for a taxpayer guarantee was especially important. In many other Olympic host cities, the national government provides an implicit guarantee to host the Games no matter the financial cost. In the United States, the federal government has refused to provide this guarantee. This means that local and state governments must promise to cover overruns. As the budget for London's 2012 Games ballooned, the UK government stepped in, at a cost to the average UK taxpayer of more than $200. But the UK has roughly ten times as many people as Massachusetts—similar overruns would have cost the state's taxpayers $2,000 per person, and close to $8,000 for a family of four.

The experiences in Lake Placid, Atlanta, and Salt Lake City were decidedly different from Los Angeles. Lake Placid 1980 experienced cost overruns of 321 percent and ultimately required a bail out from New York State. The state contributed $63 million or 17 percent of total costs and the federal government spent $179 million or 50 percent of total costs.[4] Thus, public funding was over two-thirds of the total and this allowed the Lake Placid operating committee to assert that it had balanced its books once the post-Games bailout was complete.

Atlanta 1996 had a cost overrun of 147 percent; that is, the final cost of its venue and operating budget was 2.47 times higher than the initially projected cost after adjusting for inflation. Nonetheless, the Atlanta operating committee reported a small surplus of $10 million. Approximately one-third of all spending, or $823 million, came from taxpayers. Of that, $609 million was federal.[5] Atlanta's boosters leave out this fact when they claim that the 1996 Games were a financial success. Moreover, the construction of the athletes' village and the Olympic stadium in Atlanta required the destruction of two low-income, minority communities. This, in turn, led to an increase in homelessness during the Games and a repressive response from local government to remove the homeless from the vicinity of the competition venues and, thereby, to improve the optics for the Olympics.

According to a US government report in 2001, excluding the additional security costs necessitated by the September 11, 2001, terrorist attacks, the federal government planned to spend $342 million on the 2002 Salt Lake City Winter Olympics. The Salt Lake City municipal government planned to spend $75 million and the Utah state government committed an additional $150 million.[6] The final public bill was considerably higher.

The question, therefore, is not why the US hosting experience is different; rather, it is why the economics of hosting are stacked so heavily against a positive outcome, whether in the United States or elsewhere. The answer begins by observing the economic structure of the Olympics.

The International Olympic Committee is an international monopoly that auctions off to the world's cities the "privilege" of hosting either the winter or the Summer Games every two years. The IOC wants potential Olympic host cities to think that they are entering a competition, much as marathon runners might line up at the starting line or swimmers might stand on the starting block. IOC President Thomas Bach is fond of calling the bidding process a "great race" and a "fascinating competition" in which the "best" city wins the right to host a prize even more glittery than the shiniest gold medal and more rare than a world-record-breaking performance. Cities that approach Olympic bids as a competition may well win the International Olympic Committee's race, but they are likely to lose in the long run.

Reframed not as a race but instead as an auction, the dynamics inherent in the International Olympic Committee's process become much more clear. Instead of a starting line, picture an auction room with the International Olympic Committee up front at the podium, with the former fencer Thomas Bach wielding not his old foil but instead an auctioneer's gavel. Before even beginning the auction, Bach and his team have spent a good deal of time convincing as many well-known and prosperous bidders as possible to enter the auction room. With the cities' boosters now before them, bidding paddles in hand, the International Olympic Committee can begin an auction process that maximizes its own benefit. The highest bid—in terms of its ease, comfort, opulence, and general impressiveness—wins.

Economists often refer to the likely outcome in this type of auction as a winner's curse. Imagine five cities from around the world bidding against each other. Four of the cities all believe that the economic value of hosting the Games is, say, $8 billion or below. The fifth city believes it is worth $12 billion and its bid, accordingly, boasts more gigantism, more trappings of IOC worship, fancier facilities, and so on. The fifth city bid is the outlier and, likely, overly exuberant. The fifth city has overbid and, though a winner of the auction, is cursed by its victory. It has committed to spending more than the Games are worth. In reality, the outcome for the host city is bound to be worse still because the people bidding on behalf of the city usually represent particular interests in the private sector, such as construction companies and unions, insurance companies, architectural firms, investment bankers who float the bonds, and the like. These groups will benefit handsomely from hosting and, like the IOC, will benefit from more extravagant Games. The city and its taxpayers will pay for the waste and the overruns.

Ultimately, the "most transparent bid in Olympic history" wasn't very transparent. But it was transparent enough to expose the International Olympic Committee's process as one that asks cities to take monumental risks for dubious gains.

The arguments for hosting the Games are actually quite weak. The core arguments typically fall along the following lines—all of which were offered by Boston's boosters:

1. The Games will put the host city on the map.
2. This bid will be different—it will escape the mistakes of prior hosts.
3. Olympic bids are a good planning exercise for a city's future.
4. The Games will leave behind a legacy of improved infrastructure.

Let us consider each in turn.

1. THE GAMES WILL PUT THE HOST CITY ON THE MAP. Ironically, the Olympic propagandists from all cities appear to make the claim that hosting the Games will put their city on the map. Boston 2024's proponents did. Even London's did. Yes, London!

Apart from the silliness of the map metaphor, what proponents are really asserting is that hosting, and putting images of the city on a couple billion television sets or computer screens around the globe, will increase tourism, trade, and foreign investment. The evidence that any of these salutary outcomes will occur is sketchy at best. While a few hosts over the last three decades have experienced a very modest uptick in tourism during the Games, there is little reason to expect a significant positive impact. Indeed, recent hosts Beijing 2008, London 2012, and Athens 2004, among others, have experienced notable decreases in tourism during the Games.[7]

The main reason is that normal tourists stay away from a city during the 17 days of Olympic competition. Olympic Games bring congestion, high prices, minimum stay requirements at hotels, and the heightened possibility of security incidents. All of these factors drive tourists elsewhere. In Boston, the usual horde of tourists who descend on the city in the summer months, when hotel occupancy rates are already above 90 percent, would have been displaced by Olympic visitors.[8]

Moreover, according to various worldwide tourism authorities, the best way to promote tourism over time is via word of mouth. This transmission mechanism is largely shut down during the Olympics. When normal tourists visit London, they return home to tell their friends, neighbors, and relatives about the city's tourist attractions—the theater, the National Gallery, Buckingham Palace. When Olympic tourists return home, they talk about the gymnastics or swimming competition or the thrill of the 100-meter dash. The effect, if any, is to encourage visits to future *Olympics*, not visits to prior host cities. The same is true for Olympic television viewers who might be inspired to travel—what's primarily being promoted is the Olympics, not the host city. Thus, studies have found few long-term benefits to tourism in host cities.

The notion that hosting will promote trade and foreign investment is even more puzzling. Companies don't select trading partners or investment targets based on whether a city has hosted the Olympics; rather, they select them on the basis of quality, price, proximity, reliability, workforce skills and wages, fiscal incentives, raw materials, schools, weather, and so on. Here, too, no scholarly evidence supports the fanciful claims of Olympic boosters.[9]

London 2012's propagandists averred that the Games brought a substantial inflow of new foreign investment. In particular, they boasted that a meeting with sixteen international companies occurred just prior to the Games, where multiple investment commitments were made. Were this true, it would suggest that the level of foreign investment in the United Kingdom might have risen in 2013. In fact, it decreased by £900 million. Further, during the three prefinancial crisis years (2005–2007), there was a yearly average of £91.6 billion of foreign direct investment in the United Kingdom. But during 2012 to 2013, the annual average was £44.15 billion, or less than half the previous level.

And to be sure, there is always the possibility that being on the world stage propagates negative, rather than positive, publicity. There can be bad weather, severe air or water pollution problems, traffic jams, political repression, social dislocation, terrorism, reports of corruption or poor services—all deleterious images broadcast worldwide. Just ask Rio, Beijing, Sochi, Mexico City, Munich, Athens, Nagano, or Salt Lake City about bad publicity.

2. THIS BID WILL BE DIFFERENT—IT WILL ESCAPE THE MISTAKES OF PRIOR HOSTS. This hopeful spin is a variation on the American exceptionalism theme. "We've learned from the past. We are smarter and more efficient. We'll do it right this time." The problem is that the structural realities of the worldwide auction and the enormity of the required Olympic investments in infrastructure and facilities, along with their evanescent existence, heavily stack the odds against Olympic economic success for any city.

Cost overruns are omnipresent. Why? The answer is clear. First, to gain acceptance of the Olympic project from political bodies, the proponents deliberately underestimate the likely costs and misrepresent the potential complications down the road. Second, upon entering a bid, each city must compete with the bids of other cities from around the globe, applying pressure to add more ribbons and bows to their facilities and amenities. The scope of the Olympic design expands. Third, the need to build or adapt some thirty-five different sports venues for the Summer Games, along with an Olympic village, a media and broadcasting center, transportation routes, medical clinics, and communications facilities inevitably means that the host city finds itself rushing to finish everything in time. The rush during the final two years of preparation, in turn, leads to relaxation of competitive bidding procedures, back room deals, and opportunities for corruption. General contractors and construction companies are not given the luxury of finishing each project a month or two late or even a day or two late. The opening ceremonies cannot be postponed because there are electrical or plumbing glitches at the Olympic stadium. All these pressures lead to higher prices.

Even without the need to modernize basic infrastructure, the cost of hosting the Summer Olympics rises easily to the $10–20 billion range. The revenue from the host's share of international television and sponsorships, ticket sales, domestic sponsorships, licensing, and memorabilia can approach $5 billion. (The Winter Games are generally around half the size of the Summer Games.) The direct costs, then, handily double the revenues— not a very favorable financial balance.

Hosting Olympic Games also impose considerable indirect costs. Consider first the white elephants. Whether it's an eighty-thousand-seat Olympic stadium replete with luxury boxes, club seats, and tablecloth dining, a velodrome, a bobsled run, a beach volleyball stadium or a golf course, there is a common pattern. Olympic facilities are made, after all, for the Olympics and the post-Games use is often minimal or at least insufficient to justify the millions of dollars of annual upkeep expenditures and land use.

Take, for example, Beijing's Bird's Nest Olympic stadium, which cost $460 million to build back in 2008 and boasted ninety thousand seats and 140 luxury suites. There was a plan to have a local professional soccer team play its home games there, but the team backed out over concerns that its standard ten thousand attendees would look lonely in a cavernous facility. Today, the Bird's Nest costs $10 million annually to maintain, hosts an occasional event, and serves as a rather unpopular tourist "attraction" for visitors to Beijing. According to a CBS News report from February 2014, "Few tourists are willing to pay more than $8 to tour the facility" as the memories of the 2008 Games fade.

Or consider the aftermath of the 2004 Summer Games in Athens. The *Toronto Globe and Mail* described the current condition of the former Olympic scene in Athens: "If you spend time wandering the fields and hillsides outside of Athens, as I've done, you will see rising from the scrub a very different sort of Greek ruin. There's a crumbling volleyball stadium with nomadic families living in its stands. There's a twenty-thousand-seat softball park largely reclaimed by trees. A barren, grass-covered hillside resembling a huge abandoned amphitheater turns out to have been a kayaking venue. All were built for the 2004 Olympic Games."[10] All told, twenty-one of the twenty-two sports venues from Athens 2004 were in a state of abandonment or disrepair ten years after the closing ceremonies. White elephants also take the form of excess building of hotel and residential units. Sydney, Lillehammer, and Sochi are examples.

To avoid a legacy of white elephants, cities are now spending hundreds of millions of dollars to convert Olympic facilities into regular-use venues or designing temporary venues. London's Olympic boosters loudly promised their Games would leave no white elephants. But after winning the bid, the organizers realized that their plan to convert the Olympic stadium into a smaller twenty-five-thousand-seat sporting venue was uneconomic. Instead, the organizing committee has been forced to spend more than $350 million of public funds to convert the stadium to the new home of the West Ham United soccer club. West Ham will contribute less than $30 million to total costs of conversion. It may have been cheaper to knock down the Olympic stadium and build a new one from scratch, but London's commitment to no white elephants made that approach politically impossible.[11]

Boston planned a temporary building for its Olympic stadium. If Boston 2024's optimistic projections were to come true, the stadium would have cost almost $200 million and it would have disappeared after the Games. Left unanswered was whether it made economic sense to spend $200 million on a facility that would vanish after three weeks. Besides the wasted resources, the problem with temporary venues is that they leave no sports legacy.

Next consider the indirect cost of land. Hosting the Summer Games requires a lot of real estate. The IOC guidelines for minimum surface area of venues is 1,660 acres (equivalent to 7 percent of the surface area of Barcelona). With ceremonial green space, large-scale public space, parking, transportation and communications facilities, the land area use can quadruple. Beijing 2008 used 8,400 acres of real estate (equivalent to 15 percent of the surface area of Boston).[12]

Land, of course, has an opportunity cost. Back in 2004 when New York City was bidding to host the 2012 Games, the initial plan was to build an Olympic stadium in central Manhattan between Tenth and Eleventh avenues and Thirty-first and Thirty-third streets. In order to do so, it would first have to build a $400 million concrete deck over the Long Island Rail Road yards. NYC2012 even had a legacy plan. After the Games, the stadium would become the home of the NFL New York Jets, who would play eight regular season games there each year. The problem with this plan, above all, is that once the deck was built and construction was made possible, this acreage in midtown, adjacent to Broadway and the theater district, overlooking the Hudson River, would be some of the most valuable real estate in the world. Under the NYC2012 plan, after adding two exhibition games, a possible football playoff, and a couple of concerts, the stadiums would be used maybe fifteen days each year—hardly the most economic or socially beneficial use of prime real estate.

Yet another indirect cost, related to land use, is the potential loss in property taxes. In order to find the necessary land, the Olympic organizing committee often has to buy real estate from its private owners. Those private owners pay taxes on the land. When converted to public use, that tax revenue may be lost and not replaced. It is also noteworthy that the IOC requires that no taxes on individuals and activities be connected to Olympic construction and operations. In London 2012, it is estimated that the government lost tens of millions of dollars in sales and income tax exemptions mandated by the IOC.[13]

The IOC also mandates that all billboards and advertising space in the city be cleared for use by Olympic sponsors. There are significant expenses here not only from clearing existing space and then reinstalling the ads but also from the lost revenue that would be paid by the advertisers. The space must be cleared beginning a month before the Games and remain under IOC control for several weeks after the Games.

A further indirect cost of hosting results from environmental degradation. The IOC adopted the "sustainability" mantra in the early 1990s, but it has done little beyond lip service to honor its commitment. The Russian government allowed the dumping of tons of sludge and chemicals in the Black Sea in the lead-up to Sochi. In Rio, a new golf course in the Barra da Tijuca area of the city was constructed in what was once a nature preserve. Rio has underutilized two other elite golf clubs that cater to a small class of super-rich businessmen. They will now have a third course, despoiling the ecology of the wetlands in Barra and demanding regular irrigation in a water-short city. It is hard to see how sustainability has been advanced by hosting the Olympics. Perhaps the most egregious example of blatant disregard for the environment, however, is occurring now in the plans for Beijing to host the 2022 Winter Games, discussed below.

There is also human cost. While the IOC declares its commitment to human rights, its record on this score is inconsistent at best. China's human rights records is one of the worst in the world, yet Beijing will have hosted both the Summer and Winter Olympics within a period of fourteen years.

The process of clearing space and beautifying optics for the Games results, almost universally, in displacing people from their communities and jobs. The most poignant recent example occurred in Rio de Janeiro. The Rio landscape is dotted with hundreds of shantytowns or favelas. More than 20 percent of Rio's 6.5 million inhabitants live in favelas. At the beginning of the process of hosting the 2014 World Cup and 2016 Olympics, Rio developed a plan to modernize and bring new services to its favelas, called *Morar Carioca*, along with pacifying those favelas riddled with gang and drug violence. This process was begun, but quickly abandoned. Instead, local government focused on emptying the favelas that stood in the way of Olympic venues and infrastructure projects, or that were near Olympic sites and deemed to be eyesores. An estimated 77,200 favela residents have been relocated under this program. The families typically are sent to low-income housing projects in western Rio, which, given the city's horrific transportation problems, may be two hours away from their leveled homes. These families now find themselves torn asunder from their long-standing communities, the children must find new schools, and the parents are unable to commute to their old jobs. Many residents in different favelas have resisted relocation. As Rio's opening ceremonies approached, the local government became more anxious about these recalcitrant *favelados* and resorted to increasingly violent measures. In mid-March 2016, a standoff took place at the Vila Autódromo favela next to the Olympic Park in Barra da Tijuca. In the end, roughly five hundred families were removed forcibly from Vila Autódromo.

Other than Beijing 2008, where more than one million residents reportedly were evicted, the social dislocations in Rio may be more extensive and severe than those during other Games, but they are present in practically every case.[14] These disruptions result in housing shortages, lost jobs, and attendant social problems.

Support for nonprofits is another potential casualty from hosting. Mounting an Olympic bid and staying in the competition for two to four years costs a lot of money—usually near $100 million. Olympic bid committees generally finance themselves with tax-deductible contributions from the private sector, as was the case with Boston 2024. With the allure of favorable publicity from a connection to the Olympics, and perhaps seeking jobs or political ties, individuals and companies open up their wallets to support the bid process. The problem is that their contributions to the bid organizing effort do not always come on top of other contributions they make to social causes. The result is that donations to more legitimate nonprofits diminish. The situation in London 2012 became particularly dramatic. According to the British charity Directory of Social Change (DSC), the government diverted $665 million from monies originally designated for nonprofits in order to finance the 2012 Games.

3. OLYMPIC BIDS ARE A GOOD PLANNING EXERCISE FOR A CITY'S FUTURE. Boston 2024's boosters frequently claimed that the bidding process actually was intended as an effort at envisioning what Boston might look like in the future. The group made a "commitment to align its Olympic bid efforts with [greater Boston's] long-term planning as a city and state through 2030."[15] That sentiment was echoed by the USOC's Dan Doctoroff, who wrote in a *Boston Globe* op-ed that "perhaps nothing did more to set New York on a course toward a greater future than [the failed New York's 2012 bid]."[16] In making the case that the Olympics would be a good exercise in planning the city's future, Boston's mayor Marty Walsh was quoted as

saying that hosting the Olympic Games is an opportunity that comes along once a century. If the opportunity is only going to come around once every one hundred years, it would seem prudent for cities like Boston to learn how to plan for their future without the prospect of hosting the Olympics!

The typical city that hosts the Games does not have an urban design or development strategy in place prior to taking on the massive project of preparing for the Olympics. In the absence of a coherent vision, the venue and infrastructure demands of the IOC take precedence. The city is forced to contort itself to accommodate the thirty-plus Olympic venues, even as its political leaders try to make the case that the city's long-term goals will come first. This was the case in Boston, where the Walsh administration announced an "Imagine Boston 2030" planning initiative a few months after the USOC had chosen Boston 2024.

Real planning ex ante is easy enough to detect. It happened, for instance, in Barcelona around the hosting of the 1992 Summer Games. With the death of Franco in 1975, Barcelona anticipated a new opportunity to reshape its development. A positive spirit of cooperation between capital and labor and among the municipal, regional, and national governments fostered a proactive approach. In 1976, the city produced the General Metropolitan Plan (PGM), which established a new spatial framework for the city. A major element of this framework entailed opening the city to the sea. This involved relocating rail lines that separated the Pobleneu neighborhood from the beach and placing a roadway below-grade at the bottom of the famous street, Las Ramblas. It also meant that an area of mostly abandoned warehouses and factories in Pobleneu would be razed and become the eventual site of the Olympic village, to be converted to residential housing after the games. Other parts of the plan related to improving the road network around the city, extending the metro system, redesigning the airport, renovating public spaces and museums, and modernizing the sewerage system.

Thus, an early plan for urban redevelopment was formulated by 1976 and then elaborated in the following years. In 1983, city planners put out a preliminary report on the feasibility of hosting the Olympics and concluded that the refurbishment of the 1936 stadium in Montjuic (which became the Olympic stadium) and the construction of the Sports Palace and swimming facility would be undertaken whether or not the city was selected to host the games. Of the thirty-seven sports facilities ultimately used during the 1992 Olympics, twenty-seven were already built and another five were under construction at the time Spain was selected to host the games in 1986. Thus, a central feature of the Barcelona experience is that *the plan preceded the games*, and hence the games were put at the service of the preexisting plan, rather than the typical pattern of the city development plan being put at the service of the games.[17]

So, yes, planning is desirable, but it needs to be substantial and to precede the bidding effort. If the Olympic bid initiates the planning process, as it did in Boston, the Olympics will dominate the city. This is precisely the outcome that a city needs to avoid.

4. THE GAMES WILL LEAVE BEHIND A LEGACY OF IMPROVED IN-FRASTRUCTURE. There is little question that the Games will leave a legacy. The question is whether that legacy will be positive or negative. To assess the balance, one has to consider the direct and indirect costs against the revenue benefits and calculate whether any intangible gains can be made.

The straight financial calculus is not encouraging: between $10 billion and $20 billion in costs, or more, depending on the needed infrastructure, and $3 to 5 billion in revenue. The amounts for the Winter Games are generally between 50 and 60 percent those of the Summer Games. There would have to be robust long-term gains to offset these short-term losses. Yet the scholarly literature does not reliably find such gains.

What remain are the physical infrastructure and sports venues that a host city has after the Games but did not have before them. Two issues to consider are (1) whether the roads, bridges, metro stops, and stadiums are things that the city really needed and if so, were they erected in the best places for the city's development or instead in the best places to service the Olympic clusters; and (2) if they do serve the city's development needs, why couldn't they have been built without the additional expense of hosting the Olympics.

Olympic boosters often answer the second question by saying that the Games can be a "catalyst" for needed development, that they allow city leaders to cut through slow, bureaucratic processes, and force improvements to be done on a deadline. But if a city's development and investment processes are broken, city leaders would be far better off fixing them, rather than temporarily suspending them for hosting a mega sporting event. Deadlines are a double-edged sword: they may force action, but they are also likely to raise the costs of projects or to promote shoddy work. And more important, host cities typically deliver only the infrastructure most critical to the Games, while other promises languish. Rio, for example, expects to have its Olympic sports venues completed for the Games, but some public transportation improvements once associated with the bid won't be completed until sometime after the Games are over, and a promise to clean the water in Rio's Guanabara Bay was dropped. Meanwhile, the completed projects are of dubious benefit to Rio's development.

Citizens in potential host cities should maintain a healthy skepticism about promises that an Olympic bid will improve their public transit systems. Indeed, many months after the bid's demise, Boston 2024 leader Steve Pagliuca would later tell Reuters, "you don't really need a T for the Olympics."[18]

Olympic boosters often cite noneconomic benefits: the feel-good effects, better exercise routines, among others. While it is true that the residents of many hosts cities do experience feel-good effects, the evidence suggests that these are ephemeral—they don't last very long after the Games. There is no evidence to support claims of better exercise habits or higher athletic participation rates by the population. As Boston's Olympic opponents were fond of saying, "You don't encourage physical exercise by building a stadium in which ten people run and 69,000 people sit."

THE 2022 WINTER GAMES AND HANDICAPPING THE 2024 SUMMER GAMES

Much has been made of the IOC's Agenda 2020. But for the 2022 Games, the IOC was stuck with two bids that fell far short of Agenda 2020's stated commitments and ideals.

The human rights records in both Kazakhstan and China, to put it generously, leave much to be desired. Back in 2001, the IOC had claimed that awarding the 2008 Summer Olympics to Beijing would shine a bright light on China, bring the country into the community of nations, and improve its human rights policies. Yet China's human rights ranking actually deteriorated between 2008 and 2014, according to Human Rights Watch and the Reporters Without Borders Press Freedom Index.[19] Rather than a salutary effect on human rights, the typical pattern when China has hosted international events is a clampdown on political expression, a roundup of activists, and tighter censorship.

Kazakhstan is hardly any better. It has had the same president since 1989, and Human Rights Watch has criticized the country's repression of dissent and religious freedom as well as its use of torture on detained persons.[20] Ever the soothsayer and spin artist, IOC President Thomas Bach declared: "We have two excellent candidates."[21]

Agenda 2020 also professes a concern for affordability. The Beijing organizing committee pitched its bid to the IOC by noting that it would use some of the venues left over from the 2008 Olympics. China also cooperated by excluding from its estimated Olympic budget the cost of the high-speed railroad that will link Beijing to the downhill and cross-country ski areas (54 miles and 118 miles from the capital, respectively), a project that has dubious long-term value. Chinese state media estimated the cost of the high-speed rail at $5 billion.[22] China says it did not count the rapid trains in the Olympic budget because it was going to build them anyway. Games or not, the rail line is financially and environmentally imprudent in the extreme.

Also excluded from the budget will be the substantial expense of new water diversion and desalination programs that will be necessary for drinking, icemaking, and artificial snowmaking in the water-starved northern cities. North China's climate is arid, and only 25 percent of the country's water resources lie in the north, although nearly 50 percent of the population resides there.[23] Accordingly, China launched an $80 billion water-diversion program from the south prior to the 2008 Summer Olympics. But the north's per capita water availability still remains below what the United Nations deems to be the critical level. Zhangjiakou, the site of the Nordic skiing competition, gets fewer than eight inches of snow per year. Yanqing, the site of the Alpine skiing events, gets under 15 inches of precipitation annually. Little of that snowfall remains on the ground. Both areas will require copious water supplies for artificial snowmaking.[24] Beijing, Zhangjiakou, and Yanquing are part of the North China Plain, encompassing the four provinces of Shandong, Henan, Jiangsu, and Hebei, which is China's most important agricultural region, producing sorghum, corn, winter wheat, vegetables, and cotton. The demand for water from the ski areas will divert water from these vital agricultural uses.[25]

Even without considering the lost agricultural output, it is evident that the published budget for Beijing 2022 will be understated by billions of dollars, enabling the IOC to trumpet the success of its Agenda 2020 affordability campaign. Further, China's purported legacy of creating permanent ski resorts in the mountains bordering Inner Mongolia and the Gobi Desert only threatens to worsen an acute and unsustainable water shortage. If the ski resorts survive, only China's richest residents will be able to afford them, while food supplies will be adversely affected and foodstuff prices will rise.

Another strike against Beijing 2022 is that the winter is one of the worst times for air pollution in the city. Studies have shown this pollution to be responsible for a significant increase of cardiovascular and respiratory diseases.[26] Deforestation of the northern mountains will only compound the problem. Prior to the 2008 Games, Beijing succeeded in temporarily reducing airborne particulates by placing strict controls on traffic, closing nearby factories, discouraging residents from driving, and using cloud seeding to induce rain. Similar strategies are bound to be employed again in 2022, although the negative economic impacts of these actions will never be included in the Games' budget. And even with these adjustments, it is hard to imagine that the athletes' health will not be put at some risk.

Faced with a choice between two different repressive regimes, the IOC narrowly selected Beijing over Kazakh rival Almaty, by vote of 44 to 40. "It really is a safe choice. We know China will deliver on its promises," IOC President Bach offered, just days after accusing Boston's boosters of "not delivering on promises they made to the USOC when they were selected."[27] Paired together, the quotations are revealing of the IOC's priorities.

But the bidding process for the 2022 Games started long before Agenda 2020 was passed. Thus, the significance and impact of Agenda 2020 for the Olympic Movement still remains to be tested. The selection of a host city for the 2024 Summer Games may be more revealing.

The ninety-odd voting members of the IOC will meet in Lima, Peru, in September 2017 to award the right to host the 2024 Summer Olympics to one of three remaining candidate cities: Los Angeles, Paris, or Budapest.[28] Of course, Los Angeles replaced Boston (the original US entry) and, by virtue of a November 2015 referendum, Hamburg dropped out of the race. What follows is a preliminary evaluation of the four bids based upon the first bid document ("Vision, Games Concept and Strategy") submitted to the IOC in February 2016 by each bidding city. Two more bid documents are to follow: "Governance, Legal and Venue Funding" in October 2016; and "Games Delivery, Experience and Venue Legacy" in February 2017.

The Los Angeles Bid

Unlike in Boston, the Los Angeles city council has endorsed the city's bid. On September 1, 2015, the council voted 15 to 0 to support LA 2024, with the important caveat that the council reserved the right to approve the budget in the city's execution plan. The LA county board of supervisors previously had approved an interest in seeking the Games. Also unlike in Boston, and most other cities, the inspiration and drive for the bid came from the mayor's office, not the construction industry.[29]

The Los Angeles 2024 bid bears many of the same characteristics as its 1984 bid. The city is well stocked with sports, transportation, and communication infrastructure and needs to do very little building relative to other bids. LA is in a unique position, as 97 percent of the planned competition and noncompetition venues exist, are already planned as permanent venues by private investors, or will be temporary. This means that Los Angeles will need to construct only one additional permanent venue from the ground up—the canoe slalom course.[30] The construction projects that remain to be done have private partners who are committed to handle the lion's share of the financing. Los Angeles is in the process of expanding its metro system and will have invested at least $88 billion in its development prior to 2024, according to bid documents. Los Angeles also has begun investing in the modernization of its airport (LAX) and plans to invest $14 billion in this project, also before 2024. These investments are scheduled whether or not Los Angeles hosts the Games.

The bid that Los Angeles boosters first submitted to the USOC in December 2014 proposed building a new Olympic village on rail yards just east of downtown Los Angeles, at a projected cost of at least $1 billion. But

Los Angeles 2024 has revised its plans and is now expecting to host the Olympic village in dormitories at the University of California–Los Angeles (UCLA). UCLA already is committed to expanding its student housing and has ample athletic, training, medical, dining, and entertainment facilities. It is also centrally located among the various Olympic clusters planned in the bid. Although some cost will fall on the LA organizing committee for preparing, renting, and operating the village, it likely will be a few hundred million, rather than the $2 to 3 billion that is likely to be spent for the athletes' village in Tokyo for the 2020 Summer Games. It is also probably $1 or 2 billion dollars less than what Paris, Rome, or Budapest projected to spend on their Olympic villages. Hence, the LA plan is decidedly more frugal and becomes an interesting test of the new affordability mantra in Agenda 2020. The IOC has said that it is serious about wanting economically responsible bids, rather than lavish, excessive ones. LA might be said to be calling the IOC's bluff.

Second, the Olympic stadium will be the LA Memorial Coliseum, which was the Olympic stadium for both the 1932 and the 1984 Games. The coliseum is on the University of Southern California (USC) campus and serves as the home field for its football games. The coliseum requires renovation, additional construction, and the installation of a track. USC has thus far committed $270 million to this project. The NFL's Los Angeles Rams franchise has moved from St. Louis and will play at the coliseum for the next two years while their new multibillion dollar facility is being built near the airport. It is expected that the Rams will make an additional investment in modernizing the coliseum. The LA organizing committee is likely to have to contribute several hundred million on top of the investment by USC and the Rams, but, again, relative to building a new Olympic stadium for over $1 billion, as was done in London (including the remodeling) and will be done in Tokyo, this is a modest sum.

Third, the media and broadcasting center will be built on the lot of Universal Studios, owned by Comcast/NBC. NBC is, of course, the US broadcaster of the Games and pays the IOC the highest rights fees by a healthy margin. NBC has committed to building a new facility that will be converted into a Comcast/NBC office building after the Games. Again, a modest cost will be involved for the LA organizing committee, but it is likely to be in the tens of millions, relative to the several hundred million dollars the media/broadcast center will cost elsewhere.

The village, stadium, and media/broadcasting center are, by a substantial margin, the most expensive venues involved in the summer Olympics. In each case, the LA organizing committee's expense will be very modest, at least relative to other bids. Further, LA will have minimal additional expenses for its other venues and for infrastructure.

While the LA bid necessarily involves some risks, they are very small compared to what many other hosts experience. A portion of those risks may be covered by the state. A bill was introduced in the state legislature in March 2016 to appropriate $250 million in support of the LA bid. The bill is contingent on Los Angeles agreeing to cover the first $250 million of financial shortfall, if it should occur. Should $500 million be insufficient, any remaining backstop would be provided by the city.

Further, the LA bid does depend on the US government declaring the Games a National Special Security Event. When the federal government does this, it generally picks up most of the security tab. But this outcome is not automatic. If Congress does vote to finance security at an Olympics in Los Angeles, it is likely to cost between $1 and $2 billion. Thus, although the risk for the LA or California taxpayer appears to be small, the US taxpayer will be on the hook (though only for $6.25 per person, if the security tab reaches $2 billion).

On the first page of its bid, LA 2024 writes, perhaps prophetically, that an LA Olympics "refreshes the Olympic brand around the world for a new generation." This is what LA 1984 accomplished, when it rescued the Olympics from a mega-event no one wanted to host and created a vision of desirable and possibly profitable event. Too many imponderables make it impossible to know the outcome, but LA 2024 appears to have a fighting chance to do it again.

The Paris Bid

There was considerable doubt whether Paris would bid for the 2024 Games. In November 2014, Paris mayor Anne Hidalgo shared reservations: "We are in a financial and budgetary position today that does not allow me to say that I am making this bid." By March 2015, however, Hidalgo had become a convert, and, again, unlike in Boston, the Paris bid was able to proceed because it received an endorsement from the city council.[31]

Paris last hosted the Olympics in 1924. No French city has hosted the Summer Games since (two French cities hosted Winter Games, Grenoble in 1968 and Albertville in 1992). If Paris is selected as the 2024 host, it will mark the centennial of the 1924 Games. The symmetry and symbolism in that fact will not elude the voting members of the IOC. The voting members also might be moved by a spirit of solidarity with Paris, after the series of terrorist attacks in the city over the last two years. Together, these emotional factors might rule the day, regardless of the objective basis for picking which city will run a more effective and responsible Games.

But the Paris bid also has several objective factors in its favor. Of the thirty-six sports venues, twenty-six already exist and another eight will be temporary. The Stade de France in the Saint Denis district of Paris, around six miles from the city's center, will serve as the Olympic stadium. It is a modern facility, built in 1998, with over eighty-one thousand seats and 172 executive suites. It is in the same district as one of two Olympic clusters. The Saint Denis cluster also will include a new Olympic village, to be built on and near the Ile Saint Denis on the Seine River. The new aquatic center also will be in this cluster.

The Paris plan also anticipates constructing a new arena, the media and broadcasting center, and an extensive public transportation network, along with some new roads. The new transportation network includes seven line extensions of the Paris metro, three tram lines, and two high-speed (TGV) rail lines, between Paris and Nice and Paris and Toulouse. The village and media center are slated to be funded privately—although London 2012 made these same claims and ultimately was forced to pay for the facilities with public funds when private developers backed out. The rest of Paris's bid is funded publicly. Because of the need for substantial new construction and infrastructure, the Paris bid, although relatively economical, will be substantially more costly than that of Los Angeles.

The Rome Bid

Rome last hosted the Summer Olympics in 1960. The only other Italian Olympic hosts have been Cortina d'Ampezzo and Turin for the Winter

Games in 1956 and 2006, respectively. Rome proposed to use some of the existing venues from 1960, which were all in need of renovation. In addition to very significant work needed at the Olympic stadium, the Rome bid would have required the new construction of the Olympic village, the media and broadcast center, an aquatic center, a velodrome, a basketball and hockey arena, a water park, and appreciable public works. Rome 2024's plan had thirty-five sport venues, with sixteen of them in five clusters, and nineteen stand-alone venues, quite widely dispersed. For instance, the proposed Olympic village at the University of Rome Tor Vergata campus to the southeast of the city lies seventeen miles from the proposed Olympic stadium. Public funds would have covered most of the new construction.[32] Rome's newly elected mayor, Virginia Raggi, took a strong stance against Rome's Olympic bid. Raggi argued that "garbage, transport, schools, social services and public space" are more important than hosting the Olympics. Rome officially dropped its bid in October 2016, at which point the number of bidders for the 2024 Games dropped to just three.

The Budapest Bid

Both the Budapest Assembly and the Hungarian Parliament voted to support the bid. Budapest has never hosted the Olympics, nor has any Hungarian city. Budapest entered a bid to host the Games in 1916, 1920, 1936, 1944, and 1960, losing each time.[34]

Budapest's plan requires the most new construction. Indeed, twenty-nine venues would have to be built, including the Olympic village, media and broadcasting center, Olympic stadium (proposed at sixty thousand seats), velodrome, and aquatic center. Some would be built on privately owned land that would have to be purchased. Almost all of the construction would be financed by the national government, although in some cases there is a plan to sell off the facilities to the private sector. Hungary's supreme court blocked a proposed referendum on Budapest's bid in January 2016.

The Handicap

In our view, the two most interesting bids are those of Los Angeles and Paris. Los Angeles requires less construction and less financing and entails less risk by a considerable margin. The Paris bid, however, has raw emotion and politics on its side. In the end, the IOC voters are likely to cast their preferences as much with their hearts as with their heads.

While the Los Angeles bid requires the least new investment, it also provides the least in new facilities or legacy. As with all Olympic Games, it is hard to see what any of the cities will gain by winning the Olympic auction.

TWELVE

LESSONS LEARNED

Boston 2024 hired pricey architects to design its stadiums, urban planners to design the areas around its facilities, lawyers to write its contracts, and fundraisers to track down six- and seven-figure checks from sponsors. But of all the bid's well-paid consultants, the two best compensated, Interpublic and Teneo, had little to do with mundane tasks such as helping ensure the bid had realistic cost assumptions or confirming that its designs made sense for the city once the Games left town. Instead, these firms, and a third, JTA, were paid at a rate of more than $2.5 million per year to achieve what is ultimately every bid's most important mandate: to win a majority of votes from IOC members and be awarded the rights to the Games. These were the hired guns that Boston 2024 valued more than any others. Interpublic's subsidiary Weber Shandwick advised the successful Tokyo 2020 and Beijing 2022 bids. Teneo's Olympic lead Terrence Burns was involved in the 1996 Atlanta Olympics and worked on the successful Beijing 2008, Vancouver 2010, Sochi 2014, and Pyeongchang 2018 Olympic bids. JTA's chairman is Jon Tibbs, who has worked on the 2002 Salt Lake and 2008 Beijing bids. (Tibbs, an Englishman, likes to brag that he's friendly with Vladimir Putin, who happens to controls Russia's three IOC votes.) The enduring businesses these firms have created are a testament to the fact that winning an Olympic bid is first and foremost about catering to the IOC. Sometimes that catering is literal. Burns and Tibbs can tell you a key IOC member's dietary preferences or favorite cocktail, which might come in handy when you corner him or her at the hotel bar during an IOC meeting. This is exactly the situation in which Los Angeles mayor Eric Garcetti found himself in October 2015, chatting with influential IOC member Prince Tunku Imran of Malaysia past midnight at a Washington, D.C., Hilton, as reported by the *Los Angeles*

Times' David Wharton.[1] Perhaps Garcetti was able to secure Los Angeles a vote over Paris or Rome, but one wonders whether the mayor's time with the prince was well spent, measured against any number of other issues Garcetti could have been addressing back home in Los Angeles. Both Burns and Tibbs, meanwhile, have parlayed their brief engagements with Boston 2024 into paid roles advising Los Angeles 2024.

What does it say about an Olympic bid that its best-paid consultants are charged not with preparing responsible bids, but with lobbying the ninety-odd members of the International Olympic Committee? It says that these IOC members become the boosters' true constituency. The IOC's priorities trump those of the voters and residents back home.

Over the course of the Boston 2024 debate, No Boston Olympics often pointed out that IOC members included members of royalty from Lichtenstein (population 37,000) and Monaco (population 38,000)—meaning that each of these small European nations had more influence over the IOC's choice than any individual citizen in Massachusetts (population 6.7 million), which was home to no IOC members. The entire United States has just three IOC members.[2] Princess Nora of Lichtenstein, Prince Albert of Monaco, Crown Prince Frederik of Denmark, Prince Feisal Al Hussein of Jordan, and other members of the IOC may well be very nice people, but they can hardly be relied upon to know what is best for the citizens of potential host cities. And even if they had any concept of what mattered to local residents, it likely would have little impact on how they cast their votes. "You don't win bids on facts. You win bids on emotion," bid consultant Burns has said, "You touch people's hearts."[3] IOC members don't vote with their heads, because they never face the consequences of bids gone wrong. Those risks and costs sit with the host cities.

As cities have grown wary of these bidding dynamics, the recent worldwide trend has become clear: interest in hosting the Olympic Games has diminished. When cities engage in substantive debates about the pros and cons of a bid, they mostly decide to pass on the opportunity. They decide they have more important priorities for their limited financial and civic resources. Boston, Hamburg, Kraków, Munich, Oslo, and Stockholm have all recently dropped out of the IOC's Olympic auction, with few regrets.

But as long as the International Olympic Committee can continue to induce a handful of bids, the International Olympic Committee appears to remain committed to the auction-style process it has overseen, and from which it has benefited, for more than a century. The IOC seems unwilling to make substantial and substantive changes. Instead, it trumpets slick but hollow reform programs such as Agenda 2020—which are ultimately no more than window dressing. The predictable result will be that every two years the IOC's ninety-odd voting members will continue to select bids that meet the needs of the International Olympic Committee (and its media and corporate funders) even when these bids pose substantial risks and few benefits for the IOC's prospective hosts.

And the IOC can reasonably expect to have a least a few bids survive, even in democracies. Olympic hosting has concentrated benefits and diffuse costs. The boosters have much to gain, so they work harder than opponents, who are more numerous but stand to lose less or don't realize how much they have to lose until it's too late. There is also a resources gap—the boosters have tens of millions of dollars to buy publicity and an audience with politicians, while the opponents typically have meager financial reserves and little access to the halls of power. When these dynamics hold, the IOC gets exactly the types of bids savored by Thomas Bach and his IOC colleagues. That was the case in 2005, when the IOC could select from extravagant 2012 Games bids submitted by London, New York, Madrid, Paris, and Moscow.

Bach blamed the defeat of Boston 2024 on boosters who "did not deliver on promises." Other pundits, like Boston University Associate Professor Thomas Whalen, told the *New York Times* that it confirmed Boston as a "parochial backwater" even as he blamed bid organizers for being "completely incompetent."[4] Boston 2024 bid leader Steve Pagliuca said, "I think we got defeated by Mother Nature."[5]

But it would be a mistake to conclude that Boston 2024's failure was simply the result of a hapless organizing committee, a parochial citizenry, or historic snowfall in the winter of 2015. Boston's boosters certainly made some unforced errors. And snowstorms that shut down the region's transportation network didn't give commuters confidence that their city was ready to host an Olympic Games. But those factors only hastened a fundamentally democratic process that was playing out across the Commonwealth of Massachusetts. The results of polling were very clear: the more voters learned about the Boston 2024 bid, the less they liked it. One statewide poll found that more than 50 percent of voters who were following Boston 2024 "not at all" supported a bid, while only 27 percent of those following it "a lot" did so.[6] Even if Boston 2024 had executed a flawless marketing campaign, the boosters would have had difficulty addressing questions about the taxpayer guarantee, Olympic highway lanes for IOC dignitaries, and the need to build a stadium, aquatics center, velodrome, media center, and Olympic village from scratch. What sunk Boston 2024 wasn't the snow. Instead, it was organized groups of educated and engaged citizens and a voracious, ambitious press corps that were willing to ask Boston 2024 tough questions to which Boston 2024's boosters could never find good answers. Boston's Olympic opponents were overwhelmingly outgunned by Olympic boosters, but they had the facts on their side. Defeating the bid became a matter of forcing the conversation out of the closed-door meetings favored by the boosters and the USOC, and into the public square, where citizens could make up their own minds about the bid's pros and cons. Citizens in democratic societies anywhere in the world can follow this model.

By rejecting Boston 2024's bid, the people of Boston reclaimed their right to chart their own city's future, without the costly demands and requirements of the International Olympic Committee's seventeen-day extravaganza. The path ahead for Boston, Hamburg, and other democratic cities that have rejected the Olympics is not easy or straightforward. Democracy never is. But it is a path of self-determination rather than oligarchic dictate. Bostonians wouldn't stand to have it any other way.

Former Boston mayor Ray Flynn made this point to the *Boston Herald* the day of the bid's defeat. Flynn had supported the bid in the early 1990s before stepping down to become ambassador to the Vatican and giving way to Menino. He also had been named to Boston 2024's board of directors. But like many in Boston, Flynn ultimately credited the people of Boston with Boston 2024's demise.

> I've been in politics a long time in this city, and every major decision has
> to start from the grassroots, come from the people in the communities
> affected . . . What the people who are most affected in the neighborhoods,
> how they feel about it, is always the most important aspect that I look
> for. And I saw very little support in the neighborhoods of Boston. Now I

don't know about the boardrooms in Downtown Boston and I don't know about the newsrooms in Boston either. But I'll tell you about the neighborhoods of Boston. People didn't buy it. They weren't convinced . . . The people of Boston would love to have the Olympics, but they also want to be respected. If they're not respected, if they aren't given a straight deal, how the communities are affected . . . Is there any benefit? The Olympics would have been number 51 on my list of 50 things that need to happen in Boston. Instead of that, they just jumped this issue to number one. As if it was the only issue—a panacea for Boston's problems. And the people saw right through it and they never supported it . . . People in Boston are too smart to be hoodwinked into something that people say is good for them.[7]

Even Boston 2024 bid leader John Fish reflected on this theme when he graciously telephoned Dempsey and offered his congratulations the day after Boston 2024's demise. "Democracy worked," he said.

ACKNOWLEDGMENTS

Kelley Gossett and Liam Kerr, my fellow volunteer cochairs, were the heart and soul of No Boston Olympics. None of what we did as an organization would have been possible without their generosity, strength, intelligence, and fierce commitment. I am honored to call them friends and fortunate to have had them fighting alongside me.

No Boston Olympics was a true grassroots organization, fueled by the efforts of hundreds of volunteers and contributors. I am grateful for every small-dollar contribution, letter to the editor, homemade sign, and tweet. Special thanks are due to our guardian angels Diana and Lee Humphrey, young gun Aaron Leibowitz, the sage Ray Howell, and JP dad Seth Kroll. Thanks also to supporters Joe Blair, Victor de Fontnouvelle, Charley Lax, Joe Huber, Noah McCormack, Mike Casella, Diane Simpson, and Robert Gifford.

Thank you to Massachusetts Representatives Bill Straus, Aaron Michlewitz, and Mike Moran for their support and friendship.

Jonathan Cohn and Robin Jacks of No Boston 2024 were allies who became friends—and even editors of sections of this book!

Thank you to Victor Matheson and David Luberoff, for introducing me to Professor Zimbalist and for their encouragement in the early days of No Boston Olympics.

My parents taught me the value and importance of civic engagement. They are my role models. I am grateful for their love, support, and encouragement, even though I don't tell them that enough!

Finally, my girlfriend, Anna Cilluffo, was patient and caring through many months in which Boston 2024 (and writing this book) consumed my life. Her love and affection helped me make it through.

—*Chris Dempsey*

Thanks to Ted Cartselos, Bill Straus, Jürgen Bruns-Berentelg, Joachim Thiel, Elizabeth Warren, Jim Braude, Eric Garcetti, Evan Falchuk, Manav Kumar, Derek Shearer, Chuck Collins, Art MacEwan, Liam Kerr, Kelley Gossett, Theresa Williamson, Victor Matheson, Rob Baade, Wolfgang Maennig, Julianna Barbassa, Chris Gaffney, Janice Forsyth, Dan Gardner, Brad Humphreys, Casey Wasserman, Jeff Millman, Laura Robinson, Judith Grant Long, and, with love, to Shelley, Alex, Ella, Jeff and Mike.

—*Andrew Zimbalist*

NOTES

Prologue

1. "Official Tally: Baker-Coakley Was Closest Governor's Race in 50 Years," *Politicker*, WBUR, November 20, 2014, accessed July 11, 2016, www.wbur.org /politicker/2014/11/20/baker-coakley-turnout.

2. "Governor Charlie Baker Delivers Inaugural Address," press release, January 8, 2015, accessed July 11, 2016, www.mass.gov/governor/press-office /press-releases/fy2015/governor-charlie-baker-delivers-inaugural-address.html.

3. TeamUSA, Twitter post, July 8, 2015, 3:29 p.m., accessed July 12, 2016, twitter.com/teamusa/status/553332687466156032.

4. Joan Vennochi, "Boston 2024 Adds Up to an Olympic Leap of Faith," *Boston Globe*, December 11, 2014, accessed December 11, 2014, www.bostonglobe .com/opinion/2014/12/11/boston-adds-olympic-leap-faith/87vz3hWsSLbncfhM DrYHCP/story.html.

5. Adam Vaccaro, "The 2 Big Mistakes in Boston's First Olympics Pitch," July 24, 2015, boston.com, accessed July 11, 2016, www.boston.com/news/local -news/2015/07/24/the-2-big-mistakes-in-bostons-first-olympics-pitch.

6. Although the announcement of the termination of Boston's bid was described officially as jointly made by Boston 2024 and the USOC, strong evidence indicates that it was the USOC that pulled the plug on the Boston bid. Even the joint announcement, referring to the lack of public support in Boston, notes: "Therefore, the USOC does not think that the level of support enjoyed by Boston's bid would allow it to prevail over great bids from Paris, Rome, Hamburg, Budapest or Toronto." "US Olympic Committee and Boston 2024 Jointly End Campaign for Boston to Host 2024 Olympic and Paralympic Games," TeamUSA, July 27, 2015, accessed July 11, 2016, www.teamusa.org/News/2015 /July/27/USOC-And-Boston-2024-Jointly-End-Campaign-For-Boston-To-Host -2024-Olympic-and-Paralympic-Games.

1. The IOC has used both the years 1881 and 1891 in describing this event. See Alain Ferrand, Jean-Loup Chappelet, and Benoît Séguin, *Olympic Marketing* (London: Routledge, 2012); and International Olympic Committee, "What Is the Olympic Motto?" accessed July 30, 2016, http://registration.olympic.org/en/faq/detail/id/29.

2. For Coubertin's biography, see International Olympic Committee, "Pierre de Coubertin," accessed July 11, 2016, www.olympic.org/Assets/OSC%20Section/pdf/LRes_16E.pdf. For Coubertin's first report on the Olympics and the quotation about the importance of athletics in empire building, see Pierre de Coubertin and others, "The Olympic Games: B.C. 776 – A.D. 1896: Second Part: The Olympic Games in 1896," LA84 Foundation, accessed July 11, 2016, http://library.la84.org/6oic/OfficialReports/1896/1896part2.pdf. Originally published in Athens by Charles Beck, publisher, in 1897.

3. Will Jennings, *Olympic Risks* (New York: Palgrave Macmillan, 2012), 70.

4. Coubertin and others, "The Olympic Games"; Frank Condron, *The I Olympiad: Athens 1896* (Warwick, NY: Warwick Press, 2015).

5. International Olympic Committee, "Connolly Takes a Leap into the History Books," accessed July 11, 2016, www.olympic.org/news/james-connolly-usa-triple-jump/242684.

6. Joshua Sternfeld, "The First Modern Olympics," National Endowment for the Humanities, August 2, 2012, accessed July 11, 2016, www.neh.gov/divisions/preservation/featured-project/the-first-modern-olympics. See also NewseumED, "Coverage of 1896 Olympic Athletes, US Presidential Race," accessed July 11, 2016, https://newseumed.org/artifact/coverage-of-1896-olympic-athletes-and-u-s-presidential-race/.

7. Steven Sowards, "Lecture 14: Greek Nationalism, the 'Megale Idea' and Venizelism to 1923," *Twenty-Five Lectures on Modern Balkan History,* last modified June 11, 2009, accessed July 11, 2016, http://staff.lib.msu.edu/sowards/balkan/lect14.htm.

8. Coubertin and others, "The Olympic Games."

9. The World's Fair has faded as an institution, probably because it is not nearly as engaging as television programming compared with events such as the Olympics.

10. Of course, even if the Games are always held in same city, the facilities would need to be maintained and used more than once every four years. Other international events, such as youth Olympics, track and field competitions, and the like would need to be held there. Further, the design of the facilities should eschew gigantism and opulence.

11. As we write in June 2016, the IOC has ninety-one members. A few will be unable to vote for the 2024 Summer Olympic host because they hail from countries involved in the bidding. Just eighty-four people cast ballots in the selection of the host for the 2022 Winter Games, the smallest number of voters since 1981.

12. Ben Mathis-Lilley, "The IOC Demands That Helped Push Norway out of Winter Olympic Bidding Are Hilarious," *Slate*, October 2, 2014, accessed July 11, 2016, www.slate.com/blogs/the_slatest/2014/10/02/ioc_demands_oslo_drops _bid_after_over_the_top_list_of_requirements.html.

13. For an excellent discussion of the popular defeat of the planned Denver Olympics, see Jules Boykoff, *Power Games: A Political History of the Olympics* (London: Verso, 2016), 118–23.

14. "US Groups Differ on Surplus," *New York Times*, February 11, 1985, accessed July 11, 2016, www.nytimes.com/1985/02/11/sports/us-olympic-groups -differ-on-surplus.html.

15. International Olympic Committee, "Olympic Agenda 2020," November 18, 2014, accessed July 11, 2016, www.olympic.org/Documents/Olympic_Agenda _2020/Olympic_Agenda_2020–20–20_Recommendations-ENG.pdf.

16. Moreover, the choice to build, say, a temporary $300 million Olympic stadium and then razing it hardly seems an example of prudent spending and frugality.

17. Olympic Games Study Commission, "Interim Report to the 114th IOC Session," Mexico, November 2002, accessed July 11, 2016, www.olympic.org /Documents/Reports/EN/en_report_581.pdf.

TWO *2013 and 2014*

Epigraph: Boston 2024 chairman John Fish, in an interview with the *Boston Globe,* September 2014. John Powers, "Compact Boston May Have Olympic Advantage," *Boston Globe*, September 16, 2014, accessed September 16, 2014, www.bostonglobe.com/sports/2014/09/15/why-boston-could-have-edge -bidding-for-olympics/bgGdIzqsXtFRhDPs8L7ddJ/story.html.

1. Adam Vaccaro wrote a great profile of Reddy and Dinopoulos for boston .com. Adam Vaccaro, "Meet the Guys Who Got the Boston 2024 Movement Started," boston.com, February 6, 2015, accessed February 6, 2015, www.boston .com/news/local-news/2015/02/06/meet-the-guys-who-got-the-boston-2024 -movement-started.

2. Jerry Ackerman, "Civic Pride Is Stressed as Lure for Olympics," *Boston Globe,* March 22, 1994, 39.

3. Joan Vennochi, "Olympic Glory at Much Too High a Price," *Boston Globe*, January 26, 1999, A19.

4. Alan Abrahamson, "USOC's 2024 Triple-Play Bid-City Letter," United States Olympic Committee, February 20, 2013, accessed July 11, 2016, www .teamusa.org/News/2013/February/20/USOCs-2024-Triple-Play-Bid-City-Letter .aspx. Alan Abrahamson's piece is also available on his informative 3 Wire Sports website, accessed July 12, 2016, www.3wiresports.com/2013/02/19/usocs-2024 -triple-play-bid-city-letter/.

5. Christiana Mecca, "Boston Considers Hosting Olympics in 2024," *Daily Free Press,* March 18, 2013, accessed October 10, 2015, http://dailyfreepress .com/2013/03/18/boston-ponders-hosting-olympics-in-2024/.

6. Erin Smith and Dave Wedge, "Boston Olympics Idea Torched," *Boston Herald*, March 6, 2013, accessed July 11, 2017, www.bostonherald.com/news _opinion/local_coverage/2013/03/boston_olympics_idea_torched.

7. "The Power of Ideas," *Boston Magazine,* May 2014, accessed July 11, 2016, www.bostonmagazine.com/news/article/2014/04/29/power-of-ideas/2/.

8. Special Commission Relative to the Feasibility of Hosting the Summer Olympics in the Commonwealth, "Understanding a Boston 2024 Olympics," February 27, 2014, accessed July 11, 2016, https://malegislature.gov/content/docu ments/newsitems/Special%20Commission%20Final%20Report%202.27.14.pdf.

9. Mark Arsenault, "Group Explores 2024 Olympic Bid for Boston," *Boston Globe*, November 10, 2013, accessed July 11, 2016, https://www.bostonglobe.com /metro/2013/11/10/group-business-leaders-exploring-boston-olympic-bid /GHU9h2PkeLwJHU6tm9nVvO/story.html.

10. The Olympic bid was not a major topic of conversation on the campaign trail although Connolly had been a stronger supporter of the Games during the 2013 election, telling the *Improper Bostonian*, "It would be wonderful to host the Olympics, and I support the idea." Walsh's quote to the *Improper* was more circumspect. He said, "I support taking a look at it." Matt Martinelli, "Mayoral Candidates Weigh In on Hub Sports," *Improper Bostonian*, September 10, 2014, accessed July 11, 2016, www.improper.com/blogs/mayoral-candidates-weigh-in -on-hub-sports/.

11. John Powers, "For Boston, Price Isn't Right: Hard to See City Budging on This Budget," *Boston Globe*, November 21, 2013, C4.

12. David Luberoff, "The Roads Not Taken," *Architecture Boston*, Winter 2012, accessed July 11, 2016, https://www.architects.org/architectureboston/articles /roads-not-taken.

13. Shirley Leung, "Olympic Dreams Need Public Input," *Boston Globe*, June 27, 2014, accessed July 11, 2016, https://www.bostonglobe.com/business /2014/06/26/who-gets-decide-that-boston-will-host-olympics/HM9Bj3JYmqar HyGXEoRoEM/story.html.

14. IOC Press Release, "IOC Awards Olympic Games Broadcast Rights to NBC Universal through to 2032," May 7, 2014, accessed July 11, 2016, https://www.olympic.org/news/ioc-awards-olympic-games-broadcast-rights-to-nbcuniversal-through-to-2032.

15. Smith and Wedge, "Boston Olympics Idea Torched."

16. Steve Annear, "There's an Olympic-Sized Feud Happening about Boston as Host City," *Boston Magazine*, February 21, 2014, accessed July 11, 2017, www.bostonmagazine.com/news/blog/2014/02/21/olympics-in-boston-2024-commitee/.

17. Although the most common figure coming out of Russia for the Sochi Games' cost was $51 million, a highly regarded accounting and consulting firm in Moscow cited $66.7 billion or more as the true cost. Andrew Zimbalist, *Circus Maximus: The Economic Gamble behind Hosting the Olympics and the World Cup* (Washington, D.C.: Brookings Institution Press, 2015), 83.

18. Special Commission, "Understanding a Boston 2024 Olympics."

19. See Zimbalist, *Circus Maximus*, 118.

20. Michael Levenson, "Boston Olympics in 2024 Would Be a 'Monumental Task,'" *Boston Globe*, February 26, 2014, accessed July 11, 2016, https://www.bostonglobe.com/metro/2014/02/26/draft-report-olympics-feasible-but-obstacle-are-significant/pLocVzwREMhaaAgois2hZL/story.html.

21. Chris Dempsey and Conor Yunits, "Boosters for Boston Olympics Are Asking the Wrong Question," *Boston Globe*, June 21, 2014, accessed July 11, 2016, https://www.bostonglobe.com/opinion/2014/06/20/boosters-for-boston-olympics-are-asking-wrong-question/6JktmOJI9SbCCK9T2ElBHK/story.html.

22. Dempsey met with Chicago's Olympic opponents in the summer of 2014, while visiting the city for a friend's bachelor party.

23. Koh did disclose this conflict of interest in March 2015 in response to an inquiry from the *Dorchester Reporter*'s Lauren Dezenski. "Mayor's Chief of Staff Formally Discloses Ties to 2024 Executive," *Dorchester Reporter*, March 19, 2015, accessed July 11, 2016, www.dotnews.com/2015/mayor-s-chief-staff-formally-discloses-ties-2024-executive.

24. Mark Arsenault, "Mayor Walsh Warms Up to 2024 Olympics Bid," *Boston Globe*, October 13, 2014, accessed July 11, 2016, https://www.bostonglobe.com/metro/2014/10/12/walsh-has-come-around-idea-olympics-bid/JYs1dwZ6UbRQtayoLwIQcP/story.html.

25. Peter Schworm and Sean P. Murphy, "Lawmakers Warm to Olympic Bid," *Boston Globe*, October 17, 2014, accessed July 11, 2016, https://www.bostonglobe.com/metro/2014/10/17/boston-olympic-bid-pitched-legislators/zNeGdMabeivh2Enkjdi4fI/story.html.

26. Jimmy Golen, "Boston Wants to Take Olympics Back to School," Associated Press, November 26, 2014, accessed July 11, 2016, www.masslive .com/news/boston/index.ssf/2014/11/boston_wants_to_take_olympics.html and https://www.youtube.com/watch?v=jEoN5PMUQNQ.

27. Peter Schworm and Sean P. Murphy, "Lawmakers Warm to Boston Olympic Bid," *Boston Globe*, October 17, 2014.

28. Garrett Quinn, "Next Stop: Olympics," *Boston Magazine*, February, 2014, accessed July 11, 2016, www.bostonmagazine.com/news/article/2014/01/28 /boston-olympics-mbta/.

29. Andrew Zimbalist, "Let Boston 2024 Pay for the Olympics," *Boston Globe*, October 9, 2014, accessed July 11, 2016, https://www.bostonglobe.com /opinion/2014/10/09/private-group-wants-olympics-boston-let-them-pay-for /Lhszp3SJirPrwAsrfpWz5J/story.html.

30. John Powers, "Compact Boston May Have Olympic Advantage," *Boston Globe*, September 16, 2014.

31. Jack Encarnacao, "Fish Bites Back at Olympic Foes," *Boston Herald*, October 29, 2014.

32. Yvonne Abraham, "Can We Talk about the 2024 Olympics?" *Boston Globe*, November 16, 2014, accessed July 11, 2016, https://www.bostonglobe.com /metro/2014/11/16/can-talk-about-olympics/MOuSbcW7GhA7owRaASGnLP /story.html.

33. Senator Jamie Eldridge, letter to *Boston Herald* editor, *Boston Herald*, November 3, 2014, accessed July 11, 2016, www.bostonherald.com/news_opinion /opinion/letters_to_the_editor/2014/11/letters_to_the_editor_nov_3_2014.

34. Garrett Quinn, "Analysis: Constantly on the Defensive, Boosters of Boston Olympic Bid Miss Opportunity to Present Case to Public at Forum," *MassLive*, December 9, 2014, accessed July 11, 2016, www.masslive.com/news/boston/index .ssf/2014/12/analysis_boosters_of_boston_ol.html.

35. Shirley Leung, "Olympics Opponent Becomes a Believer," *Boston Globe*, December 10, 2014, accessed July 11, 2016, https://www.bostonglobe.com /business/2014/12/10/leung/onYoWVeT7LDfsKZxUKJzKP/story.html.

36. Mark Arsenault, "Boston Makes US Short List for 2024 Olympics," *Boston Globe*, June 13, 2014, accessed July 11, 2016, https://www.bostonglobe .com/metro/2014/06/13/boston-makes-short-list-for-summer-olympics /K5EyOKkSWisfXySpNujZWI/story.html.

37. Ibid.

38. Mark Arsenault, "High-Tech Tool to Help Make Case for Boston Olympics," *Boston Globe*, October 8, 2014, accessed July 11, 2016, https://www .bostonglobe.com/metro/2014/10/07/olympic-planners-unveil-high-tech-tool -forecast-impacts/zL1qbyActTfbb5CmYlmRsM/story.html.

39. Adam Reilly, "Mayor Walsh: Polls Show the Majority of Bostonians Are in Favor of the Olympics," WGBH, December 11, 2014, accessed July, 11, 2016, https://news.wgbh.org/post/mayor-walsh-polls-show-majority-bostonians-are-favor-olympics.

40. This letter from Walsh to the USOC was included as part of Boston 2024's submission to the USOC on December 1, 2015. Adam Vaccaro, "What Would the International Olympic Committee Require of Boston?," boston.com, February 5, 2015, accessed July 11, 2016, https://www.boston.com/news/business/2015/02/05/what-would-the-international-olympic-committee-require-of-boston.

41. Adam Vaccaro, "Olympic Foes Call on Boston Bidders to Make Plans Public," *Boston Globe,* December 3, 2014.

42. Mayor Walsh interview on Boston Public Radio, WGBH, November 21, 2014, accessed July 11, 2016, http://news.wgbh.org/post/mayor-walsh-pres-obamas-immigration-plan-2024-olympics-and-bostons-displaced-homeless.

43. Harold Faber, "Winter Olympics Ending Its Deficit in Lake Placid," *New York Times,* May 26, 1981, accessed July 11, 2016, www.nytimes.com/1981/05/26/nyregion/winter-olympics-ending-its-deficit-in-lake-placid.html.

44. "Walsh: Taxpayers Won't Get Stuck with Olympics Price Tag," Fox25, December 2, 2014, accessed August 18, 2016.www.fox25boston.com/news/politics/walsh-taxpayers-wont-get-stuck-with-olympics-price-tag/142768567.

45. Public Records documents are available here: https://assets.documentcloud.org/documents/1682022/boston2024-emails.pdf, accessed July 11, 2016.

46. Matthew Futterman and Jon Kamp, "With Boston Out, Attention Shifts to Los Angeles for 2024 Olympics," *Wall Street Journal,* July 27, 2015, accessed July 11, 2016, www.wsj.com/articles/usoc-drops-boston-olympics-bid-1438024640.

THREE *January 2015*

Epigraph: Mayor Marty Walsh, USOC/Boston 2024 Press Conference, January 9, 2015. Steve Annear, "Mayor Walsh on 2024 Boston Olympic Bid: 'We Were Destined to Get Picked,'" *Boston Magazine,* January 9, 2015, accessed July 11, 2016, www.bostonmagazine.com/news/blog/2015/01/09/2024-boston-olympic-bid-marty-walsh/.

1. Thomas Bach, "A New Olympics," *Boston Globe,* January 6, 2015, accessed July 11, 2016, https://www.bostonglobe.com/opinion/2015/01/05/ioc-president-thomas-bach-new-olympics/owB08n6R9rs21ZduqyeKPM/story.html.

2. Alan Abrahamson, "A Wink, a Nod, an Op-Ed, Insurance, So Many Questions," *3 Wire Sports,* January 12, 2015, accessed July 11, 2016, www.3wiresports.com/2015/01/12/wink-nod-op-ed-many-questions/.

3. Chris Dempsey and Liam Kerr, "Boston Will Win by Losing Olympic Bid," *Boston Globe*, January 6, 2015, accessed July 11, 2016, https://www.bostonglobe.com/opinion/2015/01/05/boston-will-win-losing-olympic-bid/WpWkZ3kN3J5okpPB9ndGPM/story.html.

4. Ben Fischer, "Wasserman Offers Insight into 2024 Bid Choice," *Sports Business Daily* blog, 2015, accessed July 11, 2016, http://m.sportsbusinessdaily.com/SB-Blogs/On-The-Ground/2015/07/LAOlympics.aspx.

5. Shira Springer, "Convincing Case Made by Boston for Olympic Bid," *Boston Globe*, January 10, 2015, accessed July 11, 2016, https://www.bostonglobe.com/sports/2015/01/10/boston-nailed-its-presentation-and-olympics-nomination/MoS7i13858AK6yT9MHXIcI/story.html.

6. Scott Reid, "Casey Wasserman Says Top USOC Officials Always Preferred LA for 2024 Olympic Bid," *Orange County Register*, August 28, 2015, accessed July 11, 2016, www.ocregister.com/articles/boston-679857-bid-board.html.

7. President Barak Obama, "President Obama on Boston Being Chosen as US 2024 Olympics Nominee," *Boston Globe,* January 9, 2015, accessed July 11, 2016, https://www.bostonglobe.com/metro/2015/01/08/president-obama-boston-being-chosen-olympics-nominee/US7ycbvB3nn83vxKGtdwhI/story.html.

8. Associated Press produced a film of the press conference: Boston mayor Marty Walsh, USOC chairman Larry Probst, and Boston 2024 chairman John Fish, "US USOC Presser," *ABC News,* January 9, 2014, accessed August 27, 2016, www.aparchive.com/metadata/USUSOCPRESSER/2d036c8ce48aac9fd0dd48ada2a63457. Baker's comments start at 1:30.

9. Jim O'Sullivan, "Why Is There No Political Opposition to the Olympic Bid?" *Boston Globe*, January 16, 2015, accessed July 11, 2016, https://www.bostonglobe.com/metro/2015/01/16/capitalolympics/Ug3Pg6AsgvELDHURMdaOVN/story.html.

10. Dan O'Connell's appearance on WGBH's *Greater Boston*, January 14, 2015, accessed July 11, 2016, https://www.youtube.com/watch?v=m5_cvYcgv1U.

11. Ibid.

12. Adam Vacarro, "Boston 2024 to Release More Olympics Information Wednesday," boston.com, January 20, 2015, accessed August 27, 2016, https://www.boston.com/news/business/2015/01/20/boston-2024-to-release-more-olympics-information-wednesday.

13. Michelle Wu, "Boston City Councilor: 'Open Up the Conversation' on 2024 Olympics," WGBH, January 16, 2015, accessed July 11, 2016, http://news.wgbh.org/post/boston-city-councilor-open-conversation-2024-olympics.

14. David Bryant, letter to *Boston Globe* editor, January 18, 2015, accessed July 11, 2016, https://www.bostonglobe.com/opinion/letters/2015/12/26/the-trouble-with-olympic-bid/COqqeZtT7DPnMQVvEjxZFM/story.html.

15. WBUR's polling was conducted by the excellent MassINC Polling Group, whose staff closely followed and probed public sentiment on the bid. Asma Khalid, "WBUR Poll: Bostonians Back Olympic Bid, but Also Want a Referendum," WBUR, January 20, 2015, accessed July 11, 2016, www.wbur.org /news/2015/01/20/wbur-poll-boston-olympics.

16. Boston 2024 said the date of the opening ceremonies would be July 19, 2024. "Boston 2024 Olympic Bid Group Holds Community Meeting in Hyannis," CapeCod.com, May 14, 2015, accessed July 11, 2016, www.capecod .com/newscenter/boston-2024-olympic-bid-group-holds-community-meeting -hyannis/.

17. Brendan McKenna, "Coakley, Baker Spar in Worcester Debate," *MassLive*, October 27, 2014, accessed July 11, 2016, www.masslive.com/news/worcester /index.ssf/2014/10/coakley_baker_clash_in_worcest.html.

18. Garrett Quinn, "Olympic Documents Show Boston City Employees Barred from Speaking Negatively about Olympics, IOC, USOC," *MassLive*, January 21, 2015, accessed July 11, 2016, www.masslive.com/news/boston/index.ssf/2015/01 /recently_released_olympic_docu.html.

19. Katharine Q. Seeley, "Boston Mayor Says He Won't Try to Block Referendum on Hosting 2024 Olympics," January 20, 2015, accessed July 11, 2016, www.nytimes.com/2015/01/21/us/poll-finds-lukewarm-support-in-boston-for -summer-olympics-bid.html?_r=0.

20. Steve Annear, "City Parks Group Sounds Caution over Proposed Common Role in 2024 Games," *Boston Globe*, March 13, 2015, accessed July 11, 2016, https://www.bostonglobe.com/metro/2015/03/13/group-wants-olympic -backers-scrap-plan-host-volleyball-boston-common/xclvNjy3w671wyu1f GqVWO/story.html.

21. "Summer Olympics Openers Draw Big Crowds and Advertising Dollars," *Nielsen*, July 25, 2012, accessed July 11, 2016, www.nielsen.com/us/en/insights /news/2012/summer-olympics-openers-draw-big-crowds-and-advertising -dollars.html and www.nytimes.com/1984/08/08/arts/olympics-a-success-in -ratings-for-abc.html.

22. Bill Forry, "Key Columbia Point Property Owners Caught Off Guard by Olympic Village Plans," *Dorchester Reporter*, January 22, 2015, accessed July 11, 2016, www.dotnews.com/2015/key-columbia-point-property-owners-caught -guard-olympic-village-plans.

23. Boston 2024, "Number 6: Bid and Games Budgets," December 1, 2014, accessed July 11, 2016, http://cdn.2024boston.org/docs/USOC_Submission_6.pdf.

24. Philip Hersh, "Boston 2024 Bid Calls on Chicago Idea," *Chicago Tribune*, January 9, 2015, accessed July 11, 2016, www.chicagotribune.com/sports /international/chi-boston-2024-bid-calls-on-chicago-idea-20150109-story.html.

25. Zeninjor Enwemeka, "Former MassDOT Chief Named CEO of Boston 2024," WBUR, January 23, 2015, accessed July 11, 2016, www.wbur.org/news /2015/01/23/richard-davey-boston2024-ceo.

26. No Boston Olympics, Twitter post, October 14, 2014, 4:39 a.m., accessed July 11, 2016, https://twitter.com/NoBosOlympics/status/520539219216072704 ?ref_src=twsrc%5Etfw.

27. Adam Vaccaro, "Olympics Head Built Close Relationship with Boston 2024 while Transportation Secretary," boston.com, September 28, 2015, accessed July 11, 2016, www.boston.com/news/business/2015/09/28/olympics-head-built -close-relationship-with-boston-2024-while-transportation-secretary.

FOUR *February 2015*

Epigraph: Boston Mayor Marty Walsh, press conference, February 9, 2015. Erin McClam and Alex Johnson, "Boston Buried by Snow Again as 'Absurd' Winter Drags On," *NBC News*, February 9, 2015, www.nbcnews.com/news/weather /boston-buried-snow-again-absurd-winter-drags-n303086.

1. Jon Erdman, "New England Record Snow Tracker: Boston Breaks All Time Seasonal Snow Record in 2014–2015," Weather.com, March 23, 2015, accessed July 11, 2016, https://weather.com/news/news/new-england-boston-record-snow-tracker.

2. Sarah Higgins, "IOC President Bach Visits USOC Headquarters, Praises Boston 2024 Efforts," February 4, 2015, accessed July 11, 2016, www.teamusa .org/News/2015/February/04/IOC-President-Bach-Visits-USOC-Headquarters -Praises-Boston-2024-Efforts.

3. Bill Shipp, "Shipp: Eminent Domain Made Atlanta a Thriving Business Center," *Athens Banner Herald*, June 29, 2005, accessed July 11, 2016, http:// onlineathens.com/stories/062905/opi_20050629025.shtml#.VvcldvkrI2w.

4. Adrian Walker, "It's Another Plus for Boston 2024," *Boston Globe*, February 6, 2015, accessed July 11, 2016, https://www.bostonglobe.com/metro/2015/02 /06/another-behind-scenes-powerbroker-joins-boston/z0ChkzFA9zRBsNB m13X0TP/story.html.

5. Andrew Ryan and Mark Arsenault, "Top Mayoral Aide Joins Boston 2024," *Boston Globe*, February 5, 2015, accessed July 11, 2016, https://www.bostonglobe .com/metro/2015/02/05/top-walsh-adviser-joins-boston/1ZCJI6554s10d94 DeRQHHO/story.html.

6. Jim O'Sullivan, "Big Names Coalesce around Charlotte Golar Richie," *Boston Globe*, May 17, 2013, accessed July 11, 2016, https://www.bostonglobe.com /metro/2013/05/16/charlotte-golar-richie-campaign-lines-support-from-broad -base/WUsdbREj1iBTnFH3Q6DcFN/story.html.

7. Jim O'Sullivan, "Bill Seeks Details of Boston's Olympic Expenses," *Boston Globe,* February 11, 2015, accessed July 11, 2016, https://www.bostonglobe.com /metro/2015/02/11/legislative-push-afoot-open-olympic-books/Eb1k5DK 710HJNcJC5UigHO/story.html.

8. This language appeared in Boston 2024's bid documents submitted to the USOC on December 1, 2014. The full text, accessed August 8, 2016, is available at https://assets.documentcloud.org/documents/2179140/bostons-original-bid -games-budget-proposal.txt.

9. "Dynamic Duo," *Harvard Business School Alumni Magazine*, September 1, 2013, accessed July 11, 2016, https://www.alumni.hbs.edu/stories/Pages/story -bulletin.aspx?num=2846.

10. Theodore R. Delwiche and Mariel A. Klein, "Faust Says No to Fundraising for Boston 2024," *Harvard Crimson*, February 11, 2015, accessed July 11, 2016, www.thecrimson.com/article/2015/2/11/faust-no-olympics-fundraising/.

11. Boston Transportation Department, "Boston Today," Go Boston 2030, accessed July 11, 2016, http://goboston2030.org/flipbook/files/Boston-Today.pdf.

12. Joan Vennochi, "Davey's MBTA Ties Mean More Bad Karma for Olympics Bid," *Boston Globe,* April 12, 2015, accessed July 11, 2016, https://www.bostonglobe .com/opinion/editorials/2015/04/11/richard-davey-ties-mean-more-bad-karma -for-boston/mlZtrVnW62oFEa9WPKPKsI/story.html.

13. No Boston Olympics, "Would a Boston Olympics Fix the T?" accessed August 9, 2016, www.nobostonolympics.org/fix_the_t.

14. Nestor Ramos, "Olympics Opposition Groups Have Big Social Media Presence," *Boston Globe*, June 30, 2015, accessed July 11, 2016, https://www .bostonglobe.com/metro/2015/06/29/small-olympics-opposition-group-has-big -social-media-presence/tcHKTPaAALOLDPPuWfIBYP/story.html.

15. Hayden Bird, "Boston 2024 Thought a Satirical Article Was Real," *BostInno*, June 30, 2015, accessed July 11, 2016, http://bostinno.streetwise.co/2015/06/03 /boston-2024-twitter-mistake-cited-universal-hub satire article-photo/.

FIVE *March 2015*

Epigraph: Curt Nickisch, "Support for Boston Olympics Falls Further, WBUR Poll Finds," *WBUR News*, March 19, 2015, accessed August 9, 2016, www.wbur .org/news/2015/03/19/wbur-boston-olympics-poll-march.

1. Boston Municipal Research Bureau website, "About Us," accessed August 27, 2016, http://bmrb.org/about-us/.

2. Mark Arsenault, "Walsh Presses Case for 2024 Olympics Bid," *Boston Globe*, March 4, 2015, accessed July 11, 2016, https://www.bostonglobe.com

/metro/2015/03/04/boston-mayor-martin-walsh-delivers-impassioned-defense
-olympics-bid/1GPLZRf4I23ir28gXhoSLL/story.html.

3. Yvonne Abraham, "Walsh, Boston 2024 Too Close for Comfort," *Boston Globe,* March 8, 2015, accessed July 11, 2016, https://www.bostonglobe.com/metro /2015/03/08/too-close-for-comfort/H14yPLyvan31bIjiwURzlM/story.html.

4. Jim O'Sullivan, "Walsh Advisers Joining Olympic Effort," *Boston Globe,* March 5, 2016, accessed July 11, 2016, https://www.bostonglobe.com/metro /2015/03/05/walsh-advisers-joining-olympic-effort/9GFvDUbIq8QMBzy G9MtKTL/story.html.

5. Lauren Dezenski, "Franklin Park Key to Plans for Olympics; Its Boosters Weigh Impact," *Dorchester Reporter,* February 4, 2015, accessed August 27, 2016, www.dotnews.com/2015/franklin-park-key-plans-olympics-its-boosters-weigh -impact.

6. "Olympics Organizers Outline Improvements to Franklin Park; Some Residents Skeptical," *Dorchester Reporter,* March 6, 2015, accessed July 11, 2016, www.dotnews.com/2015/olympics-organizers-outline-improvements-franklin -park-some-residents-.

7. Shirley Leung, "Boston 2024 Needs to Show Some Humility, Shun Secrets," *Boston Globe,* March 13, 2015, accessed July 11, 2016, https://www.bostonglobe .com/business/2015/03/12/games-organizers-more-secrets/TVrwLA26Db048 ihChBPnWK/story.html.

8. Statehouse News Service, "Patrick's Olympic Pay: $7,500 a Day," *Commonweath Magazine,* March 9, 2015, accessed August 18, 2016, http:// commonwealthmagazine.org/olympics/patricks-olympic-pay-7500-per-day/.

9. Mark Arsenault, "Six Boston 2024 Employees Make over $100,000 a Year," *Boston Globe,* March 9, 2015, accessed July 11, 2016, https://www.bostonglobe .com/metro/2015/03/09/olympic-bid-organizers-pledge-release-salaries/bbowa XcuzG61dvVXbKay3N/story.html.

10. Curt Nickisch, "Support for Boston Olympics Falls Further, WBUR Poll Finds," WBUR, March 20, 2015, accessed July 11, 2016, www.wbur.org/news /2015/03/19/wbur-boston-olympics-poll-march.

11. WGBH, "Behind the Fight to Keep the Olympics out of Boston," *Scrum,* March 13, 2015, accessed July 11, 2016, http://news.wgbh.org/post/behind-fight -keep-olympics-out-boston.

12. Joana Weiss, "Is the Olympic Opposition Going to Turn?" *Boston Globe,* March 28, 2015, accessed July 11, 2016, https://www.bostonglobe.com /opinion/2015/03/27/olympic-opposition-going-turn/uxylnrLgEix7hrxlUYnAKP /story.html.

13. See Chris Faraone, "Shell Games: These Olympic Emails Show Who Actually

Runs Boston," *Dig Boston*, May 19, 2015, accessed July 11, 2016, https://digboston
.com/shell-games-these-olympic-emails-show-who-actually-runs-boston/.

14. UMass Donahue Institute Economic and Public Policy Research,
"Assessing the Olympics: Preliminary Economic Analysis of a Boston 2024
Games; Impacts, Opportunities and Risks," Boston Foundation, March 2015,
accessed July 11, 2016, https://www.tbf.org/~/media/TBFOrg/Files/Reports
/Boston%20Olympics%20Report.pdf.

15. Mark Arsenault, "Boston Olympics Would Bring Billions, Study Says,"
Boston Globe, March 18, 2015, accessed July 11, 2016, https://www.bostonglobe
.com/metro/2015/03/17/boston-olympics-will-mean-billions-city-study-says
/JQ2d6MKJub5CtdV8qKw1xM/story.html.

16. Catherine Carlock, "What Does No Boston Olympics Think about the
Boston Foundation Olympics Report?" *Boston Business Journal*, March 27, 2015,
accessed July 11, 2016, www.bizjournals.com/boston/real_estate/2015/03/what
-does-no-boston-olympics-think-about-the.html.

17. Coincidentally, both No Boston Olympics and Boston 2024 were meeting
that day with a collection of nonprofit leaders convened by the Barr Foundation,
Boston's largest philanthropic organization. The Barr Foundation was funded by
Amos and Barbara Hostetter, who were initially supporters of the bid and made
a $250,000 contribution. The couple quietly pulled their support after conclud-
ing that the bid would not improve the region's public transportation system.

18. Andrew Zimbalist, "Olympics Numbers Don't Add Up," *Boston Globe*,
March 20, 2015, accessed July 11, 2016, https://www.bostonglobe.com/opinion
/2015/03/20/olympics-numbers-don-add/BqrAaenp4tKK3Q7ASU5OrJ
/story.html.

19. See, for instance, Andrew Zimbalist, *Circus Maximus: The Economic
Gamble behind Hosting the Olympics and the World Cup* (Washington, D.C.:
Brookings Institution Press, 2015).

20. Tim Quinn, "No Boston Olympics Visits Worcester," *Worcester Magazine*,
March 13, 2015, accessed July 11, 2016, http://worcestermag.com/2015/03/13
/boston-olympics-visits-worcester/32008.

21. Richard Weir, "Walsh Hits Reset Button in Quest for Olympic Gold,"
Boston Herald, March 21, 2015.

22. Marty Walsh, interview with WBZ's Jon Keller, "Keller @ Large: Walsh
Wants New Olympic Narrative," *CBS Boston*, March 22, 2015, accessed August 27,
2016, http://boston.cbslocal.com/2015/03/22/keller-large-walsh-wants-new
-olympic-narrative/.

23. "Marty's Games," *Commonwealth Magazine*, March 23, 2015, accessed July
11, 2016, http://commonwealthmagazine.org/the-download/martys-games/.

24. Alan Abrahamson, "Boston 2024: A Cool Hand Luke Problem," *3 Wire Sports*, March 20, 2015, accessed July 11, 2016, www.3wiresports.com/2015/03/20/boston-2024-a-cool-hand-luke-problem/.

25. Alan Abrahamson, "Boston 2024 Is Doomed: Be Done with It," *3 Wire Sports*, March 30, 2016, accessed July 11, 2015, www.3wiresports.com/2015/03/30/boston-2024-is-doomed-be-done-with-it/.

26. Adam Reilly, "'Team Walsh' Meets in Dorchester to Revive Boston's Bid for the 2024 Summer Olympics," March 25, 2015, accessed July 11, 2016, https://news.wgbh.org/post/team-walsh-meets-dorchester-revive-bostons-bid-2024-summer-olympics.

27. Sarah Birnbaum, "Beacon Hill Leaders to Hire a $250K Consultant to Advise on Boston Olympic Bid," WBGH, March 24, 2015, accessed July 11, 2016, http://news.wgbh.org/post/beacon-hill-leaders-hire-250k-consultant-advise-boston-olympic-bid.

28. "Sen. Warren 'Really Concerned about' Olympics Bid," WBUR, March 30, 2015, accessed July 11, 2016, www.wbur.org/news/2015/03/30/elizabeth-warren-boston-olympics.

29. One irony in this statement is that Boston 2024's political consultant Doug Rubin was also the strategist behind Senator Warren's first campaign.

30. Jon Chesto, "Olympics Bid Has Ripple Effect for Chamber Leadership," *Boston Globe*, January 23, 2015, accessed July 11, 2016, https://www.bostonglobe.com/business/2015/01/23/olympics-bid-has-sudden-ripple-effect-for-boston-chamber-leadership/X82VnWuNc10u4HvXKwWxhI/story.html.

31. Joan Vennochi, "John Fish Is Boston 2024's Main Force—and Its Liability," *Boston Globe*, March 30, 2015, accessed August 27, 2016, https://www.bostonglobe.com/opinion/2015/03/30/john-fish-boston-main-force-and-its-liability/ZBUOr8ZxsY8CTUojkowyQL/story.html.

six *April 2015*

Epigraph: Boston 2024 chairman John Fish, speech to the CEO Breakfast Forum, hosted by Northeastern University, April 1, 2015.

1. Mark Arsenault, "Boston 2024 Offers to Open Books," *Boston Globe*, April 1, 2015, accessed July 11, 2016, https://www.bostonglobe.com/metro/2015/04/01/head-boston-says-state-and-city-accountants-can-study-group-books/zwzVXoHOSfOG1PMXQJ5ivL/story.html.

2. Jon Keller, "Keller @ Large: Mayor Walsh Sends Blunt Warning to USOC," WBZ, April 1, 2015, accessed July 11, 2016, http://boston.cbslocal.com/2015/04/01/keller-large-mayor-walsh-sends-blunt-warning-to-usoc/.

3. Ibid.

4. Jim O'Sullivan, "London Mayor Predicts Boston Olympics Opposition Will Fade," *Boston Globe*, February 9, 2015.

5. While Johnson's Boston visit did not go so well, he would soon step down from his position as London's mayor and successfully campaign for the Brexit campaign in his own country. For Johnson's Boston commentary, see Jim O'Sullivan, "London Mayor Predicts Boston Olympics Opposition Will Fade," *Boston Globe*, February 9, 2015, accessed July 11, 2016, https://www.bostonglobe.com/metro/2015/02/09/snowfall-dampens-london-mayor-boris-johnson-visit-boston/eeSvebtH19HFWoC2QAxPpN/story.html.

6. "London 2012: Olympics and Paralympics £528m under Budget," *BBC*, July 19, 2013, accessed July 11, 2016, www.bbc.com/sport/olympics/20041426.

7. The *Globe*'s Peter Abraham reported in September that when David Ortiz had been named to the Boston 2024 board of directors in April, Ortiz himself had been oblivious to the decision. His agent had arranged the deal and hadn't managed to tell Ortiz before the appointment was announced. It was another embarrassing revelation for Boston 2024. As Peter Abraham put it, "that moment was evidence at just how poorly organized Boston 2024 was. It was doomed from the start." Peter Abraham, "Red Sox Should Not Search for New Manager," *Boston Globe*, September 18, 2015, accessed July 11, 2016, www.bostonglobe.com/sports/2015/09/18/red-sox-should-not-search-for-new-manager/OKOyWJJzj8AoX1noBQngjI/story.html.

8. Of the $1.5 billion, $335 million was for security. According to Jules Boykoff, this was 1.5 times the amount that the US Treasury had spent on seven previous US Olympic Games. Jules Boykoff, *Power Games: A Political History of the Olympics* (London: Verso, 2016), 153.

9. Jack Encarnacao, "Mitt Romney Set to Give Tips on Boston 2024 Bid," *Boston Herald*, Monday, May 18, 2015, accessed July 11, 2016, www.bostonherald.com/news_opinion/local_coverage/2015/05/mitt_romney_set_to_give_tips_on_boston_2024_bid.

10. Mark Arsenault, "Red Sox Executive Larry Lucchino in Talks with Boston 2024," *Boston Globe*, April 24, 2015, accessed July 11, 2016, https://www.bostonglobe.com/metro/2015/04/23/red-sox-executive-talks-with-boston/o3CN72tNkhex71iNHns6KI/story.html.

11. Ibid.

12. Matt Pepin, "Larry Lucchino Still Considering Boston 2024 Olympics Role," *Boston Globe*, April 30, 2015, accessed July 11, 2016, https://www.bostonglobe.com/sports/2015/04/30/larry-lucchino-still-considering-boston-olympics-role/Y07w17H67SoVDqEJXKzKXP/story.html.

Epigraph: USOC and IOC board member and former Olympian Angela Ruggiero, testimony to the Boston city council, May 18, 2015.

1. Michael Levenson, "Pagliuca Takes the Reins of Struggling Olympic Bid," *Boston Globe*, May 22, 2015, accessed July 11, 2016, https://www.bostonglobe.com /metro/2015/05/21/new-boston-chief-has-turnaround-experience/qNLRWR74 LVaYs7e2cIJtJN/story.html.

2. Steve Pagliuca and Aidan Browne, "2024 Summer Games Would Be a Boon for Beantown," *Banker & Tradesman*, December 15, 2014.

3. Mark Arsenault, "Pagliuca Takes Over as Boston 2024 Chairman," *Boston Globe*, May 21, 2015, accessed May 21, 2015, https://www.bostonglobe.com/metro /2015/05/21/boston-expected-confirm-leadership-change-today/AAt2x7VyIld1 D62DpqjBpO/story.html.

4. Jim Braude, interview with Peter Roby, *Greater Boston*, WGBH, May 26, 2015, accessed August 27, 2016, http://video.wgbh.org/video/2365497715/.

5. Jack Connors, interview with Boston Public Radio, "BPR: Charlie Sennott, Sore Losers, Jack Connors, Brian McGrory, Garen Daly," WGBH *News,* June 18, 2014, accessed August 27, 2016, http://news.wgbh.org/post/bpr-charlie-sennott -sore-losers-jack-connors-brian-mcgrory-garen-daly.

6. Gintautas Dumcius, "Boston Businessman Jack Connors: Boston 2024 Is Now in Hands of Gov. Carlie Baker, Boston Mayor Marty Walsh," *MassLive,* July 8, 2015, accessed August 18, 2016, www.masslive.com/news/boston/index .ssf/2015/07/boston_businessman_jack_connor.html.

7. "Boston 2024 with Vice Chair Peter Roby and Harvard Graduate Running for President in Somalia," *Greater Boston,* WGBH News, May 26, 2015, accessed August 12, 2016, http://news.wgbh.org/post/boston-2024-vice-chair-peter-roby -and-harvard-graduate-running-president-somalia.

8. Ibid.

9. Joshua Miller, "After 100 Days, Baker's Popularity Historically High," *Boston Globe*, April 24, 2015, accessed April 24, 2015, https://www.bostonglobe.com /metro/2015/04/24/why-charlie-baker-wicked-popular/wlQiWDsjbpyUvRa 8f9653J/story.html.

10. "Boston Olympics Foes Meet with Governor, Cabinet Members," AP, *USA Today*, May 15, 2015, accessed May 16, 2015, www.usatoday.com/story/sports /olympics/2015/05/15/boston-olympics-foes-meet-with-governor-cabinet -members/27368277/.

11. Andrew Ryan and Mark Arsenault, "USOC Official Says Boston Bid Not Certain," *Boston Globe*, May 19, 2015.

12. Kyle Clauss, "Here's the Bid Book Boston 2024 Submitted to the USOC," *Boston Magazine*, May 27, 2015, accessed May 29, 2015, www.bostonmagazine .com/news/blog/2015/05/27/boston-2024-bid-book/.

Epigraph: Boston 2024 chairman Steve Pagliuca, June 29, 2015, at the unveiling of Bid 2.0.

1. Boston 2024, "Boston 2024 Partnership Q1 2015 Progress Report," June 5, 2015, accessed July 11, 2016, https://scribd.com/document/267804385/Q12015 -Boston-2024-Progress-Report.

2. Alan Abrahamson, "Big Decision but Not Difficult—Kill Boston 2024," *3 Wire Sports*, June 18, 2015, accessed July 11, 2016, www.3wiresports.com/2015 /06/18/big-decision-but-not-difficult-kill-boston-2024/.

3. Mark Arsenault, "Walsh Contradicts Himself in Remark on Olympic Bid," *Boston Globe*, June 10, 2015, accessed June 10, 2015, https://www.bostonglobe .com/metro/2015/06/09/walsh-gives-contradictory-answers-familiarity-with -olympic-bid/PbDGMhugObEsdcY8eWNqTM/story.html.

4. Kyle Clauss, "Has Anyone at City Hall Read the Boston 2024 Bid Book?" *Boston Magazine*, June 9, 2015, accessed July 11, 2016, www.bostonmagazine.com /news/blog/2015/06/09/marty-walsh-boston-2024-bid-book/.

5. Jon Chesto, Andrew Ryan, and Dan Adams, "Boston 2024 Wants Huge Tax Break for Widett Circle Deal," *Boston Globe*, June 30, 2015, accessed June 30, 2015, https:// www.bostonglobe.com/business/2015/06/29/boston-envisions-tax-break-unprece dented-scope-redevelop-widett-circle/bxANs68FfocI1FK0X5PbqL/story.html.

6. See, for instance, the Brattle Group, "Analysis of the Boston 2024 Proposed Summer Olympic Plans," August 17, 2015, 49. Available at www.mass.gov /governor/docs/news/final-brattle-report-08-17-2015.pdf.

7. Ibid., 52.

8. Ibid., 143.

9. Ibid., 65.

10. Mark Levenson and Mark Arsenault, "Insurance for Olympics Won't Cover Every Risk," *Boston Globe*, July 2, 2015, accessed July 2, 2015, https://www .bostonglobe.com/metro/2015/07/01/insurance-plan-would-cover-myriad -scenarios/PFPoPfR8jVis2VhrQsuBEP/story.html.

11. The Brattle Group, "Analysis of the Boston 2024 Proposed Summer Olympic Plans," 127.

12. Michael Levenson, "Latest Olympic Plan Leaves Media without a Home," *Boston Globe*, July 11, 2015.

Epigraph: *Boston Herald,* front-page headline, July 28, 2015.

1. Curt Nickisch, "WBUR Poll: Deadline Looming, Public Support of Boston's Olympic Bid Largely Unchanged," WBUR, July 10, 2015, accessed July 11, 2016, www.wbur.org/news/2015/07/10/wbur-july-olympics-poll.

2. John Powers, "Complexities Abound for Boston 2024's Olympic Bid," *Boston Globe,* July 17, 2015, accessed July 17, 2015, https://www.bostonglobe .com/sports/2015/07/16/complexities-abound-for-boston-olympic-bid /9885bNYAOF4PRbZo7cb2MM/story.html.

3. One exception occurred on Jim Braude's *Greater Boston* show on March 9 when Boston 2024 sent its PR consultant Doug Rubin to debate Zimbalist. Rubin perplexingly argued that Zimbalist's position was congruent with that of Boston 2024. The video and transcript of the debate are available at "The Two Sides of the Boston Olympic Debate Face Off," March 9, 2015, accessed July 11, 2016, https://www.youtube.com/watch?v=norwzdq-6hM.

4. Kristina Moore, "Power Wear: Allen & Co. Sun Valley Conference 2015," *Forbes,* June 30, 2015, accessed July 11, 2016, www.forbes.com/sites/forbesstylefile /2015/06/30/power-wear-allen-co-sun-valley-conference-2015/#1082935b52d4.

5. Tito Jackson, press conference on the steps of City Hall, July 20, 2015, accessed August 27, 2016, https://www.youtube.com/watch?v=s3E9CXCWlk4.

6. Martin J. Walsh, "USOC Olympic Games Host City Contract Update," July 27, 2015, www.cityofboston.gov/cable/video_library.asp?id=16129.

7. Garrett Quinn, Twitter post, July 27, 2015, 4:56 p.m., accessed July 11, 2016, https://twitter.com/GarrettQuinn/status/625817173672488961.

TEN *The Aftermath*

1. "Why Hosting the Olympics May Not Be a Golden Opportunity," PBS *NewsHour,* July 28, 2015, accessed July 11, 2016, www.pbs.org/newshour/bb /hosting-olympics-may-golden-opportunity/.

2. Christine Brennan, "Blame USOC for Boston's Failed Olympic Bid," *USA Today,* July 27, 2015, accessed July 27, 2015, www.usatoday.com/story/sports /olympics/2015/07/27/brennan-blame-usoc-failed-boston-bid/30735529/.

3. Scott Reid, "Casey Wasserman Says Top USOC Officials Always Preferred LA for 2024 Olympic Bid," *Orange County Register*, August 28, 2015, accessed August 28, 2015, www.ocregister.com/articles/boston-679857-bid-board.html.

4. David Wharton, "U.S. Olympic Leaders Offer Apology for Failed Boston Bid," *Los Angeles Times*, September 25, 2015, accessed August 27, 2016, www .latimes.com/sports/sportsnow/la-sp-sn-usoc-apology-20150924-story.html.

5. Yvonne Abraham, "Will Mayor Walsh Be Hurt by Olympic Debacle?" *Boston Globe*, July 30, 2015, accessed July 30, 2015, https://www.bostonglobe.com /metro/2015/07/29/lesson-learned/rH07ppIiWJq1xBHZBMA80N/story.html.

6. Mark Arsenault, "IOC Leader Says Boston Has Great Potential," *Boston Globe*, February 1, 2015, accessed February 1, 2015, https://www.bostonglobe.com /metro/2015/01/31/boston-compelling-candidate-for-olympics-says-ioc-head /8RXywz6sW1JJJ7r4i0JFqJ/story.html.

7. John Powers, "Olympic Chief, Walsh Trade Barbs over Failed Bid," *Boston Globe*, July 29, 2015, accessed July 29, 2015, https://www.bostonglobe.com /sports/2015/07/29/ioc-president-boston-failed-deliver-promises-usoc/ZgfLv Unn3RJAbewuSzMQhI/story.html.

8. Stephen Wilson, "IOC President Slams Boston for Failing to Deliver on 'Promises' to USOC," Associated Press, July 29, 2015, accessed August 27, 2016, www.theglobeandmail.com/sports/more-sports/ioc-president-slams-boston-for -failing-to-deliver-on-promises-to-usoc/article25749743/.

9. "Mark Arsenault of the *Boston Globe* on Brattle Group Olympics Report," Boston.com *Morning Show,* WRKO, August 19, 2015, accessed July 11, 2016, http://media.wrko.com/a/108411726/mark-arsenault-of-the-boston-globe-on -brattle-group-olympics-report-8-19-15.htm.

10. Kyle Clauss, "Boston 2024 Returns from Dead to Throw Shade at Brattle Group Report," *Boston Magazine,* August 19, 2015, accessed July 11, 2016, www .bostonmagazine.com/news/blog/2015/08/19/boston-2024-brattle-group -rebuttal/.

11. The terrorist at the offices of *Charlie Hebdo* in Paris prior to Hamburg's referendum probably also provided a fillip to the "no" vote.

ELEVEN *American Unexceptionalism*

1. "Walsh: Taxpayers Won't Get Stuck with Olympic Price Tag," Fox 25 News, December 2, 2014, accessed August 13, 2016, www.fox25boston.com/news /politics/walsh-taxpayers-wont-get-stuck-with-olympics-price-tag/142768567.

2. Bent Flyvberg and Allison Stewart, "Olympic Proportions: Cost and Cost Overrun at the Olympics, 1960–2012," Said Business School Working Papers, University of Oxford, 2012. This study only considers operating costs and sports venues. It does not include infrastructure costs.

3. Notably, even in LA 1984, the federal government chipped in to the tune of $78 million. US Government, GAO, *Olympic Games: Costs to Plan and Stage the Games in the United States*, November 2001, 5.

4. Ibid, 6.

5. The Brattle Group, "Analysis of the Boston 2024 Proposed Summer

Olympic Plans," August 17, 2015, 102. Available at www.mass.gov/governor/docs/news/final-brattle-report-08-17-2015.pdf. Flyvberg and Stewart, "Olympic Proportions," 10.

6. US Government, GAO, *Olympic Games,* 9.

7. Data on tourism and other economic impacts of hosting are provided in Andrew Zimbalist, *Circus Maximus: The Economic Gamble behind Hosting the Olympics and the World Cup* (Washington, D.C.: Brookings Institution Press, 2015).

8. *Greater Boston* Convention and Visitors Bureau, "Statistics and Reports," bostonusa.com, accessed July 11, 2016, www.bostonusa.com/partner/press/statistics/.

9. See, for one, Wolfgang Maennig and Felix Richter, "Exports and Olympic Games: Is There a Signal Effect?" *Journal of Sports Economics* 13, no. 6 (2012).

10. Doug Saunders, "Is the World Cup a Giant Waste of Money?" *Globe and Mail,* May 31, 2014, www.theglobeandmail.com/opinion/is-the-world-cup-a-giant-waste-of-money/article18924852/.

11. Owen Gibson, "Inside West Ham's New Home: How Football Came to 2012's Olympic Stadium," *Guardian,* July 18, 2015, accessed July 20, 2015, https://www.theguardian.com/sport/2015/jul/18/west-ham-football-2012-olympic-stadium.

12. The excessive use of urban land in Beijing required the eviction of 1.5 million residents, according to an estimate made by COHRE.

13. The Brattle Group, "Analysis of the Boston 2024 Proposed Summer Olympic Plans," 12.

14. Lindsay Beck, "Beijing to Evict 1.5 Million for Olympics," Reuters, June 5, 2007, accessed March 2, 2016, www.reuters.com/article/us-olympics-beijing-housing-idUSPEK12263220070605.

15. John Fish, "Let's Think Big," *Commonwealth Magazine,* October 9, 2014, accessed July 11, 2016, http://commonwealthmagazine.org/economy/001-lets-think-big/.

16. Dan Doctoroff, "Boston, Use the Olympic Bid to Think Bold," *Boston Globe,* May 28, 2015, accessed May 28, 2015, https://www.bostonglobe.com/opinion/2015/05/28/boston-take-olympic-lesson-from-new-york-failed-bid/4LhBBbHE6QJdxnPvrorftN/story.html.

17. See Zimbalist, *Circus Maximus,* for a more detailed discussion of Barcelona's Olympic experience.

18. Eric Levenson, "Boston 2024 Chief: 'You Don't Really Need a T for the Olympics,'" boston.com, March 28, 2016, https://www.boston.com/news/olympics/2016/03/28/boston-olympics-chief-you-dont-really-need-a-t-for-the-olympics.

19. Jules Boykoff, "Beijing and Almaty Contest Winter Olympics in Human Rights Nightmare," *Guardian*, July 30, 2015, https://www.theguardian.com /sport/2015/jul/30/china-kazakhstan-winter-olympics-2022.

20. Ibid.

21. Bach made this remark in Moscow in late July 2015. See "Rights Advocates Oppose Beijing Winter Olympics Bid," *China Digital Times*, July 28, 2015, http:// chinadigitaltimes.net/2015/07/rights-advocates-oppose-beijings-2022-winter -olympics-bid/.

22. It is claimed that the rail will cut the time to travel between Beijing and Zhangjiakou from over three hours to less than one hour. Neil Connor, "Olympics: Smooth Piste for Beijing's 2022 Bid," AFP, July 29, 2015, accessed August 13, 2016, http://sports.yahoo.com/news/olympics-smooth-piste-beijings -2022-bid-055645444.html.

23. While the geographical water distribution imbalance is acute, China has a nationwide water shortage with 21 percent of the world's population and only 6 percent of the global water resources. It is estimated that over 300 million people in China drink contaminated water on a daily basis. See http://data.worldbank .org/indicator/ER.H2o.INTR.PC; and Shannon Tiezzi, "China's Looming Water Shortage," *Diplomat*, November 30, 2014, accessed August 13, 2016, http:// thediplomat.com/2014/11/chinas-looming-water-shortage/.

24. China launched a $60 billion water diversion program from the south prior to the 2008 Summer Olympics. Zhangjiakou, the site of the Nordic skiing, only gets 8 inches of snow per year and will require copious water supplies for artificial snow making. See Lily Kuo, "Hosting the Winter Olympics in Beijing Is a Terrible Idea," Reuters, April 1, 2015, http://qz.com/373228/hosting-the-winter -olympics-in-beijing-is-a-terrible-idea/.

25. "North China Plain Groundwater: >70% Unfit for Human Touch," *China Water Risk,* February 26, 2013, accessed August 13, 2016, http://chinawaterrisk. org/notices/north-china-plain-groundwater-70-unfit-for-human-touch/. This source reports on a 2013 survey showing that the North China Plain suffers from severe groundwater pollution with over 70 percent of overall groundwater quality classified as Grade IV+, in other words, unfit for human touch.

26. See, for one, Claire Topal and Yeasol Chung, "China's off-the-Chart Air Pollution: Why It Matters (and Not Only to the Chinese)," part one, *National Bureau of Asian Research,* January 14, 2014, accessed August 13, 2016, www.nbr .org/research/activity.aspx?id=394.

27. Stephen Wilson, "Beijing It Is," *US News and World Report*, July 31, 2015, accessed August 1, 2015, www.usnews.com/news/sports/articles/2015/07/30 /almaty-beijing-make-final-pitches-ahead-of-22-olympic-vote; and "Thomas Boch Says Boston Failed to Deliver on 'Promises' to USOC," ESPN, July 29,

2015, accessed August 1, 2015, http://espn.go.com/boston/story/_/id/13336198
/ioc-president-thomas-bach-says-boston-failed-deliver-promises-usoc.

28. Since IOC members from bidding countries cannot vote, it is likely that
the number of actual votes in Lima will be in the eighty-five to eighty-seven
range.

29. See Los Angeles 2024, "Stage 1: Vision, Games Concept and Strategy,"
http://la24-prod.s3.amazonaws.com/assets/pdf/LA2024-canditature-part1
_english.pdf.

30. The cost differential in constructing a temporary and permanent canoe
course is negligible. The London course has been used post-Games for both
training and public use. It generates appreciable revenues.

31. See Paris 2024, "Candidature File: Phase 1," http://paris2024.org/medias
/presse/paris_2024_candidature_file_part_1.pdf.

32. See Project Rome 2024, "Vision and Mission," www.roma2024.org/en
/page/tag/dossier-page-en.

33. Dan Palmer "Favourite for Rome Mayor Reaffirms Opposition to 2024
Olympic Bid," *Inside the Games*, May 9, 2016, www.insidethegames.biz
/articles/1037281/favourite-for-rome-mayor-reaffirms-opposition-to-2024
-olympic-bid.

34. See Budapest 2024, "Stage 1: Vision, Games Concept and Strategy,"
February 15, 2016, www.budapest2024bid.com/Budapest_2024_Candidature
_File_Stage_1_EN.pdf.

TWELVE *Lessons Learned*

1. David Wharton, "Seeking to Bring 2024 Olympics to L.A., Officials Work
the Social Angle," *Los Angeles Times*, October 30, 2015, accessed August 27, 2016,
www.latimes.com/sports/la-sp-ioc-bid-intrigue-20151030-story.html.

2. Puerto Rico has its own Olympic Committee that is distinct from the
USOC. In 1980, when the United States boycotted the Moscow Games, Puerto
Rico still sent its athletes. It has one member on the IOC.

3. Alan Abrahamson, "No Apologies Necessary: Still the Shining City on the
Hill," *3 Wire Sports*, December 9, 2010, accessed July 11, 2016, www.3wiresports
.com/2010/12/09/no-apologies-necessary-still-the-shining-city-on-the-hill/.

4. Katharine Seelye, "Many in Boston Feel Relief as Olympic Bid Ends, but
Others See a Stagnant City," *New York Times*, July 28, 2015, accessed July 28, 2015,
www.nytimes.com/2015/07/29/us/many-in-boston-feel-relief-as-olympic-bid
-ends-but-others-see-a-stagnant-city.html.

5. Eric Levenson, "Boston 2024 Chief: 'You Don't Really Need a T for the

Olympics,'" boston.com, March 28, 2016, accessed July 11, 2016, https://www
.boston.com/news/olympics/2016/03/28/boston-olympics-chief-you-dont-really
-need-a-t-for-the-olympics.

6. Western New England University Polling Institute, "Massachusetts
Statewide Survey," April 6–14, 2015, accessed August 27, 2016, https://www1.wne
.edu/polling-institute/doc/2015-april-6-14/ma-0415-olympics-tables.pdf.

7. "Fmr. Mayor Ray Flynn—USOC Pulls Boston2024 Bid,"
BostonHeraldRadio, July 27, 2015, accessed September 3, 2016, https://
soundcloud.com/bostonherald/7-27-15-fmr-mayor-ray-flynn.

INDEX

NOTE: Page numbers in *italics* indicate figures and tables; page numbers with *n* or *nn* indicate endnotes.